"In the face of all ou ⟩pe that God has given us men like Roy ⌄. ⌄⌄⌄⌄⌄⌄.

—Ann Coulter, nationally syndicated Columnist and NY Times best-selling Author of How to Talk to a Liberal (If You Must), Treason: Liberal Treachery from the Cold War to the War on Terrorism, and Slander: Liberal Lies about the American Right

"I greatly admire Judge Roy Moore and the courageous stand he has taken to defend the principles in which so many of us believe. He has confronted formidable opposition, but not once has he wavered in his efforts to combat judicial tyranny and to uphold the Judeo-Christian foundation that undergirds our nation's system of government. Every one of us could take a cue from the sheer strength of Judge Moore's convictions and his unyielding commitment to righteousness."

—Dr. James Dobson, Founder, Focus on the Family

"Judge Moore walks in the strong tradition of Patrick Henry—a Christian who refuses to bend the knee to a tyrannical regime. His story is a must-read for those who wish for a return to the Constitution."

—Michael Farris, President, Patrick Henry College

"I am grateful that the Christian community has a champion of the caliber of Roy Moore. I look forward to seeing how God may yet use him in the future."

—Dr. D. James Kennedy, Founder, Coral Ridge Ministries and Author of What If America Were a Christian Nation Again?, The Gates of Hell Shall Not Prevail, and several other books

"There have been times in American history when the courage or understanding of one individual opened the door to the reform of major mistakes and injustices. When Chief Justice Roy Moore refused the unlawful order of a federal judge to remove the Ten Commandments from the Judicial Building in Alabama, he proved himself to be such an individual. We cannot yet know the full consequences of his principled stand, but in this book Americans will discover the knowledge and insight that made it possible. It is an invaluable resource for the work of restoration that lies ahead. Anyone who truly cares about the integrity of the United States Constitution and the preservation of our religious liberty needs to read and understand this work."

—Alan Keyes, Former Ambassador to the United Nations
and Chairman of the Declaration Foundation

"Chief Justice Moore is a man of character, integrity, and principle. His stand in defense of God's law, our entire legal system, his oath of office, and the very freedoms our nation was founded upon is a solid example of unselfish sacrifice. He is a true patriot and a true public servant."

—Joyce Meyer, internationally known
practical Bible Teacher and Author

"Throughout recorded history, brave men have been called on to stand up and take a stand—sometimes for country, sometimes for family, sometimes for the Lord above. Roy Moore is such a man."

—Hon. Zell Miller, United States Senator (Ga.)

"Chief Justice Roy Moore is a proven fighter for his faith and our freedom. This is a book that deserves to be read."

—Oliver L. North, LtCol USMC (Ret.)
and Author of NY Times best-sellers
Mission Compromised and Jericho Sanction

"This book is a must-read in order to understand how judicial supremacists have denied our inalienable right to acknowledge God."

—Phyllis Schlafly, Founder, Eagle Forum
and Author of The Supremacists:
The Tyranny of Judges and How to Stop It

"Former Chief Justice Roy Moore has raised critically important issues facing our country today regarding the acknowledgment of God. He reminds Americans that we cannot allow activist judges to continue their disregard of some of the basic principles on which our country was founded."

—Hon. Richard Shelby, United States Senator (Ala.)

SO HELP ME GOD

SO HELP ME GOD

THE TEN COMMANDMENTS, JUDICIAL TYRANNY, AND THE BATTLE FOR RELIGIOUS FREEDOM

FORMER CHIEF JUSTICE OF THE SUPREME COURT OF ALABAMA

ROY MOORE

WITH JOHN PERRY

WND Books

So Help Me God
A WND Books book

Published by WorldNetDaily
Los Angeles, CA

Dewey: B
Subject Heading: Moore, Roy
Judges—Biography
Ten Commandments—Censorship

Jacket design by Linda Daly

WND Books are distributed to the trade by:
Midpoint Trade Books, 27 West 20th Street, Suite 1102, New York, NY 10011

WND Books are available at special discounts for bulk purchases. WND Books, Inc. also
publishes books in electronic formats. For more information call (310) 961-4170 or visit www.
wndbooks.com.

First edition published 2005 by Broadman & Holman Publishers, Hardcover edition
Second edition published 2009 by WND Books, Paperback edition

ISBN 13-Digit: 9781935071228
ISBN 10-Digit: 193507122X
E-Book ISBN 13-Digit: 9781935071761
E-Book ISBN 10-Digit: 1935071769
Library of Congress Control Number: 2009927539

WND Books

Printed in the United States of America
10 9 8 7 6 5 4 3 2 1

To my darling wife, Kayla,
and children, Heather, Ory, Caleb, and Micah,
who have stood with me in this battle to
preserve the public acknowledgment of
God in our land.

To my dear mother, Evelyn,
and in memory of my father, Roy.
Their love and sacrifice inspired me to
always stand for what I believe.

To the United States Military Academy,
which taught me
"Duty, Honor, Country."

and

To God, my Creator,
to whom be glory forever.

CONTENTS

PREFACE

When Barack Hussein Obama was sworn in as President of the United States on January 20, 2009, many predicted that America was in store for some very radical changes in economic, domestic, and foreign policy. Such predictions have come to pass already within the first three months of his term.

On April 1, 2009, Obama greeted King Abdullah of Saudi Arabia by bowing at the waist, certainly improper protocol for any head of state. A few days later Obama told the Turkish press and Parliament that, "we do not consider ourselves a Christian Nation" and that America had a "deep appreciation for the Islamic faith which has done so much over the centuries to shape the world-including in my own country."

Because of such recent disparagements of our faith by the President, I have been urged to republish *So Help Me God*, which I wrote in 2004 so that people will better understand and be prepared to deal with attacks on our Christian heritage.

As I explain within the pages of this new paperback edition, our country has always been considered a Christian nation. In 1892 even the United States Supreme Court in the case of *Church of the Holy Trinity* proved beyond doubt that our institutions, culture, and law reflect our Christian foundation. The High Court opined that, "These, and many other matters which might be noticed, add a volume of unofficial declarations to the mass of organic utterances that this is a Christian nation." The Court made it clear that "'we are a Christian people, and the morality of the country is deeply engrafted upon Christianity, and not upon the doctrines or worship of those imposters," a reference to the Muslim and Buddhist beliefs. There is simply no evidence that Islam or any other foreign religion has had any significant influence in shaping our country. So how or why does Obama or any other leader of government dare to pretend otherwise?

My election in 2000 as Chief Justice of the highest court in Alabama and the placement of a monument to the Ten Commandments in the Alabama Judicial Building in Montgomery, Alabama in 2001, eventually led to my removal from office for the simple acknowledgment of the Judeo-Christian God upon Whom our nation began. It is a story of subterfuge and intrigue.

The actions of judges, religious leaders, and public officials to include the President of the United States and the Governor of Alabama in my trial and removal from office demonstrate the hypocrisy and confusion of public officials about the acknowledgment of the Judeo-Christian God. Similar hypocrisy and confusion now form the basis of Obama's recent pronouncements.

While memory of the trials, press conferences, radio and television appearances, speeches, and rallies may have faded somewhat with the passing of time, I can still clearly recall the betrayal and rejection of my colleagues and others in public office during the entire ordeal. But still the issue of recognition of God remains and is evident in Obama's denial of our Christian heritage in the implementation of foreign policy in the Mid-east.

I am often asked why God would allow His holy laws to be removed from public view and locked in a small dark room inside the Alabama Judicial Building, or how He could permit someone who sought only to acknowledge His sovereignty to be removed from the highest judicial office in the state of Alabama. Like many others in the Christian community, I had thought, at the time, that God would intervene to cause the unlawful lower court order to be reversed by the U.S. Supreme Court or use President George W. Bush as an instrument of His will to preserve the right of the state to acknowledge the Creator God from Whom all our rights and liberties flow. After all, the Bible declares that, "The King's heart is in the hand of the Lord, as the rivers of water: He turneth it whithersoever He will." (Proverbs 21:1). But God did not choose such an outcome.

We know that in Isaiah it states that God's Word does not return to Him void, but it shall accomplish that which He pleases. "For my thoughts are not your thoughts, neither are your ways my ways, saith the Lord." (Isaiah 55:8) Simply stated, God knows what he is doing.

The vivid image of four security guards rolling the Ten Commandments monument from public view is etched in the minds of many Americans. Christian resolve to preserve the knowledge of God and His law is seen in Ten Commandments displays in nearly every state. Ordinary citizens are beginning to see the hypocrisy and deception of judges and courts across America which open with prayer and religious ceremony, but then deny that we can recognize a particular God.

Furthermore, many Americans are beginning to recognize that without God's direction we have no moral law, and that without a moral foundation we suffer disastrous consequences in our schools, our businesses, and our public institutions.

For example, a recent survey of 29,760 high school students revealed that 30% admit to having stolen from a store during the past year, 64% say they cheated on a test during the past year, and 83% say they sometimes lie to their parents. And yet, 93% say they are satisfied with their own personal ethics and character, and 77% say their ethical standards are better than those of most other people they know.

Still others are beginning to understand the intricate relationship between God and our supreme law, the United States Constitution. As John Adams, our second President, so eloquently explained, "Our Constitution was made only for a moral and religious people. It is wholly inadequate for the government of any other." Clearly, we have strayed far from the principles of our founding fathers.

We face a moral, spiritual, and political crisis in our country of unprecedented proportions.

Obama and his allies in Congress are pressing for the adoption of the Freedom of Choice Act (FOCA) which would repeal modest gains achieved in the battle for the lives of unborn children.

Obama has announced his desire to lift virtually all restrictions on homosexual conduct and has voiced support for the repeal of DOMA (Defense of Marriage Act passed by Congress in 1996.)

Several UN treaties which would adversely impact the parent-child relationship are being considered by Obama and his followers.

Obama has clearly stated his disagreement with Justices like Scalia and Thomas and has begun to appoint federal judges and justices who share his liberal view of the Constitution.

Under Obama's economic stimulus plan, the public is being deceived to believe that socialism (dependence on government control of distribution and supply of goods) is preferable to the free enterprise system we know as capitalism.

Unless and until the American public is awakened to the efforts to remove the acknowledgment of God from us we will continue down a path to destruction. For this reason I pray that you will find So Help Me God enjoyable, educational, and rewarding. Read of my struggles to preserve the acknowledgment of God and how we can fight the apostasy which now sweeps our land. Then together we can say, as did Martin Luther,

Here I stand. I cannot do otherwise.
So help me God!

ACKNOWLEDGEMENTS

First and foremost, I must acknowledge God for His providence in my life and His guidance in making this book possible.

I extend my grateful appreciation to my family and friends who have been with me during the past twelve years in my battle to preserve our religious liberty. Especially deserving of recognition are two men I have known for more than thirty-five years and without whom this book would not have been possible: Dr. M. G. "Doc" Lett and Judge John Bentley, who have always been there to give me support and encouragement for which I shall forever be thankful.

To my daughter, Heather, and attorneys Greg Jones and Ben DuPré, who worked many long hours in typing, proofreading, and critiquing this work, I can only say that without your superb assistance this book would never have been published. The special ability of Ben and Greg to express complicated legal matters in a clear and concise manner will help others to understand the critical issues of our time.

Finally, I would like to thank Phillip Jauregui, Rich Hobson, Jessica Atteberry, Mel Glenn, and my wife, Kayla, who provided insight and wisdom in the final draft; their suggestions and revisions proved invaluable toward the completion of this work.

INTRODUCTION

It doesn't seem that long ago that I became a circuit judge in Etowah County and placed a small hand-made plaque of the Ten Commandments on the wall behind my bench. Yet, twelve years have now passed and much has occurred, eventually resulting in my removal from the highest judicial office in the state of Alabama.

I have received both praise and criticism for what I have done, and some have even distorted or dismissed the true issue, but my full story remains untold. This book is not only about my life; it is about the importance of the public recognition of the sovereignty of God. Although it may appear that my journey has ended, the awakening of the American people and their response to the events that occurred in Alabama over the last decade have only just begun.

To explain why this happened, I tell my story beginning on a small farm in Alabama, to the United States Military Academy at West Point, through Vietnam, and eventually to the position of chief justice of the Alabama Supreme Court. Along the way, I discuss the history of our nation and God's indispensable role in the foundation and prosperity of this country.

Federal judges who hypocritically open their courts with a prayer ("God save the United States and this honorable court)" and take their oath ("so help me God") while prohibiting public displays that acknowledge the sovereignty of God have placed themselves above the law, making their opinions the new standard of right and wrong. As a result, our country is being led to deny the existence of the Creator God.

This turning away from God is known as apostasy and, unfortunately, is nothing new. In the days of Isaiah, the people of Judah were turned from God by those who swore "by the name of the LORD, and ma[d]e mention of the God of Israel, but not in truth, nor in righteousness" (Isa. 48:1). Like America today, Judah was a nation that called upon God's name but refused to recognize His sovereignty or abide by His law. Jeremiah described the people of Judah by stating,

And though they say, The LORD liveth; surely they swear falsely.

O LORD, are not thine eyes upon the truth? thou hast stricken them, but they have not grieved; thou hast consumed them, but they have refused to receive correction: they have made their faces harder than a rock; they have refused to return. (Jer. 5:2–3)

The eyes of the Lord are still upon the truth! Although America has suffered violence in our public schools, murder of our unborn children, and disintegration of our families and public institutions, we, like Judah, have made our faces harder than a rock, refusing to return to the only hope for our land, a belief in the God of our forefathers.

Yet God has promised in His Word that if His people, which are called by His name, shall humble themselves and pray and seek His face and turn from their wicked ways, then He will hear from heaven, will forgive their sin, and will heal their land (see 2 Chron. 7:14). Only God will heal our land. But we must understand that no governing authority can place itself above God or above the law. We must remain one nation under God, or, as President Ronald Reagan so aptly stated, "we will be a nation gone under."

It is my hope that this book will help restore the moral foundation of our law and return the knowledge of God to our land. I am pleased to tell my story, *So Help Me God*.

1

CAN THE STATE ACKNOWLEDGE GOD?

J udges do not normally find themselves on trial in their own court-room, but then again, there has never been anything normal about the legal issues I have confronted. On November 12, 2003, I sat in the witness chair in front of the very bench from which, until just a couple of months before, I had presided as the chief justice of the Alabama Supreme Court. The prosecution, led by Alabama Attorney General Bill Pryor, had already asked in their written arguments that I be removed from office. Now Pryor was cross-examining me in the court-room of the Alabama Judicial Building.

The Ten Commandments monument that I had placed in the rotunda of the building to acknowledge God had already been declared unconstitutional by a federal district judge, ordered removed from the rotunda, and locked in a storage room by my colleagues on the court. But on this day, I was being questioned before an ethics panel because I had refused to move the monument.

"And your understanding," Attorney General Pryor asked me, "is that the federal court ordered that you could not acknowledge God. Isn't that right?"

"Yes," I responded.

Pryor continued in a slow and deliberate manner. "And if you resume your duties as chief justice after this proceeding, you will continue to acknowledge God as you have testified that you would today, no matter what any other official says?" I could not believe he was actually asking me this, but there was only one answer to such a question.

"Absolutely," I replied. "Without—if I can clarify that—without an acknowledgment of God, I cannot do my duty. I must acknowledge God. It says so in the Constitution of Alabama. It says so in the First Amendment to the United States Constitution. It says so in everything I've read. So . . ." Pryor was nodding his head impatiently.

"Well," he finally interjected, "the only point I'm trying to clarify, Mr. Chief Justice, is not *why*, but only that in fact if you do resume your duties as chief justice, you would continue to do that without regard to what any other official says. Isn't that right?" Pryor did not want to hear why I would continue to acknowledge God, only *whether* I would do so. But this was an ethics trial, so I figured this ethics panel—the Court of the Judiciary—was interested in hearing the reasons for my actions, even if the prosecutor was not.

"Well, I would do the same thing this court did in starting with the prayer. That's an acknowledgment of God. I would do the same thing that justices do when they place their hand on the Bible and say, 'So help me God.' It's an acknowledgment of God. The Alabama Supreme Court opens with 'God save this State and this Honorable Court.' It's an acknowledgment of God. In my opinions, [and] I have written many opinions, acknowledging God is the source—the moral source—of our law. I think you must."

There was no question that I will always acknowledge God even if another official—state or federal—tells me not to. But the more pressing issue facing this country is whether these United States and our elected officials will be permitted to acknowledge God as the moral foundation of our law and justice system.

The American Civil Liberties Union (ACLU) first sued me in 1995 in federal court for my display of a plaque of the Ten Commandments in my small Etowah County, Alabama, courtroom that I placed there in 1992. Seven years later, the ACLU again sued me for placement of a monument of the Ten Commandments in the rotunda of the Alabama Judicial Building. The federal court eventually concluded that the Ten Commandments monument was unconstitutional because it was installed "with the specific purpose and effect . . . of acknowledging the Judeo-Christian God as the moral foundation of our laws."

The court of appeals agreed with the lower court that the monument was unconstitutional because my purpose for installing the monument was "to acknowledge the law and sovereignty of the God of the Holy Scriptures." By ordering me to remove the monument, the lower federal court intended to force me to deny the sovereignty of God, which I will not do. I cannot stop acknowledging God because it violates my oath of office to the Alabama Constitution—which invokes the favor and guidance of Almighty God—and the United States Constitution, which does not give the federal government the power to censor a state's acknowledgment of God.

My refusal to remove the Ten Commandments monument angered one of the plaintiffs in the federal case so much that he filed ethics charges against me with the Alabama Judicial Inquiry Commission (JIC), a panel with which I had already developed quite an interesting history. The JIC summarily filed formal charges against me with the Court of the Judiciary, alleging that I had breached judicial ethics by refusing to follow what I considered an unlawful federal court order. By Alabama law, I was immediately suspended from the office of chief justice. By the end of August I was locked out of my office, and my colleagues on the court had taken it upon themselves to lock the Ten Commandments monument in a storage room to appease the federal court.

It was not until the trial in November 2003 that I had the chance to explain that I believed the federal court order was unlawful and required me to violate my oath. I wanted to explain to the court that the federal court was wrong on the law, that it did not have the authority to order me or the state of Alabama to stop acknowledging God, and that my action upheld rather than violated ethical standards.

But like Attorney General Pryor, the Court of the Judiciary was not interested in why I had not followed the court order, nor did it care that removing the monument would force me to violate my solemn oath. It was enough that I had disobeyed a court order. The morning after Pryor interrogated me about acknowledging God, the Court of the Judiciary decided the case, wrote a twelve-page opinion, voted, and signed an order to remove me from office.

The presiding judge read the court's judgment. He began by saying that the case was about whether, in refusing to obey a federal court order, I had violated the Canons of Judicial Ethics, and this had nothing to do with the public display of the Ten Commandments in the State Judicial Building or the acknowledgment of God.

The Court of the Judiciary apparently agreed with both federal courts that it was unconstitutional for a state official to acknowledge God publicly. The court concluded that "Chief Justice Moore not only willfully and publicly defied the orders of a United States district court, but upon direct questioning by the Court he also gave the Court no assurance that he would follow that order or any similar order in the future."

As I listened I thought, *Have these men in black robes become so vain that they will deny God simply because a higher judge has ordered them to do so?* They broke under the pressure and did to me what not even the federal court could do: They removed me from the judicial office to which I had been duly elected. "Under these circumstances," the court declared, "there is no penalty short of removal from office that would resolve this issue." For the first time in Alabama history, the chief justice of the Alabama Supreme Court was removed from his position. And for what? Daring to acknowledge God when an oppressive federal judiciary had told him not to do so.

It was that same providential God who had brought me from the hills of Gadsden, Alabama, through Vietnam, to the head of the Alabama judicial system. I could not—and never will—deny Him, and certainly not just to keep a job. Throughout our history, our country has been one nation under God, recognizing that our inalienable rights are endowed by our Creator and not by man.

Can the state acknowledge God? It certainly can—and I believe that for America to continue to enjoy the blessings of liberty it must—and we must always recognize God as the source of these liberties. And if, at the end of my journey, my life has drawn attention to that one, true God, I will stand with the apostle Paul, who said, "I have fought a good fight, I have finished my course, I have kept the faith" (2 Tim. 4:7).

But how did someone get to the highest judicial position in Alabama, only to be removed for upholding his solemn oath of office? Let's start at the beginning.

2

"CAPTAIN AMERICA"

E towah County, in the northeast part of Alabama, is home to corn and cotton fields, poultry farms, rock quarries, and abandoned iron ore mines here and there. The Coosa River flows near the eastern edge, and plateaus spread along the west. In the middle is Blount Mountain, the tail end of the Appalachian Mountain chain that runs all the way to Pennsylvania. Gadsden is the county seat and the biggest city for miles around.

February 11, 1947, was a dreary winter day in Gadsden. But to Evelyn Moore it was a beautiful day as she gave birth to her firstborn child, a son. She affectionately named him Roy Stewart Moore in honor of her husband, Roy Baxter Moore, and her maiden name, Stewart. Evelyn and Roy had met and married after his discharge from military duty at the end of World War II. Now they were starting their family with a brand-new baby boy. Two brothers and two sisters eventually followed.

My father was a hardworking man who earned barely enough to make ends meet, but he taught me more than money could ever buy. From him I learned about honesty, integrity, perseverance, and never to be ashamed of who you are or what you believe in. Early on my dad shared with me the truth about God's love and the sacrifice of His own Son, Jesus. My mother was a homemaker who was always there to help me with my schoolwork, to care for me when I was sick, and to encourage me to do the best I could. The discipline was left to my father, who was not afraid to administer it when necessary. But most of the time he made us wish for the "hickory switch" rather than his hour-long lectures.

Although most of the people of Alabama in 1947 were farmers, my father was also a construction worker and a jackhammer operator. In 1954, when work slowed down in Gadsden, we moved to Houston, Texas, where a post-war building boom was under way. After about four years in Texas, we moved back to Alabama, then to Pennsylvania, and finally back to Alabama. At one point I attended three different schools during the same year. In the years before my father died (1967), he worked for the Tennessee Valley Authority building dams in Alabama and later with Anniston Army Depot and various other employers.

During my freshman year in high school, we moved to Gallant, a quiet farming community near Gadsden. I hitchhiked sixteen miles a day to and from Emma Sansom High School in town, catching rides with local steel workers. When I began my sophomore year, I transferred to Etowah County High, where I could take the bus from my home.

For four years, beginning in the ninth grade, I cleaned tables in the school lunchroom every day to earn my lunch money. I also worked as a stock boy at a grocery store in Attalla, Alabama, earning a whopping eighty-five cents an hour. Picking beans, tomatoes, and other vegetables during the summer months provided additional money for the family. A lot of our clothing was given to us. Since I had such long arms, the shirts people gave me never seemed to fit, so I always rolled the sleeves up for a more decent appearance.

After school each day my brother Jerry and I cut wood, which we hauled by hand from a nearby wooded area. With only an axe and an old crosscut saw, we worked for hours just to get enough wood to last our family overnight, and we repeated the process nearly every day. Mr. Clarence Walker, our landlord, allowed us to milk his cow, and my mother often made butter. Plowing with a double team of mules, we broke the soil for planting in the spring and worked with our hands and an old hoe to clear weeds from the crops during the growing season. My brother Joey was much younger, but he helped as he could.

From time to time my father raised chickens for our egg supply and an occasional hog that we fed until it was ready to butcher for meat. Hunting and fishing were something we always enjoyed. On Sundays we gathered on our neighbor's yard to play touch football. W. A. Lutes and his wife Geneva were always willing to let us ruin their beautiful grass because, as he said, "The grass will always grow back."

On Sunday mornings we attended the small country church near my home. Gallant Baptist was a friendly place. On one occasion, our elderly preacher, Brother Woods, asked me about coming forward to confess my sins and receive Christ into my life. I "walked the aisle" that Sunday and returned home to tell my parents. Daddy immediately escorted me to the preacher's home where we had a two-hour discussion to make sure that I fully understood the meaning of salvation. Although I was a little embarrassed at the time, I never forgot how important that decision was in my life. I would always remember my dad's concern and my heavenly Father's sacrifice.

Life was peaceful during the mid-sixties in Gallant, Alabama. There was no violence in our school system, and children could walk the streets of nearby towns without fear of being molested or killed by strangers. Life was physically more difficult than it is today, but people actually helped others in need, expecting nothing in return.

My mother worked at home caring for the family while my father labored to provide a modest living. During the evening, we gathered around the table and gave thanks for a large bowl of pinto beans and corn bread, spaghetti, or macaroni and cheese. It was generally a one-course meal and always one God to whom we were thankful.

We rented a house from Mr. Walker and his wife Ola who treated us well. The rent was only twenty-five dollars per month, but even that was difficult to pay at times. We had no indoor toilet facility and one old 1949 Ford. Often we were seen pushing this car up and down the road when it broke down—which seemed to happen about once a week. But we were generally happy and did not think of our situation in life in negative terms. A lot of people did not have indoor plumbing and our outhouse had two seats, which we thought was rather special. During my senior year, my younger brother Jerry and I worked with our dad to dig a hole for our new septic tank and our new "indoor plumbing." Daddy worked hard and frequently had to borrow money to make ends meet, but he always paid it back.

My father always emphasized the value of a good education, perhaps because he only finished the ninth grade. Etowah High School was a great school from which I and my brothers and sisters would eventually graduate. I did well in school, and I was perceived to be studious, probably because I carried all my books from class to class and to and from school—but the real reason I did so was to avoid paying a locker fee.

I maintained an "A" grade in all subjects, had perfect attendance for four years, was selected as Boy's State representative, and was elected student body president during my senior year. But without a scholarship, college was out of the question.

During my senior year in high school, I applied to the U.S. Military Academy at West Point in New York. Standards were high and competition was tight, but I knew that if I were accepted I would receive an outstanding education, minimal pay for four years, and an officer's commission at graduation.

I had prayed for years that I would be able to attend West Point, after having seen the movie *The Long Grey Line* in the ninth grade. But it was not until my senior year that I finally got up the confidence to write my U.S. congressman, Albert Rains, seeking a recommendation. Because he was leaving office after many years of service, he referred my request to incoming representative James Martin, who was gracious enough to invite me to apply. I went to Atlanta, Georgia, for my competitive exam and then began the long wait to see if God would answer my prayers.

In the spring, a letter came from the U.S. Army, notifying me that I had been accepted at West Point and ordering me to report on July 1, 1965. That gave me less than two months to get ready, but hurrying through the summer was a small price to pay for such an honor. One practical problem was how to get from Alabama to New York. My father borrowed three hundred dollars for my ticket and traveling expenses, which I later repaid from my small income as a cadet.

Nothing could have prepared me for the sight of West Point—the beautiful gothic buildings, immaculate parade grounds, and scenic bluffs overlooking the Hudson River. It was quite a change for an Etowah County boy, but an even bigger change was living with the other cadets. Back in Gadsden, we lived modestly, but we knew a lot of people who lived the same way. Many West Point cadets, though, came from wealthier and better educated families. Some of the men had already been in college while waiting for their appointments. I guessed that very few of them had ever been inside an outhouse or had ever set their hands to a plow behind a mule.

In a matter of days I was living a very different life—early morning exercise, classes, military drill, and strict discipline designed to turn young men from a wide assortment of backgrounds into effective and strategic leaders. I soon learned that one of the academy's tools for leadership training was intimidation. Upperclassmen seldom missed an opportunity to intimidate younger cadets. If cadets withered under the verbal criticism and hazing of their fellow soldiers in training, they would probably wither under attack on the battlefield. Intimidation separated the strong, resolute, and tenacious from the rest of the pack by testing a cadet's determination to survive.

I had to learn fast how to stand up to intimidation and not to let it defeat me. I was not as well read, traveled, or experienced as some of the other cadets, and I had a heavy southern accent, so I was an easy target. All the physical activity created a healthy appetite. But when an upperclassman at the table decided I took too long to answer a question because I had too much food in my mouth, or if he thought I took too big a bite, he could order me to hand in my plate and not to eat anymore. It was tough to be ordered to pass up a meal as hungry as I was just because some third- or fourth-year cadet ordered me to do so.

I recall one time when a "yearling," or sophomore, ordered me to pass my entire meal off the table because I had about seven peas on my fork. I took some consolation from the fact that I still had my dessert, but that also met the same fate. I soon learned the truth of the old adage, "What doesn't kill you will make you stronger."

There were many instances of intimidation at West Point. It was part of the educational process. But when it was over I would be inoculated against the threat. Later in life, I noticed how often my political and spiritual opponents tried to manipulate my behavior by intimidation. But nothing could be worse than forcing a hungry young cadet to go without a meal.

As rough and uncomfortable as it seemed at the time, my training at West Point prepared me to stand up against more sinister enemies later in life. My refusal to be intimidated became one of my most effective defenses against those organizations like the ACLU that tend to get their way by forcing others to cower under pressure.

But my most powerful weapon against the ACLU and others during the coming years was the sense of duty instilled in me by the military academy. On May 12, 1962, in his farewell address to the cadets at the United States Military Academy, General Douglas MacArthur uttered those memorable words which have become the motto of my alma mater: "Duty, Honor, Country." He continued by stating, "Those three hallowed words reverently dictate what you ought to be, what you can be, what you will be. They are your rallying points; to build courage when courage seems to fail; to regain faith when there seems to be little cause for faith; to create hope when hope becomes forlorn."[1]

And that duty was clarified by the cadet prayer: "Help us to maintain the honor of the Corps untarnished and unsullied, and to show forth in our lives the ideals of West Point in doing our duty to Thee and to our Country. All of which we ask in the name of the Great Friend and Master of men. Amen."

West Point taught me not only to stand steadfastly against all attempts at intimidation, but also to do my duty to God and country whatever the cost. It is never pleasant or easy and, most often, not rewarding to do one's duty, but I believe this is required of everyone.

At the dinner table, I had no recourse if an upperclassman ordered me to turn in my plate. But there were other places at West Point where the playing field was more level. I discovered that one place where someone from Alabama with a "country" accent could get as much respect as anybody else was in the boxing ring. In the ring, money, accent, speech, and sophistication became meaningless. Here the will to win was put to the test. During boxing class I may have been bloodied, but I never quit. During some of my most trying times I always returned to the ring.

In 1971, in Da Nang, Vietnam, we actually constructed a ring where I met all challenges from soldiers in the battalion. In 1982, after a bitter political loss for the race of circuit judge, I returned to boxing and found solace in rediscovering within myself that inner resolve I experienced in the ring.

One of my goals at West Point was to obtain a varsity letter in a sport. I had always admired my dad, who was an outstanding football player in 1934 at Glencoe, Alabama. He lettered in varsity football in the ninth grade and received all-county recognition. But I had never participated in any sport or even in physical education class in high school (during my physical education class I cleaned lunchroom tables). Because I had never participated in high school football or baseball, I faced a dilemma in choosing my sport.

I had always admired gymnasts. One day I went to the gym to watch a gymnastics training session. While there were several participants in floor exercise, rings, trampoline, high bar, and parallel bars, I saw nobody at the pommel horse, so I thought I would be least embarrassed there. Never did it occur to me that there was a good reason for inactivity at that event. It proved to be extremely hard to master, but after three and a half years I obtained the Army "A" on the pommel horse, or what we referred to as the "side horse."

At one point during my first year in this sport, Coach Wells told me to pick another sport. I went back to my room, but I returned days later to ask for another chance to make the team. The coach was a hardened veteran at West Point, direct and to-the-point, but I had an ace up my sleeve. I reminded Coach Wells of a well-known gymnast of the past who was also named Roy Moore. He had developed a technique on the pommel horse called the "Moore." I thought that having the same name might entitle me to another chance at making the team. I suppose Coach Wells saw my determination and could not say no to such ridiculous logic. Probably thinking that I had no chance, he relented and gave me another shot. I was never an athletic standout, but I eventually lettered in this sport and even helped our team beat Navy during my senior year.

My father did not live to see me graduate from the academy or participate in gymnastics. He died suddenly in October 1967, at the beginning of my junior year. His life of hardship and struggle was suddenly ended by a heart attack at age forty-nine. He had worked hard to feed his family, and he was proud of what his children had accomplished. My younger brother was an outstanding football player in high school, and all the other children had done well, but they were still attending school. Being the oldest child, I had gone to college—and not just any college, but the United States Military Academy. I regret that I was not able to see my dad's pride in my graduation from West Point.

After graduation from the academy in June 1969, I completed Infantry Officers' Basic Course (IOBC) on October 14, 1969, and the airborne school at Fort Benning, Georgia, on November 7 of that year. I was assigned to the 2nd Battalion, 51st Infantry Division, United States Army in Illesheim, Germany, as a battalion staff officer in charge of the motor pool. Fortunately, I was surrounded by experienced non-commissioned and warrant officers upon whom I had to depend. I was a young, carefree lieutenant enjoying living on the German economy and traveling throughout Deutschland. Later I was assigned to the 385th MP Company at Stuttgart where I served as a first lieutenant platoon leader.

From Germany, I shipped out to Vietnam, where American involvement was declining as more South Vietnamese soldiers assumed the defense of their country. Even so, there was plenty of brutal fighting as the native troops, with American support, attacked communist North Vietnamese positions in nearby Laos, and the communists responded with strikes from Laos and Cambodia.

I was given the command of 188th Company, 504th MP Battalion, a military police company supervising the military stockade in Da Nang on the South China Sea, not far from the border between North Vietnam and South Vietnam. After West Point, I was shocked at the lack of discipline I saw there. I immediately began implementing standard regulations and operating procedures, much to the dismay of troops who had not been trained to respect strict discipline. They did not make the connection between effective discipline and survival in combat. Disapproval of the war by the American public and soldiers who had been drafted to fight such an unpopular war led to a dangerous laxity in combat.

When I arrived, drug use was widespread and insubordination was commonplace. As a result, I administered many "Article Fifteens," disciplinary charges filed against insubordinate or disobedient soldiers. I was not intimidated by the threat of "fragging" which had taken the life of many officers and senior non-commissioned officers in Vietnam. "Fragging," or the killing of officers and non-commissioned officers, often was accomplished by tossing live grenades into their quarters or vicinity. This threat from the troops under their command caused many officers to refrain from enforcing discipline.

A great deal of mischief in Vietnam was the result of rampant drug use and race problems that had become commonplace. Perimeter defense often suffered as soldiers high on drugs failed to keep a vigilant watch for the enemy. Vietcong infiltrators could explode ammunition supplies and escape without detection. Some of our men even lost their lives while the enemy was virtually free to move across lines made insecure by undisciplined guards. It was a constant struggle in which a soldier could die either from the hand of the enemy or from those with whom he served.

On one occasion, a young soldier overdosed on drugs. As the commanding officer, I was told to conduct his memorial service. I still recall the picture of his girlfriend by his bed where we found him. During the memorial, I pledged to stop the use of illegal drugs, stating that those who had given drugs to this young man were certainly not his friends. This was an open and direct affront to those soldiers who were dealing drugs and supplying troops. I became a marked man and received several threats.

Someone informed me that a known drug user by the name of Kidwell was to be given drugs while on duty as bunker guard and would be convinced to kill me during the night. I remember writing a letter home before taking precautionary measures to reinforce my quarters. I placed sandbags under the bed and in the walls of my quarters which I "borrowed" from the area around the commanding officer's headquarters.

Several weeks passed before I was called one evening and informed that Kidwell had shot First Sergeant Howard and was coming for me. Armed with an automatic rifle and my 45-caliber pistol, I proceeded to company headquarters, only to find that Kidwell had been taken into custody and was sitting in my office. I made arrangements for a prompt court martial and was relieved that First Sergeant Howard—a good soldier—had survived.

My insistence on proper procedure and discipline earned me the nickname "Captain America" by some soldiers, and they did not mean it as a compliment. Nevertheless, I had been trained as a soldier to maintain discipline. I knew there was a right way and a wrong way to go about our mission. The right way was not only what I had sworn to do as a military officer; it was also what would keep us alive. It was not necessarily the easy way or the most popular way; it was simply the best way.

I survived the dangers during those months because I maintained a high standard and did not consort with the troops. Every commander has a different approach. Nevertheless, I wanted to prove my ability and willingness to interact with the soldiers in other areas, so I chose boxing. This was an activity that I felt the soldiers could participate in to release their frustration over the change in discipline that they were experiencing under my command.

A boxing ring was constructed, and I took on all challengers. I won all of my fights, but ended up damaging my shoulder by tearing a rotator cuff in my last match. A sense of camaraderie and acceptance seemed to prevail after these competitions.

Of course, my real strength was my dependence on God. A poem, found on the body of a dead soldier, has been in my possession all these years. Entitled, "Since I Met You I'm Not Afraid to Die," it showed this man's dependence on God in the midst of fighting a war. I kept my Bible by my bed and often read its encouraging message, while looking forward to going home!

My unit was returned stateside at the end of the war, and I was assigned to the 716th MP Battalion at Ft. Riley, Kansas, as a battalion staff officer. During this time, I had decided to pursue a career in law. So in 1974, after completion of my military commitment, I resigned my regular Army commission to begin my studies at the University of Alabama School of Law. I moved my mobile home that I had used while stationed at Ft. Riley to Tuscaloosa, Alabama, to serve as my residence during law school.

Compared to the rigorous discipline at West Point or to the dangerous assignment in Vietnam, law school was a welcome relief. Although studies were demanding, I enjoyed the endless debate on legal issues. During my senior year, I worked as an intern with the Etowah County district attorney's office. In the summer months, I also had an opportunity to work for former Congressman Albert Rains, the man who had initially recommended me for West Point.

The Rains law firm in Gadsden gave me my first experience with the practice of law. Hobdy Rains, a senior partner in the firm and nephew of Congressman Rains, was eventually appointed circuit judge of Etowah County, and he later administered my oath of office as Etowah County's first full-time deputy district attorney.

Soon, the lessons I had learned as a farmer, cadet, soldier, and student of law served me well.

3

QUITE A LAWYER?

I was sworn in as Etowah County's first full-time deputy district attorney on October 1, 1977. Proud to be a state prosecutor, I would finally fulfill a goal of mine—the protection of people who had been victimized by those who disregard the laws of society. I began to work vigorously to prosecute those who broke the law.

For months, I successfully convicted murderers, rapists, thieves, and drug pushers. My conviction rate was exceptional, much to the dismay of several leading defense attorneys who had not faced such a degree of opposition before. In five years, I lost only five jury cases out of the hundreds I tried. The district attorney, Bill Rayburn, was a very honorable man and a good prosecutor, but he had been without a full-time deputy to assist him. I was the first.

I enjoyed prosecuting criminal cases, but I was saddened by so many youths who seemed to get into trouble early in life. While prosecution and punishment were necessary, I knew that many of these young people had not been taught biblical principles. During my time as deputy district attorney, I wrote a poem reflecting what I thought was needed in the system. Titled "The Faded Black Book," it was the story of two young boys who were guided away from a life of crime by an elderly man who used direct lessons from the Bible. It read:

Came an old gray-haired man down the road one day,
 Struggling in the hot summer sun.
Two boys, traveling along the way that he went,
 Decided to have some fun.

"Hey, old man," hollered one of the boys,
 "Why are you going so slow?
Move on to the side so we can pass by,
 Then on down the road you may go."

But the old man couldn't move as fast as they did,
 So they grabbed him and shoved him down.
Then one boy said, "Let's take all his money,"
 As the old man got slowly off the ground.

One held the old man as the other one searched;
 Not a place did they fail to look.
Finally one said, "He's got nothing at all,
 Just this little old faded black book."

"That little black book," the old man said,
 "It may be faded and old.
But the things you will find written within,
 Are worth more than silver and gold."

"Shut-up, old man," cried one of the lads,
 As impatient he began to grow.
"All weak and old, with clothes of rags,
 What could you possibly know?"

"Judge not that you be not judged," said he,
 "For I, too, was once young and strong.
But time and age comes the same to all,
 And you'll be here before long.

"Riches and clothes do not a man make,
  Nor in them will you find a friend.
To have a good name is what you should seek,
  For it will last 'til the end.

"Do unto others, the good book says,
  As you would have them do unto you.
If I were you, and you were I,
  Would you still want that to be true?

"Further down the road waits a band of thieves,
  I've been this way before, you see.
But I know of another path we can take,
  And you're welcome to come go with me."

"Why, old man," said one of the boys,
  "This beats all I've ever seen
For you to offer to help us now,
  After we've treated you ugly and mean."

"Even a fool," replied the old man,
  "Learns quickly to love his own kind.
But the man who returns good for evil,
  Is surely much harder to find."

"Well, old man," said one of the youths,
  "I've never really thought of things so.
And if you don't mind we will go your way,
  Perhaps more of this book we should know."[1]

It was around this time that I fashioned a plaque of the Ten Commandments on two redwood tablets. I believed that many of the young criminals whom I had to prosecute would not have committed criminal acts if they had been taught these rules as children.

One of the principles of criminal law is that judgment and punishment must be swift and certain, but that did not seem to be happening in Etowah County. I realized there were inefficiencies in the system that I could help correct. I saw serious problems with so-called "good time" laws. These were statutes intended to reward prisoners by releasing them early for good behavior.

The problem was that there were three different good time laws: one from 1939, another from 1943, and the third from 1976. Each gave a different formula for how much credit for good behavior a prisoner could earn. Instead of using one of these statutes to determine a criminal's release date, judges and district attorneys were using all three. This allowed them to release prisoners who had served only a small portion of their sentences.

One criminal was convicted on three counts of burglary and sentenced to three concurrent five-year terms, but he was released in less than a year. Two months later, he was back in jail for assault with intent to commit murder. Another early-release inmate had tried to stab one inmate and sexually assault another. A week after his release he was arrested for robbery.

In spite of these examples and many others, the State Board of Corrections insisted that the 1976 Incentive Good Time Act—the most liberal of the three laws which allowed a prisoner to reduce his sentence by two days for every day served—was an "exceptionally good program" that the board felt was "protecting the public because most [prisoners] are motivated to do better when they get out early."[2]

My view was that a criminal sentenced to serve time for the crime he had committed should not be released just because he had been "good." After all, criminal acts committed while in prison can be punished by extended sentences. Juries simply did not understand when they deliberated how quickly the defendant might get out. So I publicly criticized the 1976 law as one of the most severe blights on our state's justice system.

In 1979, I compiled statistics showing problems with the Etowah County court system and prepared recommendations on how we could correct them. It was one thing for me to point out a case here and there, or to have a general sense of some systemic problem. But I wanted to show with specific examples a pattern of inefficiency and unfairness that the judges and the district attorney's office could then remedy. I considered this part of my job.

The problems fell into three categories. First, there were delays in considering petitions for "youthful offender status," which a defendant under twenty-one years of age could request. This program offered a second chance to young offenders charged with certain types of crimes and helped them to avoid the stigma of a criminal record. But their prosecution could not proceed until a judge ruled on the youthful offender petition, which usually took more than a year. In the meantime, the offenders were not imprisoned or jailed for their offenses, and many of them were committing more crimes while awaiting an answer to their petitions.

There were numerous examples of defendants charged with grand larceny who, having filed a youthful offender petition, committed a second crime followed by another petition for youthful offender status. One defendant was arrested and charged three times, received youthful offender status all three times, and committed first-degree murder while his three petitions were still pending in court. The murder victim would never have died if the defendant had been behind bars years earlier. As I stated, "Justice delayed is justice denied."[3]

Another problem was the lax way in which Etowah County handled bail bonds. Under the law, defendants who did not appear in court when scheduled forfeited their bail. But the record showed $70,000 in outstanding final forfeitures and $45,000 more in forfeitures not yet declared final. Some attorneys had gotten by with paying only 10 percent of their clients' bonds plus court costs while having everything else discharged. The whole point of setting bail is to make sure the defendant appears in court. When it appeared that the county wasn't serious about collecting that money, defendants had no incentive to appear for court.

A third practice I found to be inefficient involved judges granting multiple continuances in cases. This discouraged state witnesses and also deprived crime victims of a fair and efficient trial. Defense attorneys' requests for delays were routinely granted even as witnesses died or moved away and evidence gradually disappeared. Everyone in the judicial system should work together to make sure justice is swift and sure so the innocent may be vindicated and the guilty may receive their just punishment. The willingness of judges to grant so many continuances undermined these goals.

I had met and befriended a newspaper reporter, M. D. Garmon. In an effort to inform the public and make the system better, I reported my findings to him. On Sunday, December 2, 1979, the headline of Garmon's article in the local newspaper read, "Deputy D.A. Lists Court Problems."[4] Using the same enthusiasm for attacking problems that I had learned in the military, I assumed that everyone would be pleased. But I had forgotten one major difference between civilian and military life—*politics.*

My frankness and enthusiasm didn't generate the groundswell of reform I thought it would. I was rocking the boat, and none of the other passengers seemed happy. I should have known that when you rock the boat you can get tossed overboard by people who don't like the waves. My opponents were looking for an excuse to attack me, and they soon found one.

Etowah County was densely populated. The county sheriff, Roy McDowell, always had his hands full answering calls and protecting the lives and property of the people. I rarely saw a county sheriff's car out in Gallant in those days; the sheriff needed more employees, patrol cars, and equipment. In the summer of 1981, the county budget for the next year came up for review. Because county receipts were down, many departments had to take budget cuts, including the sheriff. The sheriff told me he didn't know how he would be able to run his department and do his duty with the money the county commission had allocated to his department.

To me, public safety was at stake. I believed that if people in county government knew what was happening, they would reallocate the available resources and give our sheriff what he needed to do his job. Since it was the grand jury's job to oversee the law enforcement process in the county, I brought the matter up with them. When I did, I stepped into a hornet's nest.

The Etowah County Commission, chaired by Robert "Booley" Hitt, took my action as a slap in the face and insisted it was not the grand jury's place to criticize the commission's budget. The presiding circuit court judge was even more angry. Not only had I embarrassed the courts with an article about inefficiency; I had now offended the entire county commission.

Of course, that was not my intent or desire. I liked Booley Hitt and was friendly with the commissioners. Looking back on the situation now, I can understand their feelings. My actions were justified but not politically astute.

On October 15, 1981, the presiding judge summoned me to a meeting of the circuit court judges, Commissioner Hitt, and the district attorney. Although it was only an informal gathering, the judge's court reporter was there at his request to take down everything for the record. It seemed the judge was taking it upon himself to decide what would stay in the grand jury record and what would be expunged.

The presiding judge began by insisting that the grand jury had no authority over the county budget, and that by questioning it, they were publicly criticizing Commissioner Hitt. I countered that law enforcement was part of the grand jury's job. The judge asked me if my boss, the district attorney, had approved my actions. I answered that he had been in the room when I made statements to the grand jury. The judge asked if I really thought the grand jury was allowed to criticize the county budget. I said I did. "You're quite a lawyer," he snapped sarcastically.[5]

I explained to him that I never intended any criticism of Commissioner Hitt or any other public official, and that I would do the same thing again. "No, you won't do it again!" the judge interrupted.[6] The judges insisted my remarks were critical and considered expunging them from the record. I countered that, if they did, I would consider taking legal action to let the Court of Criminal Appeals decide the issue.

I then added, "I don't appreciate the fact that you made on the record the statement that I'm not much of a lawyer. And I will tell you how much of a lawyer I am. I'm lawyer enough to stand behind what I say and what I do. And I have done something, and if you feel it incorrect, then as judge, presiding judge or anything else, you take whatever action you will."[7] Those were strong words to a presiding judge, but I had to stand my ground. In essence, I was telling him, "If you think I'm wrong, let's settle this above board, in the light of day, not in a private meeting where you and your colleagues can try to scare me into submission."

The presiding judge was now trying to convince me I had done some-thing wrong. In light of those facts, his next words were a surprise: "I'm letting this thing die now because I think that's best for all purposes."[8]

I responded, "Well, I think that's wrong, judge. I think it's wrong for you to bring me in here and try to intimidate me and tell me I did something wrong and then let it die."[9] He wasn't going to frighten me into doing what he wanted, and he knew he couldn't win this argument in an open forum, so suddenly he was ready to let the thing die.

On October 26, the presiding judge formally requested that the disciplinary commission of the Alabama State Bar Association investigate me for "suspect conduct."[10] A few days later, I received notice from the disciplinary commission that they were investigating a complaint against me. Clearly the local political establishment didn't like some young assistant district attorney looking under rocks and asking hard questions. The judge and the county commission were trying to shut me up.

In his complaint, the judge accused me of going to the grand jury "against the advice of the District Attorney."[11] That was completely untrue. He also insisted that I was criticizing the county commission, which was also untrue. I didn't criticize anybody. I highlighted a problem of concern to the grand jury and to me, as assistant district attorney, because it affected our ability to do our jobs.

On May 7, 1982, the disciplinary commission notified me that the complaint against me had been "dismissed without further action."[12] I had won my first battle with the courts and with those who tried, through intimidation, to keep me from doing my job.

I had learned that battling for a good court system involved fighting against judges, so I decided to level the playing field. After nearly five years as assistant district attorney, and after seeing how the judicial system operated—both good and bad—from the inside out, I decided that the place where I could do the most to change the system for the better was as a circuit court judge. Then, instead of struggling with the judges on the sixteenth judicial circuit bench, I would be one of them, and in a far better position to initiate improvements I thought were needed.

As I explained in my resignation letter to the district attorney, "I have long been disturbed by numerous continuances of criminal trials and repeated grants of probation to criminal defendants. Having served during these past five years in the district attorney's office, I feel that I can better correct such problems as a circuit judge."[13]

On June 22, 1982, I officially launched my campaign for Etowah County circuit judge. I said in my first press release that our court system was not created to serve the interests of a handful of lawyers, and that neither money nor influence should sway the equal application of justice to all people, rich and poor alike. As the campaign went on, I made no secret of the fact that I saw favoritism and cronyism deeply rooted in the legal system and that if I were elected I would deal with it definitively. I would restore the rights of victims and get convicted criminals off the streets.

The lawyers who ran the show in Etowah County took offense at my campaign and saw me as a threat to their usual way of doing business. They lost no time throwing their support behind my opponents. When the county commission, on the advice of the county attorney (a criminal defense lawyer), stopped the raises to my salary prescribed by law, I decided to take legal action. Mr. Rayburn, the district attorney, told me I was right, but that there would be political repercussions for taking such action. He was right!

My opponents began to run newspaper ads claiming I was "suing the taxpayers" because I was greedy and dissatisfied with my salary. Certain criminal defense lawyers wrote defamatory articles about me. But in spite of all the falsehoods they could muster, I was successful in getting into a runoff with another local attorney, Donald Stewart. Each of us received 38 percent of the vote in a three-way race. Donald Stewart is an honorable man for whom I have much respect, and he eventually became a close friend. Although he was not the pick of the defense bar, they were more afraid of me and what I might do.

The third candidate, George White, threw his support behind Stewart, but I still thought I could win if I could only make the voters realize how a handful of lawyers had the entire county justice system in their hip pockets, and how bad that was for the community in general and for each of them individually. But in the September 28 runoff, Stewart won with 57 percent of the vote.

The story in the next day's *Gadsden Times* began, "Former Deputy District Attorney Roy Moore won't break up 'the courthouse crowd,' at least not from the inside out. . . . Moore had courted voters with the promise to 'break up the trend which has allowed lawyers to monopolize the courts and justice system' and courthouse 'cronyism,' but he lost to Stewart's more intense campaign."[14] I was a threat to the system, and the system had closed ranks to defeat me.

My accusations against "the courthouse crowd" once again raised the hackles of the circuit court judges, who accused me of slandering them and expressing contempt for the court system. They were particularly upset by a campaign radio spot that said, "If you are tired of a court system controlled by a certain few lawyers where money and political influence control many decisions . . . elect Roy Moore."

The judges filed another complaint against me with the disciplinary commission. When the commission asked me to comment, I wrote that my observations were an expression of my "basic freedom of speech guaranteed under the Constitution."[15] I also wrote, "If the judges of Etowah County are personally offended, that is their problem, not mine. The guilty flee when no man pursueth."[16]

In a scathing commentary on my letter, the presiding judge led the other judges to complain to the disciplinary commission of my "utter contempt for the legal profession, its institution, its courts," and that my reply to their complaint affirmed my "slander."[17] The judges continued: "Gentlemen, the decision rests with you. If we are to condone this type of puerile behavior, this irresponsibility, this dishonesty—your commission, the Judicial Inquiry Commission, our Code of Professional Responsibility, our Judicial Canons stand for nothing. . . . Locally we will long bear the scars inflicted by Moore's scurrilous campaign."[18]

In February of 1983, the Alabama Bar Disciplinary Commission responded to the accusations against me, concluding, "Mr. Moore's conduct would not warrant discipline under either the Code of Professional Responsibility or the Alabama State Bar or the Alabama Canons of Judicial Ethics," and recommended that no action be taken.[19] In a press release, the judges, in order to save face, now said that their letter to the commission had been an "inquiry," not a complaint, and that they were satisfied with the result. But it had not read like an inquiry to me.

After the election, I successfully won the case regarding my back pay and was also awarded interest on what I had lost. Nevertheless, the tactics of my political opponents had been successful. They had purposefully confused the public into believing that I was greedy and did not care for the taxpayers, and I had lost the election as a result.

Although vindicated on the pay issue, I was forced to fight against an attack on my license to practice law. If the attack had been successful, it would have prevented me from ever again causing "problems" in the court system. My opponents not only wanted to defeat me in an election; they also wanted to prevent me from ever interfering in "their business," that is, the business of the public. The judges' complaint, filed by all former circuit judges and two district court (county) judges, had been referred to the Alabama State Bar by the chief justice of the Alabama Supreme Court, C. C. "Bo" Torbert. The state bar subsequently dismissed all charges against me.

Little did I know that the entire process would be repeated twenty-one years later when I was chief justice of the Supreme Court. I would be taken before another commission, the Judicial Inquiry Commission, and charged with violations of the Canons of Judicial

Ethics for refusing to follow what I knew to be an unlawful court order of a federal district court which had violated the First Amendment's protection of religious freedom.

On December 5, 1982, the title of an article about me in the *Anniston Star* read, "Defeated but not forgotten by his enemies."[20] They should have left me alone after the election. Instead, they continued to pursue me. In doing so they strengthened my resolve to fight.

But how could I continue? I was out of a job, and with all of Etowah County's judges against me, how could I practice law in the county? Gadsden was my home. My family and friends lived here. Although I had successfully defended against all attempts to silence me, it felt like a hollow victory. I had lost the election and my job, and I was tired of fighting.

4

THE FOUNDATION HOLDS

Home for me was sixteen acres of land in Gallant, Alabama, which I had purchased from Lacy Dean Galloway, the deputy sheriff of Marshall County. His family had deep roots in Gallant, and my family had become acquainted with the Galloways when we moved there in 1962. During law school, the aged mobile home I had purchased at Ft. Riley served me well. After graduation, I moved the mobile home to a densely wooded rock bluff several hundred yards from the main road in Gallant.

I wanted something more stable than a mobile home that was almost twenty years old, but I could not afford an architect or builder. I knew that if I were to have a house, I would have to build it myself. Having never built a structure of any kind, however, I knew it would be difficult. Something on which everyone agreed was that a house is only as good as its foundation. So, with pick and shovel in hand, and a heavy sledge hammer for breaking rocks that I could not move, I began a foundation.

I knew well the story of the man in the Bible who built his house "and laid the foundation on a rock: and when the flood arose, the stream beat vehemently upon that house, and could not shake it: for it was founded upon a rock" (Luke 6:48). Of course, I knew Jesus was speaking of a person's life and a moral foundation, but this example applied to a house as well.

My dad had been in construction. My brothers, Jerry and Joey, had more or less followed in his footsteps, so I had some help in getting started. With a little practice, I learned the art of laying concrete blocks. Mixing sand, gravel, and cement in an old wheelbarrow, I poured concrete into blocks to build solid walls. I added the first room to the rear of my mobile home and then a second floor, which became my bedroom.

With no family of my own, I had plenty of free time to work. I purchased material as money became available. Working slowly, without a plan or blueprint, I labored for days, then weeks, and ultimately years. My company during this project was an old German shepherd named Hans. From daylight until dusk I spent every weekend building my new house.

I made plenty of mistakes, including having to dig a sewer line four times before I got it right. Cutting trees and clearing land was hard work, but the most difficult task was moving large rocks with the leverage of iron bars. I had to become somewhat proficient in the skills of brick masonry, carpentry, plumbing, and even electrical wiring. Fortunately, my first cousins, Dennis and Edward Mason, were both accomplished electricians, while my brother and brothers-in-law were there to help with welding, roofing, and framing. We were a close family, with all of my brothers and sisters living next door to one another.

While I served as deputy district attorney, I spent every extra dollar and every spare moment I had on the construction of this house. By 1982, I had four rooms and two large porches added to the mobile home. I later removed the mobile home and salvaged from it what material I could use on the house.

After my unsuccessful campaign for circuit judge in 1982, I could no longer work on my house because of a lack of financial resources. It became a struggle just to earn a meager living doing odd jobs. My practice of law in Etowah County came to an end because of the opposition of the judges, who had pursued disciplinary proceedings against me before the state bar. Although they had been unsuccessful, the resentment remained. I was frustrated and nursed a growing anger for their unfair tactics during the campaign. I am embarrassed to admit that there were times when I could think of nothing but revenge.

Such feelings were not part of my spiritual makeup. I had always been taught to love my enemies, to pray for those who reviled me and persecuted me. As superintendent of the nursery department of the Protestant Sunday school while attending West Point, I had taught these principles to four- and five-year-old children. Now it was time to see if my foundation would hold.

The storms of life had blown fiercely, and the teaching of Jesus had a new meaning for me. Was my life founded on a rock? Or, like the foolish man, had I built on the sand, doomed to fall? A bitter political defeat had broken my spirit, leaving me with nowhere to turn. I had always been successful, but now I had lost my job, my profession, and my direction in life. This was a battle I could not win. I knew that I could not continue this way. I knelt in prayer one evening and asked God to take away the anger I felt for my enemies and to give me the peace that passes all understanding.

God answered my prayer immediately! I can now identify with those who experience a closer relationship with God in the valleys of their lives. From that day forward, I knew forgiveness for my enemies. The hurt remained, but there was a peace within. Although I knew I had been defeated in a political campaign, it was only a temporary setback. I would live to fight another day—but only if God was on my side.

My first priority was to show others that I had not given up in defeat. And just like I had done at West Point, in Germany, and later in Vietnam, I turned to the ring, but this time to the more demanding sport of full-contact karate. This sport—also called kick boxing—is an all-out physical contest that tests a person's physical condition and mental stamina. At the same time it demands that you follow ancient art forms and proper discipline. I wanted to learn from the best, a real master.

I had heard of Ishmael Robles of Galveston, Texas. He had been named world karate champion in his weight classification by one of the major organizations of the Professional Karate Association (PKA). So with only three hundred dollars and a new determination, I set out to find him and learn the art of full-contact fighting.

I found Robles to be a well-educated, polite, and sincere young man who was very skilled in his profession. Ishmael was a college graduate who ran his own private karate school. It was difficult to explain to a complete stranger why a thirty-five-year-old West Point graduate and former deputy district attorney had traveled from Alabama to Texas to learn full-contact fighting. But in spite of their early reservations about me, I became close friends with Ishmael's entire family.

For over nine months I trained as I had never trained before. I got a job supervising the maintenance and construction of various condominiums damaged by Hurricane Alicia, which had devastated the coastline of Texas. I devoted every free minute to running, physical exercise, and sparring. I wanted to return to Gadsden and fight in the Greater Gadsden Tournament of Champions. After approximately nine months of hard physical training, I did return. On February 25, 1984, I fought my first big fight against an experienced second-degree black belt—and I won!

It was a symbolic victory and one I needed. It was a physical contest, not a political competition. This time the result was not a bitter defeat but an unquestioned victory. In the ring, money and talk did not control the outcome. Truth prevailed. Mentally and physically I was refreshed, restored, and ready to fight again. But more importantly, God had taken the bitterness and anger from me and had given me a new resolve. Still, I had no direction.

In Vietnam, after a stressful tour in a combat zone, soldiers were given an opportunity to take "R & R" (rest and relaxation) in a friendly country like Thailand or Australia. I had looked forward to going to Australia but was denied the opportunity because of the early withdrawal of several combat units, including the 188th MP Company which I commanded. I now needed some "R & R," so I decided to take the trip I had missed.

I had saved some money from my job in Texas that I used to travel to Sydney, Australia, and then went north to the city of Brisbane where I lived with the family of friends from back home. After a short stay in Brisbane, I traveled further north to Ayr, where I lived for two weeks on sugar cane farms. From there I moved on to Cairns (pronounced *Kans*), a fishing village near the famous Great Barrier Reef.

I was thrilled to scuba dive off St. Crispin's Reef and view a beautiful assortment of marine life, including coral shell fish, star fish, and an occasional shark. St. Crispin's Reef is one of the best-known portions of the Great Barrier Reef and a place where great white sharks live.

But my real desire was to work in the Australian Outback. So after a few weeks I left the coastal area and traveled westward through Rockhampton to Emerald in Queensland. With little money left, I found myself sitting in a small restaurant without a place to spend the night. As if by the hand of providence, I became engaged in a conversation with a cattle rancher, Colin Rolfe. Our mutual interest in poetry led to an invitation from him to visit his "small" property (57,000 acres), which indeed was small in Australia.

I accepted and found myself living with the Rolfe family. Colin and his wife Cleone had several children. They were wonderful hosts and devout Christians who read the Bible to one another before bedtime. For months I worked "mustering beasts" (rounding up cattle) and branding and inoculating cattle. The terrain was dry and rough, with plenty of koala bears, kangaroos, iguana, and even deadly brown snakes.

Building stockyards and holding areas for cattle was hard work, but the most difficult task was "rock picking"—gathering stones by hand from the fields. For six days a week we labored, but the seventh was a day of rest.

Colin was a man of great faith who helped restore my confidence and determination to do God's will. He was preparing to become an Anglican deacon when he contracted stomach cancer shortly before I left Australia. He died soon after that, but I will never forget the man whom God placed in my path that day in Emerald when I thought I had reached the end of my journey.

The land "down under" was a wonderful experience, but I knew it was time to return home to resume my chosen profession. Those unforgettable months in the Australian Outback were a blessing, and they gave me a new perspective. I grew in faith and confidence, knowing that God was leading me—but little did I know where.

I returned to Gadsden determined that nothing would stop me from practicing law. When I returned, I approached the judges of Etowah County with respect, but with firm resolve to continue the practice of law in my hometown. I made it clear that I would not dwell on past differences. I was pleased to find that the judges had also mellowed and were not given to holding grudges. Even the presiding judge with whom I had clashed was polite, kind, and even helpful.

My younger sister Toni had been working for an attorney, Myron Allenstein. I had known him casually while I was a prosecutor. I had a high regard for his ability and character, and he and his wife Gloria were both wonderful Christian people. Myron agreed to let me open a law office at his location on Ninth Street in Gadsden. So the week after Thanksgiving in 1984, I opened my first law office, and my sister became my first legal secretary. She proved to be quite efficient, and we soon became busy with wills, deeds, domestic issues, and, occasionally, criminal defense cases.

It was difficult at first because all of my experience had been as a criminal prosecutor, and I had a limited knowledge of civil practice. But with help from a few attorneys and the workers in a friendly clerk's office, I soon established a thriving practice. I was excited to be back in Gadsden working again in the legal profession. I discovered my house was just as I had left it nearly two years before. My foundation had withstood the storms, and so had I.

5

PROVIDENTIAL DESIGN

It was the week before Christmas in 1984, a slow time for legal work in Etowah County. People were more interested in shopping than going to court. Myron and Gloria Allenstein had become my good friends. They had asked me to attend a church Christmas party at the home of one of the members of Emmanuel Lutheran Church, where they attended, and to recite some of the Christmas poems I had written.

Christmas is a joyous time, but sometimes it is filled with sadness as we reflect on loved ones who have passed away. My father died shortly before Christmas in 1967 during my junior year at West Point. The academy was a lonely place anyway, but for me—a young man separated from my family by more than a thousand miles—it became nearly unbearable when my dad died unexpectedly.

My father had literally worked himself to death trying to provide for his family. He did not own much, but he always shared the little he had with anyone in need. I had written a poem about him entitled "The Stranger." This poem had a special significance and had received a lot of attention in the Gadsden area. Several radio stations had broadcast it during the Christmas season.

THE STRANGER
The old man was alone by the fire that night;
    His wife and his kids were in bed.

Christmas was near, but he was out of a job
    And could barely keep his family fed.

It was snowing outside and cold in the room,
    Because he had little wood left to burn.
This would be a sad Christmas with cupboards so bare,
    For he had run out of places to turn.

In the firelight dim, he folded his hands,
    And knelt by an old chair to pray.
"Dear Lord," he said, as a tear he shed,
    "I don't know just what I should say."

Then came a knock on the door; he could pray no more;
    'Twas a young man in the shivering night.
His coat was old and his shoes were worn;
    He was really quite a pitiful sight.

"I've been walking all night," the young man said,
    "And my home is still far away.
If I may warm by your fire for a while,
    Only a minute will I stay."

The old man threw a log on the fire,
    And made him a bite to eat.
"You're very kind, sir," said the young lad,
    As the old man gave him his seat.

"Where are you bound on this cold winter night,
    Dressed so ragged and bare?"
"I'm headed home," replied the young man,
    "My father waits for me there.

"I wouldn't care about this ragged old coat,
    If only his face I could see.

When I get home, I'll have all I need,
    For there with my father I'll be."

He then went to leave, so the old man got up,
    And brought out the only coat that he had.
"Here, take my coat," he said with a smile,
    "For the weather is exceptionally bad."

The lad said good-bye before the old man could ask,
    For he wanted his name to know.
But when he looked out the door, the stranger had vanished,
    And not a trace could be found in the snow.

But there in the yard was a new stack of wood,
    Higher than a man could build.
And when he looked in the kitchen, he couldn't believe
    That all the cupboards were filled.

The chair in which the stranger had sat,
    Was now one made of pure gold.
On the back of the chair, a note was hung,
    And this is the message it told.

"My Father and yours are one and the same,
    You've been a good brother to me.
What a man sows, so shall he reap,
    And thus, it shall always be.

"When I knocked on the door, you opened it to me,
    And gave me what you needed too.
As you have done for a stranger in need,
    So shall it be done unto you."[1]

When Myron Allenstein asked me to recite a poem, I chose this
one about my father at Christmas because I knew it well, having

recited it many times before. But this occasion was different. Sitting with her mother on the sofa against the wall was a beautiful young woman. I learned that her name was Kayla. She was the daughter of Mack and Della Kisor, from Southside, Alabama.

Many years before, I had attended a dance recital at Gadsden State Junior College. I remembered one of the special dances performed by a young woman whose first and last names began with the letter "K." It was something I had never forgotten. Could that young woman have been Kayla Kisor? Anxious to meet her, I began with the line, "Haven't we met somewhere before?"

"I don't think so," she replied.

Soon after that, I was called on to recite my poem, several portions of which I forgot during the recitation. I knew Kayla was going to be a special person in my life. Long afterward, I would learn that Kayla had, in fact, performed a special dance routine at Gadsden State years before.

I was determined to get to know her, but Kayla, divorced and with a beautiful little girl, Heather, who was nearly a year old, was not interested in a relationship with anyone. She had worked as a model and with her father in the restaurant business after graduation from Southside High School. She had attended college at the University of Alabama, which I also had attended as a law student years before.

Early in the new year, Kayla came to see Mr. Allenstein about legal business for her dad. Myron just happened to be away on business, and I was the only attorney available. And I was very available! We began to date soon after that. After about a year we became engaged and were married on December 14, 1985. My partially finished house became our home as we began our new life together.

Because I had never needed a kitchen, Kayla had to adjust to an electric skillet in a washroom for cooking. It was a couple of years before I finally added a kitchen, but Kayla did a remarkable job transforming my cold, uninviting house into a warm, comfortable home. She even added curtains over the solid wooden shutters I had used as windows.

During my years as a bachelor, I built much of my furniture. With the help of Milford Smith, a farmer down the road who owned a lathe, I fashioned a poster bed, an eight-foot dining table, and several lamps—all of which I still own today. Kayla never complained about such rustic furniture, but she soon added more elegant pieces of her own choosing.

But we definitely agreed on one thing: We would continue to display in our home the Ten Commandments plaque I had made by hand in 1980.

Fifteen years had passed since I had first observed a simple metal-covered wooden plaque containing the Ten Commandments in my mother's home. My first thought was, *I could make one better.* I knew that God's law was something to be revered and that a more fitting display was within my ability. From two pieces of redwood I formed two wooden tablets of the law. The words were taken from Exodus 20 and were written in calligraphy on a paper overlay by an attorney at my request. I then traced the words on to the wood and used a wood-burning set to burn the words permanently into the plaque. With the aid of an accomplished artist and friend, Leo Reynolds of Gadsden, I sketched on the back of one of the plaques a scene of Moses descending Mt. Sinai, and the words "The Law" on the back of the other plaque.

Kayla and I decided at the beginning of our marriage that if we were going to have a family, there could be no better guide than the Ten Commandments. I had worked hard to build a house on a firm foundation that would withstand the fiercest storms. I could do no less in the lives of my children. Today we have many different displays of the Ten Commandments throughout our home. Our children are taught not only the letter but the spirit of the law. And I eventually came to understand how the Ten Commandments are not only a personal guide to living, but the moral foundation of our nation's law and justice system.

The same year I was busy creating the carved plaque of the Ten Commandments, the United States Supreme Court was busy taking them off the wall of a Kentucky schoolhouse. The court in *Stone v. Graham*[2] stated:

> The Ten Commandments are undeniably a sacred text in the Jewish and Christian faith, and no legislative recitation of a supposed secular purpose can blind us to that fact. . . . If the posted copies of the Ten Commandments are to have any effect at all, it will be to induce the school children to read, meditate upon, perhaps to venerate and obey, the Commandments. However desirable this might be as a matter of private devotion, it is not a permissible state objective under the Establishment Clause.

How could the Supreme Court of the United States draw such a ridiculous conclusion? Surely judges and justices should regard laws against killing, adultery, stealing, lying, and disregard of parental authority as desirable rules. And certainly a callous disregard of God's law today has fostered an atmosphere in which murder, rape, robbery, and all forms of disobedience of authority are more commonplace in our public schools than they were in 1980.

The Ten Commandments are not only a sacred text in the Jewish and Christian faiths, as the Supreme Court stated in *Stone v. Graham*. They are God's revealed, divine law and the basis on which our morality depends. The commandments are divided into two tables: the first table consists of the first four commandments. These prescribe the duties we owe to God. The second table lists the remaining six commandments. These comprise the duties we owe to one another.[3] The second table encompasses our virtue or morality. "Hence we often speak of religion and virtue, as different branches of one system, or the duties of the first and second tables of the law."[4]

In the Farewell Address, George Washington, at the conclusion of his second term as our nation's first president, reminded the people that virtue or morality is important to the welfare of our nation, and that attempts to destroy or take lightly this foundation of popular government would be detrimental to the country. He stated, "'Tis substantially true that virtue or morality is a necessary spring of popular government. . . . Who that is a sincere friend to it can look with indifference upon attempts to shake the foundation of the fabric? Promote, then, as an object of primary importance, institutions for the general diffusion of knowledge."[5]

President Washington implied that our institutions of learning (schools) should promote the teaching of virtue or morality. Where can that virtue be found? In God's law, the Ten Commandments!

The knowledge of God was essential to promoting morality in government. Our first Congress certainly must have believed this, as the Northwest Ordinance indicates. The Northwest Ordinance was the governing document of the new territories of the United States northwest of the Ohio River in the late eighteenth century. This ordinance was first adopted on July 13, 1787, prior to the adopting of the Constitution, and the ordinance was reenacted after the ratification of the Constitution on July 21, 1789. The same day the Congress approved the wording of the Establishment Clause of the First Amendment.[6] Article III of the Northwest Ordinance stated, "Religion, morality, and knowledge being necessary to good government and the happiness of mankind, *schools* and the means of education shall forever be encouraged."[7]

What President Washington and our other founding fathers believed we should never disregard, the United States Supreme Court explicitly rejected in *Stone v. Graham* in 1980. In his first inaugural address, Washington observed that "we ought to be no less persuaded that the propitious smiles of Heaven can never be expected on a nation that disregards the eternal rules of order and right which Heaven itself has ordained."[8] Today, the foundation of the fabric has been shaken as we have discarded those eternal rules of order and right.

But what about the first table of the law? Can we legally recognize a particular God above all other gods? Historically, we certainly did! In the Declaration of Independence, we appealed to the "Supreme Judge of the World for the rectitude of our intentions" in declaring that we were free from English rule. In his *Second Treatise of Civil Government*, written in 1689, John Locke, who influenced the writers of the declaration, including Jefferson, discussed the biblical leader Jephthah, who appealed to the same Supreme Judge as described in Judges 11:30–36.[9] Thus, it was no coincidence that this reference resurfaced in the founding charter of our nation.

When and how did our courts and our law begin to "shake the foundation of the fabric"? On February 10, 1947, the United States Supreme Court announced its decision in the case of *Everson v. Board of Education*.[10] On the surface, this was simply a case about taxpayer-funded busing of children to a parochial school in New Jersey, which the court allowed. But very few people understood at the time that *Everson* marked the first time the high court had applied the establishment clause of the First Amendment to one of the states in addressing a religious question.

Strangely enough, it was Hugo Black, an associate justice from Alabama, who authored the *Everson* opinion, stating that "the First Amendment has erected a wall between church and state. That wall must be kept high and impregnable. We could not approve the slightest breach."[11] Those simple words inaugurated half a century of misguided jurisprudence in which a recognition of God was confused with "religion" and "the separation of church and state" separated God and government.

A new vocabulary had been created. A seemingly innocent expression was introduced not only into Supreme Court jurisprudence but also into the public arena. During this time, "wall of separation" came to overshadow the very purpose and text of the First Amendment, misleading the American people and the Christian church into believing that the public acknowledgment of God was contrary to law and to scriptural doctrine.

I was born on February 11, 1947, the day after the *Everson* decision was handed down. I could never have known then that more than fifty years later my life would become intertwined with that infamous phrase, and that I would be accused of violating that "historic" doctrine by acknowledging the God upon whom our nation was founded. Nor could I have imagined that I would ultimately be elected as the chief justice of the Alabama Supreme Court, only to be removed for refusing to deny the God and those laws upon which our morality is based.

During my childhood, *Everson* had little effect on the public recognition of God. We had prayer and Bible reading in school, and there was no prohibition against displaying the Ten Commandments in classrooms. Religious symbols of our faith abounded. When I was only seven years old, President Dwight D. Eisenhower, a fellow graduate of the United States Military Academy, and supreme Allied commander during World War II, together with the United States Congress, put the words "under God" in the Pledge of Allegiance. On June 14, 1954, President Eisenhower declared:

> From this day forward, the millions of our school children will daily proclaim in every city and town, every village and rural schoolhouse, the dedication of our nation and our

people to the Almighty. To anyone who truly loves America, nothing could be more inspiring than to contemplate this rededication of our youth, on each school morning to our country's true meaning. . . . In this way we are reaffirming the transcendence of religious faith in America's heritage and future; in this way we shall constantly strengthen those spiritual weapons which forever will be our country's most powerful resource, in peace or in war.[12]

On the same date as President Eisenhower's remarks, Mr. Burke in the Senate record said, "We see the pledge, as it now stands, as a formal declaration of our duty to serve God and our firm reliance, now as in 1776, on the protection of divine providence."[13]

But soon after that, *Everson* and the Supreme Court's misconstrued concept of separation of church and state began to take its toll. In 1962, Hugo Black authored another opinion in *Engel v. Vitale*,[14] which declared a simple twenty-two-word prayer unconstitutional because it acknowledged God. That prayer simply implored: "Almighty God, we acknowledge our dependence upon Thee and we beg Thy blessings upon us, our parents, our teachers, and our Country."[15] In 1963, *Abington v. Schempp*[16] eliminated Bible reading from public schools. By 1985, an Alabama legislative enactment allowing a moment of silence "or voluntary prayer" was declared unconstitutional by the Supreme Court, thereby prohibiting the concept that there existed a God whom people could worship voluntarily, even in silence.[17]

By 1986, I had decided to again run for political office in order to do what I could to preserve our moral heritage. Prosecution of the criminal laws seemed like a good way to do that. The local district attorney, Bill Rayburn, was retiring after twenty-four years. I was well qualified for the office, having served for five years as a full-time prosecutor. But the Etowah County political system had not yet recovered from my previous campaign. The criminal defense bar united against me, and the opposition among political insiders was too strong to overcome.

On the night of the primary election, the polls reported the results, which declared my opponent to be the winner. I was again thwarted in my attempt to attain public office, but this time I was not alone. I had a darling wife and a little girl, and I still had a thriving law practice. The sting of defeat was short-lived and caused me to believe that political office was not my calling. I could no longer identify with the Democratic Party, as a liberal trend had developed among Democrats in the South, and special interests seemed to control their decisions. The South had been solidly Democratic since the end of Reconstruction, but things were beginning to change.

Guy Hunt was elected governor of Alabama in 1986, becoming the first Republican to hold the office since 1872. In 1987, I switched my affiliation to the Republican Party, for no other reason than to give those who believed as I did another choice. I was certain that I had no future in politics, and I was making a statement to the people of Etowah County.

The race for district attorney of Etowah County marked the end of my political aspirations. It seemed that God had other plans for my life. The next five years were perhaps the most enjoyable of my life. My law practice became very successful and financially rewarding, and I enjoyed helping others with their legal problems. I even had the opportunity to defend my fellow attorney, Myron Allenstein, against a charge of legal malpractice. After a four-day trial in federal court, the jury concluded that Myron had done nothing wrong and rendered a verdict in his favor. He was elated, and I was happy that I could repay him for his kindness.

I won many other cases, both civil and criminal. In October of 1992, I was successful in helping an older black couple who stood by

and watched their house burn to the ground while the city water supply could provide only a trickle of water because of low pressure. The
owners were devastated as they saw everything they owned go up in
flames. They had initially hired Birmingham attorneys as their legal
counsel. These attorneys eventually dropped their case, saying they did
not have a claim.

I went to work on their behalf. After diligent investigation I found
that irregular inspections and improper records should have led officials of the city fire department to discover deficits in the water supply
which, if corrected, could have saved the home. The trial in federal
court lasted several days and resulted in a verdict of $100,000. The
money was secondary to the hope and joy I saw in the wife's eyes when
she realized the future was looking brighter.

During this time my family increased with the birth of my first son
on July 10, 1987. We named him Roy Baxter (Ory), after my father.
Soon after that, Caleb Elisha was born on September 25, 1990. We
named him after the biblical Caleb, who was rewarded by the Lord for
his faith and boldness in the face of adversity, and Elisha, a mighty
prophet of God. I hoped that my sons would live up to their names.

Kayla and I were very happy, and we knew that God had blessed our
lives. I had even acquired a bigger office and began to practice with
Kathleen Warren, an excellent attorney and someone with whom I
worked well. Together we hired a young lady, Delbra Adams, as our legal
secretary. Delbra remained my secretary for the next thirteen years.

I was in my office one warm September day in 1992 when I was
notified of the untimely death of the presiding judge in our county. The
judge had become a good friend. In spite of our differences ten years
before, he treated me very fairly and especially so in the last jury trial
he had presided over before his death.

Two of my close friends, State Senator Roy Smith and Mr. George
Hundley, approached me and asked me to consider an appointment to

the vacant judgeship, but the prospect of becoming a judge seemed frightening. On two occasions I had put all my efforts into a campaign and had fallen short, and after devastating losses I had been blessed beyond measure. If it was not the will of God that I become a circuit judge, I feared the consequences.

Still, I was intrigued with the prospect. Two well-known and qualified attorneys began to vie for the appointment. Both had high-level connections to the state capitol in Montgomery. I had never met Governor Hunt, so receiving the appointment seemed impossible. I decided that the only thing I could do was to pray that God's will would be done. I asked for no letters of recommendation to the governor and sought no inside influence. I was satisfied that Senator Smith had recommended me and Mr. Hundley was there to give me encouragement.

A week went by, then two, then three. After a month, all of us began to be more anxious. Rumors began to surface that appointment would go to Jim Wilson, then it was Alice Pruett, then Jim again. Finally, I was told that a group was planning a party for the new judge. I concluded that it would not be me. Even so, I was curious. After a few days I called my friend, George Hundley, to see if he would contact Governor Hunt to end the suspense. But neither he nor Senator Smith could get through to the governor's office.

My neighbor's father, John Gibbs, had been a friend of Governor Hunt for many years. I went to see Gibbs to request that he make contact with the governor, but even he found the channels of communication closed. Then God intervened. During a trip to the Cullman stockyards, Gibbs ran across Governor Hunt. During a brief conversation, he was able to discuss my qualifications with the governor. But there was still no word on the appointment.

There was nothing to do but wait. I had finally made some effort to obtain the appointment, but I felt that it was too little, too late. Still, whatever happened would be God's will, and I would be satisfied.

6

THE BATTLE BEGINS

I was honored to be invited to the Veteran's Day Program at Emma Sansom High School in November of 1992 and to sit with the veterans of World War II and Korea who were to be recognized for their service in the military. Having served my country as a captain and company commander of a military police unit in Da Nang, South Vietnam, I was proud to return to the school that I had attended in the ninth grade.

As I sat there in the auditorium that day, the flags displayed around the gym along with the patriotic music caused my mind to reflect on the past thirty years. I had accomplished much, from West Point, to military service in Germany and Vietnam, then on to law school and becoming a lawyer. After working five years as a deputy district attorney and eight in private practice, I had now been married for six years and had three small children: Heather, Roy, and Caleb. But this day would mark a new chapter in my life.

About halfway through the program, I was summoned to a side door where I received news that I had just been appointed circuit judge of Etowah County by Governor Guy Hunt. I was elated and could not wait to tell Kayla. I knew that God had finally given me direction. I had prayed fervently not to be appointed unless it was the will of God. The impossible had happened! God had given me something that I had not been able to obtain through my own efforts many years before.

Within a few days I entered my new courtroom. After the presiding judge's untimely death, the judges of Etowah County had exchanged offices, leaving me the smallest courtroom available. I had tried many cases in that courtroom. Kayla had even attended a jury trial there as a spectator in 1985 when I tried one of my first civil trials before the presiding judge after my return to practice. I hadn't realized how dilapidated it had become over the years. The furnishings were worn, ceiling tiles were missing, counsel tables were stained and chipped, and even the American flag had only forty-eight stars. Nevertheless, I was determined to decorate this courtroom better than all the others.

First, a good cleaning was in order. With mops, brooms, cloths, and cleaning supplies in hand, my secretary Delbra, my court reporter Larry Cross, and I began the process. Delbra had now been my secretary for nearly eight years while I was in private practice, and she had done an exceptional job. She was loyal, innovative, and efficient. I knew she would be an excellent contribution to the court system. After serving with the previous judge for many years, Larry Cross also proved to be a very devoted assistant. Kayla, too, helped with cleaning and decorating my new courtroom. After an initial cleaning, we installed new carpet and repaired the furniture. Next came the decorations.

The courtroom was small, having only one window, a plain judge's bench, two tables for attorneys, juror chairs, and several rows of benches for spectators. With a low ceiling adorned with buzzing fluorescent lights, it presented a solemn appearance—as well it should. I thought that pictures of presidents and judicial scenes would add a sense of dignity. After all, the only portrait in the courtroom was that of Judge Hobdy Rains, a good friend and honorable judge who seemed to be casting a watchful eye over my proceedings.

I began by obtaining a great seal of Alabama, and a new flag from the administrative office of courts. A friend gave me a brass eagle for the window and a small set of the scales of justice. I used these to decorate the bookshelves behind my bench. Another friend furnished a gavel for my desk.

But finding portraits of sufficient size and quality for a courtroom was difficult. One day as I was standing in the dining room of my home, the Ten Commandments plaque I had made twelve years before caught my eye. Through the years, I had displayed that plaque in my home and in my office. I was proud of the only wood burning I had ever done. It was not elaborate, but it represented the moral foundation of the law I was sworn to uphold.

My first thought was that the plaque would be perfect behind my chair to reflect my belief in the Supreme Lawgiver of the universe. The plaque seemed to be the answer to my quest for something fitting on the wall behind my bench. But surely attorneys would object to such a "religious" display. If I was sued and forced to remove such a display, I knew there would be both political and spiritual consequences. On the other hand, I reasoned, what a hypocrite I would be if I failed to acknowledge the God who was responsible for my new job. The choice was not difficult: I would display God's law.

Later I also obtained prints of Washington and Lincoln for my courtroom walls, as well as a print of the Declaration of Independence and a copy of the Magna Charta. These completed my effort to decorate that small courtroom. But the Ten Commandments hung alone on the wall behind my bench. The display of God's law was not done to make any bold statement, to intimidate or offend anyone, or to push any particular religion. It was simply a reminder that this country was established on a particular God and His divine, revealed laws; it reflected the Christian faith of our founders.

But something more was at stake. The Ten Commandments represented the moral law on which the statutory law I was required to apply was predicated. "Thou shall not kill," "thou shall not steal," "thou shall not bear false witness," and "honor thy father and thy mother" formed the moral basis of Alabama law and American law in general.

Not long after my appointment I began work on the caseload, which had grown tremendously since the presiding judge's death. Murders, robberies, rapes, assaults, as well as civil and domestic matters overwhelmed me at the beginning. One thing was immediately apparent: People were losing touch with their moral foundation. Years of teaching evolution in school had caused our youth to forget that they were created by God with a purpose for life. The failure to recognize this simple principle had resulted in an escalating breakdown of our morality.

One case that demonstrated these moral problems was the murder of a drug addict, Joseph Lee Sims. Twin brothers who worked in Atlanta as male strippers were accused of shooting Sims in the head when he tried to panhandle two dollars from them. Known as "Silk" and "Satin"—their professional names—the defendants pled "not guilty," claiming that Sims had pulled a pistol and that it had accidentally fired when they tried to take it from him.

The assistant district attorney, Keith Pitts, who would later run against me for the office of circuit judge, was the prosecutor. Pitts argued to the jury that Sims was not on trial and should not be judged by the fact that he was drinking and using cocaine when he died. The defense countered that it would likewise be improper to convict the two defendants simply because of their moral beliefs—because they were strippers from Atlanta. Both attorneys were correct. The law should be administered impartially without regard to a person's background or religious beliefs.

In our justice system, defendants are to be judged on what they have done, not on their lifestyles, habits, or opinions. How persons view God and their relationships to Him are irrelevant to the court; therefore, Jews, Christians, or atheists stand on equal footing before the court. In his "Bill for Establishing Religious Freedom," Thomas Jefferson recognized this basic principle when he stated that "all attempts to influence [the mind] by temporal punishments, or burthens, or by civil incapacitations, tend only to beget habits of hypocrisy and meanness."[1] What a person believes with respect to God is a matter between him and God. Because it is God's business, man must not interfere. The duties we owe to God under the first table of the law (the first four commandments) are simply outside the realm of government control.

The Constitution of Alabama recognizes that our justice system is established "invoking the favor and guidance of Almighty God."[2] Religious liberty is therefore a principle that applies even to our court system.

The defendants in the Sims case were acquitted. Their attorney objected to the Ten Commandments displayed behind my bench. But even the charge to the jury reflected those principles explicitly and implicitly contained in the Ten Commandments—that murder was a criminal act, but that defendants are tried for what they have done, not for what they think or believe. In retrospect, counsel for the defendants never should have objected to the principles underlying our nation's law.

One of the more serious cases I handled during my eight years on the bench involved a woman who had drowned her own daughter in a bathtub. Seated between the mother's legs with her face looking up toward her mother, the little girl was held under water until she died. Only two years old, the little girl was the product of a failed marriage and a custody situation that had ended in tragedy. The mother had taken the life of her own daughter to prevent the father from taking custody. The little girl's last words, according to her mother's confession, were, "Don't cry, Mama. I love you." How our society has deteriorated!

During my first year on the bench, I was determined to improve the local judicial system so trials could be conducted quicker and delays could be eliminated. Because no Republican had been elected as a judge in Etowah County during the twentieth century, some attorneys were sure that I would be defeated in the next general election, so they resisted my reform efforts.

One of my first jobs was to select a bailiff of court, and I chose George Hundley, a man for whom I had great admiration. His professional demeanor was instrumental in maintaining an orderly court. George never flinched in the face of criticism or ridicule by those who tried to undermine my efforts at reform. As a longtime political observer, he knew that any weakness was a political liability, and he was a model of strength.

One of the problems I encountered in court was that defendants were not accustomed to appearing for docket calls or pretrial conferences. Attorneys routinely continued cases for frivolous reasons. I began to require the appearance of defendants in criminal cases that facilitated plea negotiations between the district attorney and attorneys for the defense. Likewise, in civil cases, I required *all parties* to be present, with the result that settlements were sometimes reached more frequently. These efforts greatly reduced pending caseloads. Despite complaints by attorneys, issues were resolved more expeditiously and to the satisfaction of the public.

I encouraged, as well as ordered, parties to participate in mediation at non-binding conferences before an impartial mediator. This helped reduce civil caseloads. It also reduced costs for subpoenas and court appearances. At the end of my term of office, I had the lowest pending caseloads in all areas of court business within the Sixteenth Judicial Circuit.

Another area of that which had been neglected was the collection of court costs and fines. Upon sentencing, I required scheduled appearances of criminal defendants who were fined or required to pay restitution to victims. This ensured that whatever they owed was promptly paid. This was also something new, but it proved effective in collecting outstanding court costs, fines, and restitution. As other judges saw the benefits, they also began to implement similar procedures.

From the very beginning of my time on the bench, I fell under the watchful eye of the American Civil Liberties Union. On June 9, 1993, Joel Sogol, a Tuscaloosa-based attorney and a member of the ACLU, wrote to the chief justice of Alabama, Sonny Hornsby, threatening suit against anyone who continued to pray in court.[3] Of course, opening the initial jury session with prayer had been a custom long before I arrived on the scene. But because I displayed the Ten Commandments, I became doubly offensive to the ACLU.

A local attorney with the ACLU even deposited on my desk a recent case entitled *Harvey v. Cobb County*,[4] which involved the removal of a Ten Commandments display from a Georgia courthouse. This was the first time the ACLU attempted to intimidate me. But I continued to maintain the display, and I also continued to open court with prayer. I would not be a party to changing this long-standing practice. In fact, the overwhelming majority of people in Etowah County voiced their agreement with this practice.

Less than six months after I was sworn into office, I received a call from a local ACLU attorney asking if I would allow a court reporter hired by the ACLU to attend and record the opening prayer before my court. I gave my permission. On June 20, 1994, the ACLU was there and so was the press. The ACLU began to threaten a lawsuit unless such practices were stopped. Those in the general public who supported my action responded with letters and editorials in the local paper.

Despite all of the positive improvements I had made in the local judicial system, the overriding controversy about the Ten Commandments display in my courtroom monopolized the media. I began speaking to civic clubs, schools, churches, and business organizations about the importance of God's law to our society. The more I studied, the more I learned about the intimate relationship between history, law, and God. I wanted to share that knowledge with others.

I obtained a large display of the Declaration of Independence and placed it on the wall above the jury. As I contemplated its words, I thought about how it plainly contradicted what I had been taught about the First Amendment, especially in law school. How could the Declaration of Independence, an "organic" law of our nation according to the present United States Code Annotated—a compilation of the laws of the United States—declare God to be the Author of our rights and Creator of all mankind, while the acknowledgment of God is considered a violation of the First Amendment, according to judges and lawyers?

Thomas Jefferson stated in the very first sentence of the Declaration of Independence that America is entitled to exist as a power on earth because of the "Laws of Nature and of Nature's God." As John Quincy Adams, the sixth president of the United States, later explained, "'The laws of nature and nature's God' . . . of course presupposes the existence of God, the moral ruler of the universe, and a rule of right and wrong, of just and unjust, binding upon man, preceding all institutions of human society and of government."[5] Jefferson and John Quincy Adams agreed that God's law formed the basis for America's law and government. Jefferson went on to say in the Declaration that it was self-evident that God was our Creator, and the grantor of rights such as "life, liberty, and the pursuit of happiness," and that the only role of government was to secure those rights for us. A government that did not effectively secure those rights was to be abolished.

More than 150 years before the Declaration of Independence, our Pilgrim fathers wrote the Mayflower Compact before they landed at Plymouth harbor. In that compact, the Pilgrims declared that their purpose in coming to this new land was for the "glory of God and the advancement of the Christian faith."[6] And when they reached shore, their first act was to thank God.

> Being thus arrived in a good harbor, and brought safe to land, they fell upon their knees and blessed the God of Heaven who had brought them over the vast and furious ocean, and delivered them from all the perils and miseries thereof, again to rest their feet on the firm and stable earth, their proper element.[7]

Someone has said that our future is certain; the only thing that changes is our past. There certainly are many people who have tried to change our past. Textbooks for our children have been rewritten to state that the Pilgrims and the Puritan fathers came to America to get away from religion. While they never wanted government to tell them how they should worship God, they certainly were not running from God. Their acknowledgment of God was the reason why they came. And when they gave thanks at the first Thanksgiving, it was not to the Indians who had befriended them, as some in our educational system would have us believe. Thanks was given to Almighty God who had provided for them. Their faith sustained them and gave them purpose in life.

Losing that purpose in life will lead people to become like "Silk" and "Satin" or Joseph Lee Sims. Then drugs, sex, and criminal activity will become commonplace. Without God as the foundation, *good* and *evil* become relativistic, meaningless terms. Children who are taught evolution are, in essence, being taught that there is no Creator God who designed them for service to Him and to one another.

As a circuit judge, I saw firsthand that our criminal justice system would continue to be filled with defendants without direction in their lives unless we returned to God's truth. This is not a matter of religion, or faith, but of reality. Every parent understands that it matters what children are taught. As a society, how have we failed to realize that truth? More importantly, why have we turned our back on the truth about God?

By the summer of 1994, I was campaigning for election to the office to which I had been appointed. The ACLU had not yet filed a suit against me, calculating that if I were not elected the controversy would be resolved. I knew the campaign would be a battle, and that certainly turned out to be the case. Keith Pitts was a worthy opponent. His family was well known in the community, and his wife served as tax assessor for Etowah County. I was honored to have been appointed circuit judge. But without a mandate from the people, something was missing.

When the race for circuit judge began, the ACLU had already made an issue of prayer in court and the display of the Ten Commandments. It was an issue that would not go away, and the people were angry with the ACLU. One of the more vocal members of the community was Dean Young. He and I had become friends when he spoke at a Christian Coalition meeting in Gadsden. He was outspoken, articulate, and not afraid of controversy. Dean's boldness and confrontational nature were positive traits, but also ones that caused some resentment with certain groups. On June 20, 1994, he spoke out against the ACLU to the *Gadsden Times*, stating, "This is another time when the ACLU has stepped out of its bounds. We think this country was founded by men who believe there's a right to have prayer."[8]

When the ACLU threatened litigation, I decided to fight them with all I could muster. I continued to remind jury panels of the history of the jury system and how different it was from what they had seen on TV. I advised them of what I called the "five Ps": be prompt, patient, polite, professional, and prayerful. I told them to listen, because God answers prayers in His own quiet way. I'm sure that did not please the

ACLU, which had been trying for more than eighty years to eliminate any kind of recognition of God from our public life.

The ACLU began in 1917 as the National Civil Liberties Bureau to defend World War I draftees who claimed deferment as conscientious objectors. Founder Roger Baldwin was a member of the Communist Party who spent nine months in prison for refusing to report for his own draft physical exam. In 1920, the bureau reorganized as the American Civil Liberties Union, supposedly to defend civil rights.[9] But one of its chief goals was the rejection of God and religion. Embracing atheism and a materialistic view of life, the ACLU undermined those absolute rights that Thomas Jefferson declared had come from God. By denying the existence of God, the ACLU denied the source of our rights of life, liberty, and the pursuit of happiness.

The definition of the term *life* in the due process clauses of the Fifth and Fourteenth amendments to the United States Constitution was taken from the book of Genesis in the Bible. Life is the "immediate gift of God, a right inherent by nature in every individual; and it begins in contemplation of law as soon as the infant is able to stir in the mother's womb."[10] When the acknowledgment of God is removed from public life, life itself is not defined as a gift of God, but it begins when government says it does. That is the reason why we have such immoral procedures as partial birth abortion.

Although the ACLU would not actually file a suit until they knew how the election would be resolved, by the spring of 1994 they had made it clear that action would be taken. The *Gadsden Times* reported a "dark cloud" on my horizon "in the form of litigation from the American Civil Liberties Union."[11]

Dean Young, who represented the Christian Coalition, circulated a petition supporting prayer in court. It was signed by more than 6,800 people and was presented to me on August 2, 1994, on the steps of the Etowah County Courthouse. Upon accepting the petition, I indicated my intention to continue prayer in the courtroom because "[i]t has been going on since this judicial system was established."[12]

Joel Sogol responded on behalf of the ACLU: "Judges are representatives of the state and the state is not supposed to support a religion of any sort. . . . Judge Moore has made this his personal crusade."[13]

But the opposite was true. I was only doing what judges in Etowah County had always done. The ACLU had singled me out as an example and was determined to make me back down. I was just as determined not to be intimidated. Because I did not cower into submission, they labeled it my "crusade." After all, the United States Supreme Court opened with what Justice Douglas had called a prayer in *Engel v. Vitale:* "God save the United States and this Honorable Court."[14] Not only does the highest court of our land open with prayer, but so does the United States Congress in both houses.

The first act by the first president of the United States, George Washington, in his inaugural address on April 30, 1789, was a public prayer. In his words:

> Such being the impression under which I have in obedience to the public summons, repaired to the present station, it would be peculiarly improper to omit, in this first official act, my fervent supplication to the Almighty Being, who rules over the universe, who presides in the councils of nations, and whose providential aids can supply every human defect.[15]

My opponent Keith Pitts ran a good campaign and refused to turn prayer or the Ten Commandments into a campaign issue. He did have a picture taken with the former head of the Etowah County Baptist Association, to counter my support from many people in Baptist churches in the county. Some who supported Keith accused me of using religion for political reasons. But they failed to recognize it was the ACLU that started the entire controversy over prayer when they sent a reporter into my court to record the opening jury session. The ACLU had hired a court reporter as a threat or act of intimidation long before the campaign for circuit judge had begun. It was a move they came to regret.

My family worked hard in the campaign. Kayla and the children helped distribute pamphlets and brochures. At a campaign rally they helped serve lemonade and hot dogs to supporters. Even my brothers and sisters contributed by personally soliciting votes. My dear mother did as she had always done, giving me support by encouraging me to do what I believed.

Christians, conservatives, and concerned citizens who wanted to fight the ACLU began to lend me their support and to speak out against threats to undermine their basic freedom. The battle lines were drawn, not so much between me and my opponent, but between me and the ACLU. Since no Republican had been elected as a circuit judge in Etowah County in the last one hundred years, it would be a miracle if it happened this time.

But God is the author of such miracles. On November 8, 1994, I was elected as an Etowah County circuit judge by almost 60 percent of the thirty thousand votes cast. My first act was to acknowledge the providence of Almighty God and thank Him for all His blessings. God had been my strength and my shield against all that had come against me in the previous two years since my appointment, and He had given me a great victory. But the battle had just begun.

7

THE ACLU: "WE'VE JUST BEEN WAITING"

About a year before my election as circuit judge, our last son was born on October 1, 1993. He was named Micah Joseph Moore in memory of my paternal grandfather, Michael Joseph Moore, with a slight variation of his first name to honor the prophet Micah. Kayla and I were happy to be blessed with another son, and life seemed wonderful. On December 14, our anniversary, I wrote a poem to Kayla that used my experiences in the court system to express my feelings for her. It was published in the local newspaper around Valentine's Day in 1994.

THE VERDICT
Condemned to a life of marital bliss,
My fate was sealed by our very first kiss.
For the terrible crime of loving you, dear,
I now must repay with a rose for each year.

You captured my heart with your beautiful smile,
And I was found guilty without even a trial.
Shackled by the bonds of true love,
My only appeal is to heaven above.

From the Lord of creation no mercy I'll get,
Judgment was rendered, the sentence was set.
The verdict was clear right from the start,
I'm guilty of love, 'til death do us part.[1]

But tragedy struck our family in March of that year with the sudden death of Kayla's mother, Della. She had campaigned hard for my election, and she would have been very pleased with the results. Della was a wonderful mother-in-law. She loved her family and was a loving grandmother for the children, who called her "Nana."

The race for governor of Alabama in 1994 was much closer than my race had been. Forrest "Fob" James won over Jim Folsom by approximately 1 percent of the vote. Republicans were still something of a novelty in state politics in the South, and I was glad to see a godly man like Fob elected. Fob James knew that God had a rightful place in public life. He also knew that the Tenth Amendment still had a purpose.[2] At his inauguration, he proudly displayed a banner indicating his belief in our Constitution. I requested that the new governor administer my oath of office. On January 17, 1995, he graciously made it his first official act.

My staff and their families, together with my family, assembled in the governor's office as Governor James made it official. I was now the first elected Republican circuit judge in Etowah County in the last one hundred years.

But the press seemed to concentrate on only one thing: the controversy over the Ten Commandments. In one account of my swearing in I was identified only as "the Republican who is threatened with a lawsuit by the Civil Liberties Union for displaying the Ten Commandments in his courtroom."[3] It had been seven months since that court reporter had been sent into my courtroom by the ACLU. My name seldom appeared in the media without some reference to prayer, the Ten Commandments, or the ACLU.

The *Gadsden Times* carried a quote by Joel Sogol about the pro-posed lawsuit: "We've just been waiting on the inauguration here and haven't really done anything with it. It's going to be coming."[4] And I would have to wait patiently.

The long wait began as I tried to concentrate on the business of my court. The attitude of the attorneys improved dramatically after I was elected. Things were much more orderly after the enormous caseloads I inherited were reduced to a manageable level. Then George Hundley decided to retire. I knew I would miss George because he had been such a good friend. His loyalty and devoted service would be difficult to replace.

In an effort to find a new bailiff, I began interviewing applicants in late January of 1995. After weeks of interviews, I became frustrated at my inability to find a replacement for George. Then Scott Barnett paid a visit.

Scott was only fourteen years old when I first met him in Gallant, Alabama, in 1981. I had seen him only three or four times during the intervening years. He had been working with the Red Cross in Birmingham, but he had recently decided to move back to Gadsden where he was married and began his search for new employment. Scott asked me for a recommendation. I thought to myself, *What a coinci-dence.* But of course, God does not need coincidence to fulfill His plans. Both Scott and I soon learned that God had been in charge from the very beginning.

I told Scott that I had been looking for a bailiff, but I was trying to find someone with legal experience who was proficient in computers and technology. To my surprise, Scott was in his second year of law school at the Birmingham School of Law and was familiar with com-puter systems. I began to think that perhaps God had answered my search for a new bailiff, so I decided to give Scott the job.

During casual conversation I asked Scott to step into my court-room to see what had created such a controversy in the media.

Standing behind my bench, I pointed to my plaque of the Ten Commandments on the wall. Scott remarked without hesitation, "I have one like that." My first thought was that Scott was trying to impress me. This was not necessary because I had just informed him that he was hired. I replied, "Scott, you couldn't have one like that because I made this one."

But Scott assured me that his plaque was also made of two pieces of redwood, with identical words and design. I took the tablets off the wall, turned them over, and pointed to the back. "But yours can't have a picture of Moses descending the mountain on the back of one tablet and the words 'The Law' written on the other tablet." He replied excitedly, "Mine does too!"

At once we were silenced and amazed! We could only look at each other in bewilderment. I asked Scott if he could bring his plaque to the office the next day. Sure enough, his plaque consisted of two tablets exactly like mine. He explained that fourteen years before, he had purchased a wood-burning tool and had used a "diagram" to create his own plaque that he had given to his grandparents. It was the only wood burning he had ever done. After his grandfather's death, his grandmother decided to return the plaque to him two weeks before he came to see me. He had never seen my plaque, and I had never seen the one he had made.

I faintly recalled that his father Willie had visited my home and had borrowed my drawings back in 1980, and had later returned them to me. The puzzle had been solved, but only God could have designed these circumstances. The fact that Scott Barnett, a young boy of fourteen when I met him in 1981 and now as a young man in law school, visited me looking for a job was strange enough. But to have carved a Ten Commandments plaque identical to mine fourteen years before was beyond all probability.

Neither of us have forgotten that moment when I sharply rebuked Scott by saying that he "couldn't have one like that." I had always thought that the Ten Commandments plaque was my own idea, but now I knew the truth. This was God's plan, not mine!

During the next six years I alternated the plaques on my wall, and nobody ever knew the difference. But God's law made a difference in the hearts and minds of those who saw it, dividing and identifying those who acknowledge God from those who do not. The Bible says, "The word of God is quick, and powerful, and sharper than any two-edged sword, piercing even to the dividing asunder of soul and spirit, and of the joints and marrow, and is a discerner of the thoughts and intents of the heart" (Heb. 4:12).

And divide it did as people began to identify where they stood on this issue. On one side was a circuit court judge who believed in a sovereign God, who had the support of a great number of the people in Etowah County and beyond. On the other side was the ACLU, which professed the sovereignty of man, with virtually no support among the people.

Those who believed in God recognized that God was the grantor of rights and freedoms, especially the freedom to choose to believe or not believe in Him without the interference of government. Those who believed in man as the superior power saw man as the grantor of rights and freedoms, that a government of men guaranteed freedom of conscience. A public official who openly acknowledged God and God's law was certainly an offense to those who believed in man as sovereign.

And the division continued as pastors, lawyers, judges, governors, and other politicians chose sides. It often surprised and shocked me where some people stood. But I never doubted that God had chosen this time and this place to stir His people to a new awakening and a new commitment.

Perhaps the ACLU thought that just the threat of a lawsuit would be sufficient. Martin McCaffrey, vice president of the Alabama ACLU board of directors, told reporters that Chief Justice Sonny Hornsby had already advised state judges that the ACLU intended to sue if judges continued to open courts with prayer. Many judges across Alabama had decided to discontinue the practice of opening courts with prayer rather than risk being sued. But threats were not enough in Etowah County. Now that the ACLU had seen I could be elected, they proceeded with their plan to make me an example to others.

On Friday, March 31, 1995, a little more than two months after my first full term in office began, the ACLU filed their lawsuit in U.S. district court against me personally on behalf of the Alabama Freethought Association.[5] Three people declared they had been illegally subjected to my personal religious beliefs because of my Ten Commandments plaque and courtroom prayer. The ACLU claimed prayer was "a religious test." Their goal was to "stop religious practices led by or initiated by judges in Alabama's courtrooms"—though I was the only one of those judges they were suing.[6] They requested removal of the plaque and a permanent injunction to stop me from "leading, conducting, or promoting the recitation of prayers in the courtroom."[7]

At a press conference after the ACLU announcement, I explained that I wouldn't change anything I was doing. When asked by reporters if I would remove the Ten Commandments, I replied, "I wouldn't have put them up if I intended to take them down.[8] . . . There is definitely a doctrine that the state should stay out of the affairs of the church," I explained, "[b]ut now that is being interpreted that anything mentioning God is [forbidden]."[9]

This is a misunderstanding of the First Amendment that has festered in our courts and our culture for more than a generation. If the ACLU had been around when America was founded, they would have tried to block the very law that allowed them freedom of conscience.

The First Amendment provides, "Congress shall make no law respecting an establishment of religion, or prohibiting the free exercise thereof; or abridging the freedom of speech, or of the press; or the right of the people peaceably to assemble, and to petition the government for a redress of grievances."[10]

The often-quoted "establishment clause" at the beginning does not mean "the government shall not recognize God." The first thing Congress did on September 25, 1789—the day they adopted the wording of the First Amendment—was to direct a joint committee of both houses to request President Washington to recommend a day of public thanksgiving and prayer to Almighty God for the peaceful manner in which the Constitution had been established.[11] Acknowledging God is not the same as establishing a religion. The establishment of a religion means setting up a state church or state-supported church bureaucracy.

The founders were familiar with established state churches, and they knew that a national church would curb freedom of conscience. As British subjects, American colonists paid homage to a king who was also the head of the Church of England. This church had been formed in 1529 by an act of Parliament to appease King Henry VIII. Henry wanted to divorce his wife Catherine of Aragon because she had failed to produce a male heir. Pope Clement VII refused to allow it, so Henry formed a new church with himself as head.

From the time of Elizabeth I, all British monarchs took the dual role as head of the church and head of the state. Any person who was not a member of the Church of England or the "established church" forfeited many civil rights, including, for Jews, the right to serve in Parliament. The established church in England was (and is today) supported by the government. The same is true for the Catholic Church in South American countries such as Argentina, Bolivia, and Peru and the Lutheran Church in the Scandinavian countries of Norway, Sweden, and Finland, and in other nations around the world where the church is a publicly funded bureaucracy.

Establishing a religion means setting up a church bureaucracy—houses of worship, schools, seminaries, liturgies, creeds, and so forth—

at government expense and giving it special powers denied to other types of churches. This was the British system of establishment that the First Amendment was specifically written to avoid. Steering clear of an official religion was consistent with Article VI of the U.S. Constitution, which states that "no religious Tests shall ever be required as a Qualification to any Office or public Trust under the United States."[12] But acknowledging God was not the establishment of a religion.

One of the first acts of Congress was the Judiciary Act of 1789 which required all federal judges to take an oath of office that ended with "so help me God."[13] Does displaying the Ten Commandments or taking an oath or saying a prayer in a courtroom constitute a religion? No. This simply acknowledges that America is founded on a belief in the God of the Bible.

In the Declaration of Independence, the founders of our nation explained to the world that their break with England was due to "the Laws of Nature and of Nature's God," and that all rights came from a Creator God. With their lives, fortunes, and sacred honor at stake, they declared their independence not with a massive army of enormous resources, but with "a firm Reliance on the protection of Divine Providence."

Here is the essential point: The United States of America is founded on a belief in a particular God—the God of the Holy Scriptures. Americans are free to believe anything they want because God has given them that freedom of conscience. The Constitution guarantees everyone freedom of thought as well as equal treatment under the law. "One nation under God with liberty and justice for all" is a truth that Americans can understand and with which they can identify.

No government entity can force us to worship a certain way—or to worship at all. Our relationship to God belongs to God and not to government. The government cannot set up an "established church" at public expense or discriminate against people because of their beliefs or opinions. But the fabric of America is woven on the loom of Judeo-Christian laws, principles, and traditions. This is the biblical God whose standards define the framework of American government. Since the Mayflower Compact of 1620, Americans have consistently affirmed this connection between God and government. That is not my opinion; that is history.

But because the ACLU and its supporters were either unfamiliar with history or chose to ignore it, they pressed ahead with their suit against me. On April 3, 1995, the Monday after the ACLU filed its complaint against me, county officials—both Democrat and Republican—gathered on the courthouse steps and announced their support for prayer in court.

Sheriff James Hayes was there, along with state legislators and judicial officers, including revenue commissioner Judy Pitts, wife of my former opponent, Keith Pitts. Dean Young announced the formation of the Roy Moore Defense Fund, managed by a local accounting firm, to help pay my legal expenses.

Alabama Attorney General Jeff Sessions announced that his office would handle my defense, but I decided that I ought to be responsible for my own legal team. By the end of the week, the governor offered to contribute a flat rate toward my own lawyer's hourly fee; the rest would be my responsibility. I accepted his generous offer until the end of the year. By then I saw that the case might go on indefinitely. I could not in good conscience rely on public funds.

On April 10 there was a rally at the courthouse, with a crowd of four hundred to five hundred people assembled outside the building. People had gathered before court opened. They stood on the front steps and lined the hallway to my courtroom to see if I would still begin my proceedings with a prayer. Much to the dismay of the ACLU, I did. When I called on Pastor Maurice Wright to offer thanks to the

Creator, they had their answer. Other pastors, including Phillip Ellen and Stephen Owenby, spoke to the crowd outside, showing their support for keeping God in government.

The enthusiastic crowd sang "God Bless America" and "Amazing Grace." I walked to a lectern at the top of the courthouse steps and looked out at small American flags waving back and forth and at the hundreds of people who were there to show that the ACLU did not speak for them. Kayla was on the steps with Caleb and Micah (the older kids were in school), all standing by my side. It was a wonderful and humbling experience to feel the support of my fellow citizens.

I began by expressing the same simple, familiar thoughts I had shared before and would express so many times again. "The ACLU would have you believe that it is wrong for a public official in the performance of his duty to acknowledge Almighty God. I submit to you it's wrong not to.[14] . . . This is a nation founded under God. We have a duty to acknowledge His providence."[15]

Before the week was over, state legislators had set up their own fund to help with my legal bills. State Senator Gerald Dial, a Democrat from Lineville, told his colleagues that this was not a partisan matter. "It's time to stand up again for Alabama," he said.[16] His check was the first contribution. Governor James left no doubt about his views. At a press conference in Montgomery, he said, "I do not stand with the pigmy-headed, pea-brained, so-called jurists of perhaps the last four or five decades which have been more void of classical explanation and real scholarship than any period in the history of the United States."[17]

Jeff Sessions wasted no time responding to the suit on my behalf. On April 21, 1995, he filed a declaratory judgment action in the Montgomery County Circuit Court on behalf of Governor James, arguing that neither prayer nor the Ten Commandments violated the state or federal constitutions. He quoted from the state constitution that Alabamians sought "the favor and guidance of Almighty God," and noted that opening "sessions of deliberative bodies with prayer is deeply embedded in the history and tradition of this Country."[18]

Sessions contended that the suit belonged in state court, not federal court, because it raised questions about the state law. He also pointed out that Alabama's Constitution prohibited the "establishment of religion by law, giving preference to any religious sect, compelling anyone to attend religious services, imposing taxes for religious purposes, requiring religious beliefs as a qualification for holding public office, and affecting the civil liberties of citizens because of their religious beliefs."[19] He concluded by observing that I had done none of those things. Thus, the suit was without merit.

The issue was now before both a federal and state court. Would we continue to acknowledge God as sovereign, or had man taken His place in our lives? It was a question that was as old as the sun, a conflict that existed in the Garden of Eden, and an issue that needed a resolution. Was Governor Fob James correct? Were jurists of the past fifty years devoid of scholarship and classical explanation?

Perhaps it is time to look at some facts which your history teacher may have failed to tell you or was forbidden to tell you about God's law and His relationship to our country and our own law.

8

UNDER WHOSE AUTHORITY?

During the reign of King Darius in the Mede-Persian Empire, around six hundred years before the birth of Christ, a Jewish man named Daniel rose to a position of authority in the government. In fact, Daniel was second only to the king in authority and power. Daniel's ascendancy angered some other officials, who resented his powerful position and foreign birth. Seeking a way to remove him was difficult, but his enemies came up with a plan.

Daniel believed in the God of his fathers and in a higher law. This was something that King Darius did not profess. In order to create a conflict, Daniel's enemies obtained a decree from King Darius that whoever should bow down to any god or man except King Darius should be killed by being thrown into a den of lions. Under the law of the kingdom, this rule could not be changed or altered.

When Daniel learned of the decree, he proceeded to do what he had always done: at his home's windows, which opened toward Jerusalem, he knelt in prayer to Almighty God. Daniel knew that no king or man was above God and that no king or government could control what a person believes about God. Finally, Daniel's enemies had their chance to accuse him.

King Darius was deeply disturbed by the thought of Daniel having to pay the ultimate price for his violation of the decree. He had a great regard for Daniel, but the law could not be altered or changed. Daniel was cast into the den of lions, but he was miraculously delivered by the Lord from what seemed to be certain death. Thereafter, King Darius destroyed Daniel's enemies, restored Daniel to his position of authority, and recognized the ultimate authority of God (see Dan. 6).

In 1776, when Thomas Jefferson wrote the Declaration of Independence, he recognized a Creator God and a law higher than that of an earthly king. He wrote that the American colonies had a right to "dissolve the Political Bands" that had bound them to Great Britain and to "assume among the Powers of the Earth, the separate and equal Station to which the Laws of Nature and Nature's God" entitled them. King George III had become a tyrant by placing himself above the law of God by usurping the colonists' God-given rights.

In the Declaration of Independence, Jefferson wrote, "A prince, whose Character is thus marked by every act which may define a tyrant, is unfit to be the Ruler of a free People." Jefferson explained it was "self-evident" that rights came from God which no man or king could overthrow. Like Daniel, our forefathers did not close their shutters to the world, boldly proclaiming that "to prove this let facts be submitted to a candid World."

Throughout the centuries, the issue has remained the same: *Under whose authority will we be governed?* Our forefathers knew the lesson of Daniel—that no king could place himself above God and His holy law, and "with a firm Reliance on the Protection of Divine Providence, [they] mutually pledge[d] to each other [their] Lives, [their] Fortunes, and [their] sacred Honor." They would soon face their own lion's den, but first they would make their position clear.

In the first sentence of the Declaration of Independence, our forefathers justified the colonies' existence as a new nation under the laws of

God. Jefferson and other delegates to the Continental Congress did not invent this connection between God's law and the state. They adapted it from an understanding of their biblical history and in part from one of the best-known and important legal treatises of their time—the *Commentaries on the Laws of England* by Sir William Blackstone.

As legal counselor to the king, law professor at Oxford, and judge of the Court of Common Pleas, Blackstone was one of the noted legal scholars of his time. Drawing on earlier works from John Locke and other recognized thinkers, Blackstone wrote that the laws of nature and of nature's God came not only through God-given reason and conscience, but also by direct revelation of divine law, found only in the Bible.

Blackstone wrote the *Commentaries* from 1765 to 1769. A Philadelphia printer, Robert Bell, published the first American edition of Blackstone's *Commentaries* in 1771 for a select group of one thousand subscribers, including John Adams, Roger Sherman, and Robert Livingston. These men were three of the four lawyers on the drafting committee for the Declaration of Independence. Thomas Jefferson already owned a set of the *Commentaries* according to a letter he wrote from his home in Monticello to Robert Skipwith on August 3, 1771.[1]

Other noted American forefathers who also subscribed to Robert Bell's publication were John Jay, the first chief justice of the United States Supreme Court, and James Wilson, who signed both the Declaration of Independence and the United States Constitution. At least fourteen of the fifty-six men who signed the Declaration of Independence, and others who helped fashion the Constitution, were subscribers to Bell's printing of the *Commentaries*.[2]

But in America even those not trained in law were well acquainted with Blackstone's *Commentaries*. The great English philosopher and orator Edmund Burke, on the floor of Parliament on March 22, 1775, noted that an education in law from reading the *Commentaries* had

given rise to a "fierce spirit of liberty among the colonists."³ Burke
explained:

> In no country perhaps in the world is the law so general
> a study [as in America]. The profession itself is numerous
> and powerful; and in most provinces it takes the lead. The
> greatest number of the deputies sent to the Congress were
> lawyers. But all who read, and most do read, endeavor to
> obtain some smattering in that science. I have been told by
> an eminent bookseller that in no branch of business, after
> tracts of popular devotion, were so many books as those on
> the law exported to the plantations. The colonists have now
> fallen into the way of printing them for their own use. I hear
> that they have sold nearly as many Blackstone's
> *Commentaries* in America as in England.⁴

Thus, even the British recognized how the American Continental
Congress was filled with lawyers, many of whom had been influenced
by Blackstone's writings. Blackstone was fiercely loyal to the British
king, but he inadvertently inspired a spirit of liberty that eventually led
to revolution in the American colonies.

Blackstone's work involved the compilation of the common law. It
was predicated on the fact that law was based on an understanding of
God and His authority. In his chapter entitled "Of the Nature of Laws
in General," he explained that "when the Supreme Being formed the
universe, and created matter out of nothing, he impressed certain principles upon matter from which it can never depart and without which
it would cease to be. . . . Man, considered as a creature, must necessarily be subject to the laws of his Creator, for he is entirely a dependent
being. . . . And consequently as man depends absolutely upon his
Maker for everything, it is necessary that he should in all points con-

form to his Maker's will. The will of his Maker is called the *law of nature*."[5]

Thomas Jefferson began our organic document of government, the Declaration of Independence, with the statement that this law of nature together with the law of God gave the colonies the right to exist as a new nation. In 1788, James Madison, the chief architect of the Constitution, in a letter published in a New York newspaper—a work we now know as "Federalist No. 43"—explained to the people of that state that the Constitutional Convention's authority for drafting a new Constitution was the same laws of nature and nature's God about which Jefferson had spoken.

Madison stated that under Article VII of the Constitution only nine states, instead of the thirteen that had signed the Articles of Confederation, would be required for ratification of the new Constitution simply because of "the transcendent law of nature and of nature's God, which declares that the safety and happiness of society are the objects at which all political institutions aim, and to which all such institutions must be sacrificed."[6]

Today, professors of law from major universities like Harvard and Yale have misled the political and legal establishment into believing that God has no relationship to our government or to our law. The truth is that without a belief in God we would have no country and no Constitution. Still others, professing themselves to be wise, have confused the American people into thinking that the law of nature had nothing to do with the Bible and revealed divine law.

But Blackstone stated clearly that man's reason became clouded and impaired after the fall of our first ancestor, Adam, so God intervened and gave us "revealed or divine law, found only in the Holy Scriptures. These precepts, when revealed, are found upon comparison to be a part of the original law of nature."[7] Blackstone was not stating anything new; he was summing up a truth known for centuries by philosophers such as John Locke and legal scholars and judges such as Sir Edward Coke. The law of nature written on our hearts by God was the same law written in the Holy Scriptures, and more explicitly by God's own finger on two tablets of stone on Mt. Sinai.

Blackstone further explained that "undoubtedly the revealed law is (humanly speaking) of infinitely more authority than what we generally call the natural law. Because one is the law of nature, expressly declared so to be by God himself [the Ten Commandments]; the other is only what, by the assistance of human reason, we imagine to be that law."[8]

The conclusion is both powerful and compelling: "Upon these two foundations, the *law of nature* and the *law of revelation* depend all human laws; that is to say, no human law should be suffered to contradict these."[9] In other words, because man's law must be based on God's law, it cannot contradict God's law. This might come as a shock to many people in our legal establishment and certainly to the ACLU and organizations like it which would never concede that all laws made by men are to be under the authority of God's law.

This is not a novel concept. In 1690, John Locke wrote in his *Second Treatise of Civil Government* that "the Law of Nature, stands as an eternal rule to all men, *legislators* as well as others."[10] The laws made by legislators must therefore be conformable to the law of nature—that is, to the will of God.

Working through the eighteenth-century prose, the message here is simple: The laws of man originate with God, and man is consequently bound by the law of God. This was a truth understood by our founding fathers and especially by men like Associate Justice James Wilson, who stated, "Human law must rest its authority ultimately upon the authority of that law which is divine."[11]

Today, if a teacher of history in the public schools tells her students that our law comes from the law of God and from the Bible, she might be fired. If a law professor maintaining a true allegiance to centuries of legal jurisprudence tells his students that law is based upon God, he might soon be looking for a new job. Indeed, the law school itself might be in jeopardy of losing accreditation if it consistently maintained such a philosophy rejected by the legal establishment. But how do we change history? Are we to erase those references to God and God's law found in the Declaration of Independence and in the writings of those men who wrote our Constitution?

Here I stood, a circuit court judge in the state of Alabama in 1995, having learned these truths and now having to defend them before a federal district court. I was charged with a violation of the First Amendment, and it was a scene repeated often as I stood before judges who had not been taught these truths. In grade school our children are not taught these concepts which were once commonplace in America. For example, using the *Elementary Catechism of the Constitution of the United States* by Arthur Stansbury, school children in 1828 were taught that the purpose of the First Amendment was religious freedom. The following excerpt from the *Elementary Catechism* is a series of questions and answers posed to elementary school children:

Q: What was the subject of the First Amendment?

A: The subject of religious freedom.

Q: What do you mean by that?

A: I mean the right that every man has to worship God in such way as he thinks fit, without being called to account for his opinions, or punished for them.

Q: Is this a sacred right, which ought to be guarded with the greatest care?

A: Certainly. God alone is the judge of our religious belief and service, and no man has a right to interfere with it, so long as it does not lead us to injure or disturb our neighbor. A great part of the misery and oppression which has existed in the world, began with forcing men to do what their conscience disapproved.[12]

Yet, in our day even judges do not understand what children in years past were taught—that our religious freedom comes from God, *not* from man. Joel Sogol and the ACLU alleged in newspapers across Alabama that I was "pushing my religion" on others. But I was neither pushing religion nor professing religion by acknowledging God. No juror was required to pray or to participate in prayer in my court. And certainly the mere acknowledgment of God is not considered religion, but the very source of religious freedom.

In *United States v. Macintosh*,[13] the United States Supreme Court in 1931 recognized in a majority opinion that Americans were a "Christian people . . . according to one another the equal right of religious freedom, and acknowledging with reverence the duty of obedience to the will of God."[14]

Both the prayer in my courtroom and the display of the Ten Commandments had been challenged by the Alabama Freethought Association. My friend, Myron Allenstein, initially represented me as I had represented him while in private practice. And the issue was simple: the acknowledgment of God. How Americans have been deceived! Children were once taught in school that our country began with an acknowledgment of God. Our first president in his first official act during his inaugural address on April 30, 1789, acknowledged God by prayer and supplication. He firmly insisted that "no People can be bound to acknowledge and adore the Invisible Hand which conducts the affairs of men more than those of the United States."[15]

Even the venerable Benjamin Franklin at age eighty-one rose to his feet during the Constitutional Convention and declared, "I have lived, Sir, a long time, and the longer I live, the more convincing proofs I see of this truth, that God governs in the affairs of men. And if a sparrow cannot fall to the ground without his notice, is it probable that an empire can rise without his aid?"[16]

Our school children were even taught that America was presumed to have a divine foundation. Noah Webster, the original author of the *American Dictionary of the English Language* of 1828, said in the preface to his dictionary, "The United States commenced their existence under circumstances wholly novel and unexampled in the history of the nations. They commenced a civilization with learning, with science, with constitutions of free government, and with the best gift of God to man, the Christian religion."[17]

And how strange it was to be sued by an organization calling itself the "Alabama Freethought Association." I believe as strongly as any American in liberty of conscience—the freedom to think and believe what you wish—but I also know that freedom was given by God. Thomas Jefferson, in his *Notes on the State of Virginia*, echoed this same sentiment when he asked, "Can the liberties of a nation be thought secure when we have removed their only firm basis, a conviction in the minds of the people that these liberties are the gift of God?"[18]

The Alabama Freethought Association did not want freedom of thought; they wanted to suppress freedom of thought by denying its very source—God. The Christian, the Jew, and people of all faiths—or no faith—have a right to believe as they choose, but only because God has given that freedom and because the First Amendment has secured that freedom for them. Our forefathers recognized this truth.

President Washington, for example, wrote to a synagogue in Newport, Rhode Island, on August 17, 1790, that "[a]ll possess alike liberty of conscience and immunities of citizenship. . . . May the children of the Stock of Abraham, who dwell in this land, continue to merit and enjoy the goodwill of the other inhabitants . . . . May the Father of all mercies scatter light, and not darkness, upon our paths."[19]

Washington understood that freedom of conscience comes from God and thus is available to all people, no matter what their background or beliefs.

With regard to freedom of conscience, James Madison observed that, "Whilst we assert for ourselves a freedom to embrace, to profess and to observe the Religion which we believe to be of divine origin, we cannot deny an equal freedom to those whose minds have not yet yielded to the evidence which has convinced us. If this freedom be abused, it is an offense against God, not against man: To God, therefore, not to men, must an account of it be rendered."[20] Madison, in these words from the *Memorial and Remonstrance*, stated unequivocally that man could never interfere with freedom of conscience, and any human attempt to do so is an offense against God.

The First Amendment was never meant to suppress the acknowledgment of God, but to secure that freedom of conscience given by Him. Perhaps Jefferson said it best in his Bill for Establishing Religious Freedom, written more than ten years before the Constitution and the First Amendment: "Almighty God hath created the mind free, and manifested His supreme will that free it shall remain by making it altogether insusceptible of restraint."[21] The First Amendment was written to secure that freedom of conscience by restraining Congress from making any law regarding the establishment of religion—how we worship God.

That simple truth that was taught to our forefathers, legal scholars, and even school children well into the nineteenth century has been lost to this generation because it is no longer acceptable in our public school system.

Why have Americans, and particularly Christian Americans, been so easily deceived? Perhaps we are seeing what the apostle Paul predicted: "For the time will come when they will not endure sound doctrine; but after their own lusts shall they heap to themselves teachers, having itching ears; and they shall turn away their ears from the truth, and shall be turned unto fables" (2 Tim. 4:3–4). Have we turned from sound doctrine to fables?

America was founded on a belief in God and God's law. This truth was recognized in *McGowan v. Maryland*[22] by William O. Douglas, an associate justice of the United States Supreme Court: "The institutions of our society are founded on the belief that there is an authority higher than the authority of the State; that there is a moral law which the state is powerless to alter; that the individual possesses rights, conferred by the Creator, which government must respect. . . . And the body of the Constitution as well as the Bill of Rights enshrined those principles."[23]

The men who drafted the Declaration of Independence and the U.S. Constitution were godly men who consciously, respectfully, and overtly acknowledged the providence of God. They were men of faith who believed that God was the author of all rights, including liberty of conscience. They intended to preserve that right in the First Amendment. Grade-school children, as well as law students, were taught these principles.

But during the past one hundred years there has been a lapse in instruction on these basic concepts. Today, the ACLU, Freethought Association, Americans United for Separation of Church and State, and other such groups are seeking to remove the knowledge of God from our land. It is our right, indeed our duty, to resist. Citizens are called on to obey civil authority, but when that civil authority rejects the God on whom our nation was founded, we must stand firm in our convictions. Under whose authority will we be governed?

9

Moore, 1; ACLU, 0

By the middle of May 1995, six weeks after the ACLU filed its lawsuit against me, the Ten Commandments issue had generated so much publicity that it became almost impossible to handle all the letters and telephone calls of encouragement. Even Governor Fob James came to Gadsden to show his support. On the afternoon of May 16, Governor James spoke to several thousand people who had gathered at Coosa Christian School's football field.

With a huge American flag behind him and a set of the Ten Commandments beside him, Governor James spoke forcefully about history and American law: "The early Christian Anglo-Saxon King Alfred the Great based his entire legal system on a much more ancient set of laws—the Ten Commandments. These biblical laws formed the foundation of what became English common law and eventually led to a major check of monarchical power, the Magna Charta [1215], the forerunner of our Constitution."[1]

Governor James continued, tracing the unbroken line between the United States code and all state laws back to the Constitution, from there to the Declaration of Independence, and then through centuries of British law directly back to the law of God as revealed in the Bible.

"I say to you the time is right," James declared. "I say to you the judge has taken a stand that first is morally right, and second is legally proper and thirdly is constitutional. Are we going to allow in this

Country an insidious, back door, by-the-night attack in the courts to take freedoms that no other armed country has been able to take?"[2]

The audience roared back, "NO!"

Governor James warned that victory would not be easy, quick, or without frustration (how right he was!), but that "if we understand the law, if we cling to the Constitution, if we have faith in the good Lord above, we shall maintain ourselves as free people."[3] The people stood and cheered, waving Bibles, copies of the Ten Commandments, signs, and whatever else they could. Governor James was a man of conviction and was not afraid to stand for the right of all Alabamians to acknowledge God. An all-American halfback from Auburn University, Fob governed like he ran the ball—straight ahead and without fear.

The pretrial hearing for the ACLU case came about a month later, in the court of U.S. District Judge Robert Propst in Birmingham. The bailiff called out, "Hear ye! Hear ye! The United States District Court of the Northern District of Alabama is now open according to law. May God save the United States and this honorable court." If the ACLU saw any irony in that prayer they did not mention it, nor did they file a lawsuit against Judge Propst for acknowledging God like the United States Supreme Court does in the same manner.

Albert Jordan, a good friend and an outstanding lawyer, represented me as an assistant attorney general appointed by Attorney General Jeff Sessions. The judge questioned whether the case belonged in federal court because the plaintiffs did not ask for damages but disagreed with the actions of a state judge. The ACLU naturally wanted the case to be tried in the more liberal federal courts. These courts have provided a generous cash flow to lawyers who create their own constitutional violations by being offended at any religious expression or recognition of God.

An interesting moment occurred when two of the three plaintiffs, Gloria Hershiser and Barbara Stappenbeck, admitted they had never been called before me for jury duty. They had both been in the court-room over which I eventually presided, but it was long before I had been appointed a judge. Back then the plaque in question was still hanging on my dining room wall. Hershiser had been subpoenaed before me as a witness, but she admitted she could not read my plaque without her glasses and only recognized it by its shape. The ACLU has no hesitation suing over something even if it just looks "religious" by its shape.

My attorney asked Hershiser if she remembered any of the other items on my courtroom walls—the picture of Washington, Lincoln, the seal of Alabama, and so forth. She could not remember anything else, even though the plaque was the smallest item on display.

Hershiser said she had attended the jury organizing session on April 10, 1995. That was the first session after the lawsuit was filed, when people rallied on the Etowah County Courthouse steps and when I opened court with prayer. But she had not been subpoenaed that day. The judge asked Hershiser if an attorney told her to attend in prepara-tion for this lawsuit. One of her attorneys objected, saying that the question violated attorney-client privilege. The judge agreed.

Stappenbeck then took the stand. She testified that she had never been in my courtroom and had never seen the plaque. But she insisted that if she had, she certainly would have been offended and would have felt "singled out" by leaving the room during the opening prayer.

This was the first legal test of my position. The judge's ruling would not change what I did, but I figured it would make a big difference in how long and rocky the road ahead would be. On July 7, 1995, Judge Propst dismissed the ACLU suit. As good as that news was, it wasn't a clean victory because the court ruled on a technicality. Judge Propst did not decide whether it was legal to acknowledge God in court; instead, he ruled only that the plaintiffs had no legal standing to file the suit. He said in part:

[T]here is neither allegation nor evidence that plaintiffs have been called to defendant's court with such regularity that it is reasonable to expect that they will be so called in the immediate future. In sum, none of these allegations present the "real and immediate threat of future harm" required in order to find that plaintiffs have standing to maintain this action.[4]

The banner headline on the front of the next morning's *Gadsden Times* read, "Moore 1, ACLU 0."[5] But the ACLU never gives up that easily.

Joel Sogol of the ACLU told the press that his next step would be to "contact some of the people who have contacted us since we filed this action and refile."[6] Looking for a quick victory that might intimidate me, or hoping that the mere act of filing would scare me into changing my mind, the ACLU had gone to court accusing me of displaying something the plaintiffs hadn't even seen. I had no doubt they would be back.

Though we had won on technical grounds, our supporters were elated at what they considered to be a legal victory. In interviews I did my best to explain that the ACLU had taken an extremely confusing position. They kept saying the First Amendment gave people freedom of religion (true) and that acknowledging God in government deprived them of that freedom (not true). They argued that if we included God or Christian thinking in government, we were going to lose our rights.

Just the opposite is true: God is the source and defender of our rights. The role of government is to secure those rights for us. Government cannot be "neutral" toward God especially when it presumes to take His place and grant us our rights, one of which is the right of conscience—the right to worship God in any manner we choose. The ACLU promoted the notion that every man is a god in his own eyes, whatever each person does is right because he's free to do it, and there are no rights greater than the right to privacy.

The acknowledgment of God by the state was an obstacle to such a philosophy because it implied a higher law by which all people are bound and within which freedom exists. Those who wish to be free of God's law are "offended" by the recognition of a higher moral code that restricts their behavior.

With the federal court case dismissed, the governor's suit could now continue in state court. The ACLU was shocked that state judges and state courts might decide the issue. First, instead of "caving in," I had fought them; now, they were in a venue to which they were not accustomed. The standard intimidation procedure had failed to work.

Still trying to stay in federal court, the ACLU attempted to remove the case to federal court. But on October 16, U.S. District Judge Harold Albritton returned the case to state court—to Circuit Judge Charles Price in Montgomery, Alabama. I was named a codefendant along with the ACLU, although Governor James supported my position. Joining me in the suit was a legal strategy devised to put an end to the ACLU's attempt to control state courts. Finally, a state government had taken a stand against those who were trying to eliminate any recognition of God in favor of secular humanism.

I was eager to help. I cross-claimed (sued) the ACLU, seeking injunctive relief (an order of court to stop their harassment). I charged that their actions "have resulted in numerous expenses, much inconvenience, and increased workload" and requested a ruling defining my "rights and freedoms as a public official," plus a halt to "further legal action and any threats, actions or proceedings to intimidate, coerce or deny the public acknowledgment of God."[7]

As 1996 began, the battle for the Ten Commandments in Alabama became more and more of a national story. USA Today had already put the story on the front page, and features appeared in the Los Angeles

Times, Boston Globe, and elsewhere. Reporters called every day with questions, and I answered as many as I could. When asked if I would ever give up or back down, I responded that I was sworn to do my duty, "so help me God," that this nation was established on an acknowledgment of God (the Declaration of Independence) and a higher moral law, and that it was not within the jurisdiction of courts to stop such recognition. Furthermore, if we failed to stand up for the God who gave us our rights, we would soon lose them.

Ironically, the First Amendment was designed to be a shield to *protect Americans from* religious persecution, although groups such as the ACLU use it as a sword to take our rights from us. The central purpose of the First Amendment is to allow the freedom to worship God according to the dictates of one's conscience. In other words, without the acknowledgment of God, there would be no First Amendment.

On August 15, 1789, during the debate over the wording of the First Amendment, James Madison, the man known as "the Father of the Constitution" and who proposed the amendment in Congress, stated that he "apprehended the meaning of the words to be, that Congress should not establish a religion, and enforce the legal observation of it by law, nor compel men to worship God in any manner contrary to their conscience."[8]

Several of the delegates to the Constitutional Convention foresaw the very tactics the ACLU would use one day. Delegate Peter Sylvester of New York said, "He apprehended that it was liable to a construction different from what had been made by the committee. He feared it might be thought to have a tendency to abolish religion altogether."[9] Delegate Benjamin Huntington of Connecticut said:

> He feared, with the gentleman first up on this subject [Sylvester], that the words might be taken in such latitude as to be extremely hurtful to the cause of religion. . . . He

hoped, therefore, the amendment would be made in such a way as to secure the rights of conscience, and a free exercise of the rights of religion, but not to patronize those who professed no religion at all.[10]

Today, the ACLU and other groups have put another spin on the First Amendment, an interpretation that has nearly destroyed its original meaning. Instead of allowing for the freedom to worship God, these groups have used the First Amendment to eliminate even the acknowledgment that there is a God entitled to be worshipped. In an attempt to establish secular humanism (the belief that mankind is god), judges, educators, and government leaders have certainly patronized those who profess no religion at all.

I was determined to stop the threats and intimidation of ACLU lawyers to muzzle the voice of truth and to prevent interference with a recognition of God and His law in Alabama. I was pleased to have a governor with equal determination standing with me.

10

"I WILL NOT STOP PRAYER!"

The fight with the ACLU intensified in 1996. On Tuesday, January 9, 1996, the *Birmingham News* reported, "ACLU says it's ready to fight judge over religious issues." James Tucker, a Montgomery lawyer with the ACLU, said, "By filing this document [their answer to my complaint] we are letting the courts, the governor, the attorney general, and Judge Moore know that if this is where they want to litigate these issues, we're ready to do that."[1]

I had undertaken my own legal defense and had decided to pay all of my own legal expenses with contributions to a legal defense fund rather than accept a state-funded defense to which I was entitled. This was done to blunt any protest the ACLU would surely make if I allowed public funds to be spent on my behalf. No taxpayer funds were used for my defense, even though Alabama law allows such a defense when a public official is sued in his official capacity.

And indeed, the defense became very expensive. Since the filing of the original complaint by the ACLU in April 1996, the bill was estimated to be more than one hundred thousand dollars, and Dean Young, my defense coordinator, anticipated that the actual cost would exceed half a million dollars. Rallies were being held to raise money, and donations from churches and individuals were gladly and thankfully accepted.

In early March of 1995, I spoke at Coral Ridge Ministries' "Reclaiming America for Christ" conference in Fort Lauderdale, Florida, to an audience of more than nine hundred people from at least thirty-nine states. Other speakers included Janet Parshall, a Christian radio talk show host from Washington, D.C., then-U.S. Senator John Ashcroft, and Gary Bauer of the Family Research Council. "If we just stand up for the thing in which we believe," I told the audience confidently, "we can't lose. I repeat, we can't lose."[2] Dr. D. James Kennedy and Coral Ridge Ministries agreed to assist in raising funds for my defense.

In June of 1996, Dean Young left as defense coordinator to head a state organization for the American Family Association, where he continued to help raise money for my defense. By this time, the story was making the national news, being reported in such papers as the *Boston Globe*,[3] the *Buffalo News*,[4] the *Tallahassee Democrat*,[5] the *Los Angeles Times*,[6] the *New York Times*, the *Atlanta Journal-Constitution*, the *Houston Chronicle*, the *Washington Post*, the *Washington Times*, and many others.

ACLU lawyers and other lawyers in Gadsden who took advantage of the publicity began to file motions for dismissal of cases before my court based on my "religious" beliefs. In July of 1996, a woman who had lost custody of her two daughters because of an extramarital affair with another woman, which she publicly acknowledged, filed to have me removed from her case in part because her attorney was a member of the ACLU, and in part because she asserted that I would not decide her case in an unbiased fashion. But under the law an extramarital affair by itself was proper grounds for a change in custody.

On September 11, 1996, my trial over the Ten Commandments and prayer finally began, and I was glad to get my day in court. It was rather strange to sit in a fellow circuit court judge's courtroom and to be on trial for the manner in which I had decorated my own courtroom by displaying the Ten Commandments. Nobody seemed to note that a Bible verse adorned the wall outside his own courtroom. Both sides filed for a summary judgment, asking for a judgment in their favor before the commencement of a trial because, they argued, the issue could be decided on the law alone.

I had met a very sharp attorney well versed in the law who was now representing me. I had engaged several previous attorneys, but none had come more highly recommended than Steve Melchior. The National Legal Foundation had recommended him to me, and I had great respect for their opinion. Steve did an excellent job representing me before not only the circuit court and the Alabama Supreme Court, but also later in another federal district court, and eventually the United States Supreme Court. Bobby Segall, a Montgomery attorney, represented the ACLU.

The arguments made before the circuit court were very familiar. Segall said the issue was separation of church and state. Melchior replied that this was about the acknowledgment of God. The issue *was* simple: Did the display of the Ten Commandments and opening of court with voluntary prayer led by clergy violate the First Amendment's prohibition against the "establishment of religion"? Then-Assistant Attorney General Bill Pryor argued on behalf of the state by saying, "The United States Supreme Court in 1983 said the Nebraska Legislature can open its sessions with prayer because the practice was steeped in tradition."[7]

Pryor continued by pointing out that the United States Supreme Court displays a copy of the Ten Commandments: "If you are going to remove it from Moore's courtroom you are going to have to remove it from the Supreme Court."[8] Pryor, who had not yet been appointed as attorney general, was arguing the position taken by Governor James.

People had assembled on the steps of the Montgomery County Courthouse. They came from various parts of the state, including a bus caravan from Gadsden. Others had gathered on lawns and sidewalks to pray and display signs with such messages as: "If you don't stand for something you'll fall for anything."[9] The Reverend James Granger, a black minister of Tabernacle Baptist Church in Gadsden, gave a fiery speech. Reverend Granger and I had become good friends, and I appreciated his understanding that Americans were losing our morality by removing the acknowledgment of God from our land.

As always, my biggest support came from my family. Sitting in the crowd was my wife Kayla and youngest son Micah. My other children remained in school in Gadsden. My mother, my oldest sister Nancy, my two brothers Jerry and Joey, and a couple of cousins were also present. My sister told the press that "he always fights for what he believes in."[10] Like so many other non-lawyers, Nancy did not understand that the issue was more about law than it was about my personal beliefs; but her support and that of others like her was crucial in this battle.

Judge Charles Price ruled quickly on the matter. The next day he said that the Ten Commandments could remain in my courtroom but that opening court with prayer was unconstitutional. Judge Price initially ruled that the Ten Commandments plaque, when viewed from a distance, did not appear to promote religion. Therefore, he did not find the plaque of the Ten Commandments to be unconstitutional at that time.

But Judge Price also ruled that "the prayers at issue in this case, including those in Judge Moore's Court, in the courts of other circuit court judges in Etowah County, and in other Alabama courts where judges conduct or arrange prayer before jurors summoned for jury duty, violated the Constitution of Alabama and the United States."[11] Price enjoined the governor and the attorney general to "take all reasonable steps to prevent the conduct of unconstitutional prayer in the public courts of this State and to take all reasonable steps to have Judge Roy S. Moore and any and all other judges of the State of Alabama to immediately cease and desist from acting in this unlawful manner."[12]

At a press conference immediately following the ruling, I gave my response to Judge Price's ruling: "I will not stop prayer!"[13] My explanation for my resolve then remains true today: "I don't know what it might mean to my job. I don't know what it might mean to my future. I know what it means to me personally. I know that it means my children may look back someday and say their daddy didn't give up the acknowledgment of God. That's enough for me. That's all I need."[14]

It really did mean something to my children. When told of the ruling, my nine-year-old son Ory told the *Birmingham News* that he wished the court had ruled against the Ten Commandments instead of the prayer "because we like to pray."[15] Actually it was not just about prayer; it was about the acknowledgment of God.

That point was made perfectly clear when the ACLU asked Judge Price to reconsider his ruling about the Ten Commandments display. In his original order, Judge Price had said that the Ten Commandments could stay in my courtroom as long as it was part of a historical display. But in response to questioning from the press, I stated that "[i]t's not there as a historical item; it's not there as a secular item; it's there as an acknowledgment of God."[16] I would not be party to an intentional deception of the public about our inalienable right to acknowledge God. *This is the very issue that continued to be crucial to an understanding of the controversy over the public display of the Ten Commandments.*

Bill Pryor, who had by now been appointed state attorney general by the governor, commented, "This case is about whether an acknowledgment of God by government is unconstitutional."[17]

On Friday, February 7, 1997, Judge Price visited my courtroom in Etowah County, spending approximately fifteen minutes viewing the

plaque. I left the courthouse to allow him to do his job without interference. The following Monday, February 10, he decided that the
plaque would have to be removed within ten days to comply with his
order unless I surrounded the plaque with appropriate historical documents. On February 11, which happened to be my fiftieth birthday, I
awoke to read the headline in the *Gadsden Times:* "Moore gets 10 days
to change display."[18]

There is no doubt that my previous statement to the press of my
intention to defy Judge Price's order to stop prayer in my courtroom
had greatly angered him, as did my statement that nothing was ever
placed around the plaque to deny the acknowledgment of a sovereign
God. The next jury session over which I presided and opened with
prayer was February 24, 1997. Two other judges in Etowah County had
already stopped prayer in response to Judge Price's ruling, but I had
made it clear that I would not cease prayer.

On the very day Judge Price came to view the plaque in my courtroom, the Alabama Supreme Court issued a stay (order of a higher
court temporarily stopping the order of a lower court) of his order.
This allowed me to continue the practice of opening courtroom sessions with prayer. It is my opinion that obviously aware of that affront
to his authority Judge Price had responded immediately by reversing
his earlier order about the Ten Commandments plaque, and insisting
that I surround the plaque with historical documents to "secularize"
God's law.

In other words, what Judge Price was actually saying was that if I
would admit that the display was just reflective of history and not really
an acknowledgment of God, I could keep the plaque on the wall of my
courtroom. This I refused to do.

Because the Alabama Supreme Court's stay of Judge Price's order
had removed any possibility that I could be in violation of his earlier
order regarding prayer, the only threat I now faced was a deadline for

removal of the plaque of the Ten Commandments. The news media waited anxiously each day to see if I would change the display.

Governor Fob James had intensified the controversy by stating that he would use all legal means, including the National Guard, to prevent the removal of the plaque. Explaining his position, Governor James told the *New York Times*, "If we accept all judges' orders, we don't have a government of law, we have a government of men."[19] Governor James asked rhetorically, "What would have happened if Lincoln obeyed slavery laws?"[20]

On Tuesday, February 18, 1997, the Alabama House of Representatives approved a resolution by a vote of 61 to 14 supporting my display of the Ten Commandments. The very next day the Alabama Supreme Court again stayed (prevented the order from taking effect) the order of Judge Price until the case could be heard by them. It was a last-minute ruling that averted what could have been a significant confrontation. By the grace of God I had stood firm and had been successful in defending the acknowledgment of God through the display of the Ten Commandments and prayer in court. I had done my duty; I had upheld my oath.

On Friday morning I was flown to Rockefeller Center in New York City to appear on the *Today* show with Katie Couric along with my attorney. Joel Sogol appeared for the ACLU by satellite from Birmingham. I argued forcefully that the acknowledgment of God was not the establishment of religion. If that were so, I said, "In God We Trust" on our money is unconstitutional. Sogol countered by contending that phrases such as "so help me God" refer to a "general god."[21]

The following Sunday, on February 23, 1997, at Gadsden State Community College, more than two thousand people packed Wallace Hall auditorium while two thousand more stood outside watching on a giant television screen. I told the crowd:

This is not about me. This is about something far more important. It transcends race, it transcends politics, it transcends gender. This is about the laws of God. The eyes of the nation are not on me or the governor, the eyes of the nation are on the people of Alabama. It's time to stand up and say, "We have the right to acknowledge God."[22]

It *was* about liberty and the freedom to acknowledge God. Thomas Jefferson once put it this way: "The God who gave us life gave us liberty at the same time; the hand of force may destroy, but cannot disjoin them."[23] Liberty to worship God according to the dictates of our conscience comes not from man but from God, so we must be steadfast in maintaining our right and duty to acknowledge Him publicly.

The following Monday was the date of my next courtroom session. Reporters crowded the room as I called on my friend and pastor from Crosspoint Community Church, the Reverend Phillip Ellen, to open with prayer. This time I was not required to disobey a court order, but I wondered what I would have done if the order had been enforced against me. Would I have followed an unlawful order? Would I have violated my conscience and my oath to keep my job?

We had won in the eyes of the people, and the people seemed to be pleased. But still I wondered whether they would have been as supportive if I had been forced to disobey a court order that prohibited me from opening court with prayer or displaying the Ten Commandments.

A poll taken at that time showed that nearly 90 percent of Alabamians believed that I had the right to display the Ten Commandments in my courtroom.[24] I was not surprised by the poll results. This indicated that many Alabamians understood what freedom of religion actually means, and it certainly does *not* mean that we have to deny God.

On March 5, 1997, the United States House of Representatives approved a resolution by a vote of 295 to 125 in my support. Sponsored by Representative Robert Aderholt and supported by the entire Alabama delegation with the exception of Representative Earl Hilliard of Birmingham, the resolution supported the display of the Ten Commandments in government offices and courthouses and described the commandments as "a declaration of fundamental principles that are the cornerstone of a fair and just society."[25]

On March 20, 1997, I was invited to Washington, D.C., to receive a framed copy of the resolution presented by the National Clergy Council, an independent network of pastors and laity headed by the Reverend Rob Schenck, a devout Christian and close friend who had supported me over the years. While in Washington, D.C., I spoke to area churches and appeared on the Christian Broadcasting Network's *700 Club*. People everywhere wanted to hear how we had successfully fought the ACLU.

But the case was still pending before the Alabama Supreme Court. A petition with more than two hundred thousand signatures had just been filed in that court by the Christian Family Association, asking the court to allow judges to acknowledge God.

11

A COURT DILEMMA

It has been said that you will rarely see God coming, but you can always see where He has been. That was certainly the case when about twenty-five thousand people came from across the country on April 12, 1997, to Montgomery, Alabama, to show their support for the public acknowledgment of God. Several organizations from outside the state assisted in putting the rally together. But in Alabama the main rally organizers were John Giles, head of the Alabama Christian Coalition, and Tom Blackerby with the Alabama chapter of the American Family Association. The crowd was diverse. The people came by plane, bus, van, car, and even by motorcycle from states as far away as New York, California, Illinois, and Florida.

For more than a generation the ACLU and similar organizations have been chipping away at our right to acknowledge God, and now people had seen enough. A line had been drawn in Montgomery, the home of states' rights, civil rights, and now religious liberty. Just a block away from where Martin Luther King Jr. preached at his home church on Dexter Avenue, a varied group of people—ranging from pastors to legislators to bikers—stood shoulder to shoulder in support of God's law. Waving signs and placards supporting the Ten Commandments of God, wearing T-shirts and necklaces proclaiming their faith in the God of creation, people from all walks of life gathered to sing, pray, and acknowledge the God upon whom our country was founded.[1]

The weather was bad the previous evening, with constant rain and lightning. But by midday the clouds lifted and the sun appeared, much to the delight of the jubilant throng. The local newspaper reported, "A storm front moved through as the rally got under way and skies cleared for the remainder of the three-hour gathering."[2] The reports I heard were that according to the radar screen the clouds from the west divided going north and south of Montgomery, leaving blue skies above the city. Many people felt that God blessed this gathering for His own purpose.

One by one, nationally known speakers took their turns exhorting and encouraging the crowd. Among them were Ralph Reed, executive director of the Christian Coalition; Donald Wildmon, head of the American Family Association; George Grant, author and director of King's Meadow Study Center; Governor Fob James; and Alan Keyes, former ambassador to the United Nations and chairman of the Declaration Foundation.

As Keyes's voice rose with emotion, he proclaimed, "The greatest danger we face today is from those who in the name of freedom tell us we must turn our backs on God. When judges decide they should legislate from the bench, our legislatures should impeach them.[3] . . . I came here today because we must hold Governor James and Judge Moore up so that every governor, every decent judge, and every legislator can see that we will not let our freedom be destroyed. We will stand with these two men through thick and thin, and we will prevail."[4]

Governor Fob James, who had campaigned for office on upholding states' rights through the Tenth Amendment, stood on the steps leading to the spot where Jefferson Davis had once taken his oath as president of the Confederacy. The governor had stood with me in this fight and had at one time threatened to call out the National Guard to prevent removal of the plaque of the Ten Commandments.

The governor exhorted the crowd: "Let us not rest until we can say that this was the day when the American people set their minds and hearts to return to the principles that served them so well for so long.[5] . . . When Judge Moore decided to preserve his freedom and not compromise, he was preserving freedom for all of us. Never doubt my resolve. We are with you."[6]

Even newly appointed Alabama Attorney General Bill Pryor addressed the crowd, stating that he had become a lawyer because he was "concerned that we were losing constitutional democracy in this country" and he wanted to oppose the American Civil Liberties Union.[7]

I was impressed with such a large turnout in support of God's law, and I wanted everyone to remember why they were there. When it was my turn, I started my speech by reminding the crowd, "This rally is not about me or about the Governor. It is much bigger than that. This rally is not about politics. This rally is about you and the future of our children. We must have God back in America again."[8]

I also wanted the crowd to know the importance of their coming to this event: "[Coming here] means more than you can know," I assured them, "for your presence today will send a message across this Nation. It's a message that will resound in every house, and every church, and every office, from the schoolhouse to the statehouse and even to the halls of Congress. I'm not running for anything, but I'm not running away either," I vowed. "The ACLU began this controversy. With God's help, we will finish it."[9]

The ACLU initiated this battle, but thus far they were losing in the court of law as well as the court of public opinion. Cards, letters, and telephone calls poured into my office at the Etowah County Courthouse. People were getting the message and were responding by demonstrating a willingness to fight for their right to acknowledge God.

The ACLU and others were not happy. Olivia Turner, executive director of the ACLU of Alabama, related that she had "never heard of a governor or a judge endorsing and supporting unlawful and unconstitutional behavior. It can't be good for the State when the Governor threatens to use force of arms for any citizen who says they plan to disobey a court order and flagrantly break the law."[10]

Barry Lynn, executive director of Americans United for Separation of Church and State and a former ACLU attorney, never misses an opportunity to criticize the public recognition of God. He stated, "Many Christians have been fooled into thinking this rally is about support for the Ten Commandments. In fact, it's about opposition to the rule of law and church-state separation. The Religious Right's crusaders won't rest until they impose their religion on all of us."[11]

Despite Lynn's rhetoric, this was not about imposing a religion on anyone; it was simply about the acknowledgment of the God on whom our country was founded.

In an interview, Rabbi Daniel Lapin of Toward Tradition, which cosponsored the rally, stated, "America has provided Jews with the most tranquil and prosperous haven they have enjoyed for the last 2,000 years. This is because America is a Christian nation. It is incumbent on all Jews, the people to whom God gave the Ten Commandments in the first place, to rise to the defense of Judge Roy Moore as he champions the founding document of American civilization."[12]

Susan Mowbray, a messianic Jew who came with friends from Springfield, Illinois, observed, "That's what's wrong with kids today. They don't have any standards to go by. The judge is setting a standard we all can follow."[13] Both Christians and Jews recognized the guiding principles of the Ten Commandments.

A Shelby County anesthesiologist came in support of the Ten Commandments. He said, "Our Country has to decide whether we're going to obey the laws of God or the laws of man. . . . Our founding fathers knew what they believed in, and our Constitution came from that belief. Every law in our system of government was created on some moral basis."[14]

Several days after the rally, things returned to normal as we were criticized by several groups which filed friend of the court briefs (briefs of non-parties allowed by courts to clarify the issue) supporting the ACLU's position. People for the American Way, Americans United for Separation of Church and State, and the American Jewish Congress were only a few organizations that opposed our position.

But the opposition that really surprised me was that of fifty-two ministers, rabbis, and priests. Their puzzling position was exemplified by the statements of Howard Roberts, pastor of First Baptist Church of Auburn, Alabama. Pastor Roberts explained, "It is imperative nothing be done by the government to promote a religious faith."[15]

But as I have already explained, the acknowledgment of God is not equivalent to the definition of religion that was used by our forefathers in the First Amendment. What Pastor Roberts was really objecting to was the fact that the Ten Commandments acknowledged a particular God. Many Christian theologians like him have been misled to believe that our government must be neutral toward God for others to have freedom of conscience. But our founding fathers believed it was a particular God—the God of the Holy Scriptures—who gave man freedom of conscience with which the government could not interfere.

Joseph Story was an associate justice of the United States Supreme Court in the early nineteenth century and author of the *Commentaries on the Constitution of the United States*, first published in 1833. He wrote about the First Amendment: "The rights of conscience are, indeed, beyond the just reach of any human power. They are given by God, and cannot be encroached upon by human authority, without a criminal disobedience of the precepts of natural, as well as of revealed religion."[16] Government cannot interfere with freedom of conscience because that is a right given by God and is beyond the reach of human power.

Another Christian leader who voiced opposition was Dr. Richard Land, executive director of the Christian Life Commission (later the Ethics and Religious Liberty Commission) of the Southern Baptist Convention. He told the *Alabama Baptist* that he would not support me on prayer in court unless people were given the option to leave the courtroom and other prayers of different faiths were accepted.[17] Following this thinking, one would not accept a courtroom in which a Baptist minister opened with prayer unless court sessions could also be opened by Buddhists, Hindus, and Muslims. That same logic could lead one to protest even the use of the Bible by the president of the United States in inaugural ceremonies, unless the Koran and Buddhist manuscripts were also made available.

Nevertheless, the great majority of those participating in prayer before court, like those attending inaugural ceremonies, recognize that the God of the Bible is the basis for America's religious and civil liberty. It is a historic and legal fact that America was founded by Christians on the God of the Holy Scriptures who gave the Ten Commandments to Moses on Mt. Sinai. It is this God who gives freedom of conscience and the right to worship as one chooses. Nobody is ever forced to pray, and people are not commanded to participate or even to remain in the courtroom during prayer.

To acknowledge the false gods of foreign lands is to deny the freedom of conscience which Dr. Land highly regards. The god of Islam commands that no other faiths are to be tolerated by the government. In contrast, the God of the Christian faith prohibits government from interfering in that relationship which lies solely between God and His creation. Our forefathers recognized that essential truth and adopted the First Amendment to protect freedom of conscience from government interference. They followed strictly the command of Jesus to "render therefore unto Caesar the things which are Caesar's; and unto God the things that are God's" (Matt. 22:21).

Freedom of conscience does not belong to Caesar or any government; it belongs to God.

Without acknowledgment of God by governing authorities, we have no moral basis and no freedom of conscience. After spending more than thirty-four years on the Supreme Court of the United States, Joseph Story knew this basic truth. He would have explained to religious leaders of our day who do not understand the First Amendment that "the real object of the [F]irst [A]mendment was, not to countenance, much less to advance Mahometanism, or Judaism, or infidelity, by prostrating Christianity; but to exclude all rivalry among Christian sects, and to prevent any national ecclesiastical establishment, which should give to a hierarchy the exclusive patronage of the national government."[18] If judges today would see the issue so clearly, then perhaps Christian leaders could better understand the propriety of the public acknowledgment of God.

In May, shortly after the rally, Judge Charles Price received the Profile in Courage Award at the John F. Kennedy Library and Museum in Boston for his courage in declaring prayer and the display of the Ten Commandments unconstitutional. To me, these actions did not require courage but a gross misunderstanding of the First Amendment.

Prayer and the Ten Commandments merely acknowledge the same sovereign God who, ironically, John F. Kennedy acknowledged when, as a United States congressman on June 22, 1954, he offered a resolution from the Massachusetts House of Representatives supporting the inclusion of the phrase "under God" in the Pledge of Allegiance.[19] Part of that resolution quoted Senator Homer Ferguson of Michigan: "Our Nation is founded on a fundamental belief in God, and the first and most important reason for the existence of our Government is to protect the God-given rights of our citizens."[20]

In September of 1997, I was invited to Washington, D.C., to accept the Christian Statesman of the Year award from the D. James

Kennedy Center for Christian Statesmanship. In accepting the award, I again stated my position: "An acknowledgment of God was the first thing Congress did after they approved the final wording of the First Amendment."[21] I reminded the audience that one of the first acts of John Jay, the first chief justice of the United States Supreme Court, was to authorize opening jury selection by inviting clergy to pray.[22]

In early December, I requested that the Alabama Supreme Court rule expeditiously on the pending case between me, the state of Alabama, and the ACLU. To the surprise and shock of both sides, the Alabama Supreme Court suddenly dismissed the case on Friday, January 23, 1998, citing technical grounds. The court concluded that "the State was seeking to use the tribunal for an advisory ruling on a politically volatile issue, but there [did not exist an actual] controversy between the Governor, Attorney General and Judge."[23]

I was pleased that Judge Price's unlawful orders had finally been set aside and that prayer in the courtroom and the display of the Ten Commandments would continue. Nevertheless, the highest court in our state had avoided the biggest controversy in the state and the nation: Does the acknowledgment of God through such practices as prayer and the posting of Ten Commandments displays violate the First Amendment? We would have to wait for the answer to that question.

The ACLU had again failed to stop the acknowledgment of God. Bobby Segall, one of the ACLU attorneys, said that "he was disappointed the case was not resolved on the merits."[24] Joel Sogol, another ACLU attorney, commented, "It appears that six years of litigation has been ordered to start over. . . . In a practical sense, it seems the emotions run high enough on both sides of the issue to bring another lawsuit."[25]

Perhaps the most insightful analysis of the ruling came from Tom Berg, a law professor at Samford University: "By deciding the case on a technical issue, justices don't have to address the main legal issues and don't have to worry about angering voters who support Moore. . . . This was a tough case for the Alabama Supreme Court justices."[26] But the court should not avoid "tough" cases. It is their duty to resolve existing conflicts and especially where fundamental rights are involved. Judges should never consider politics in making their decisions, but they sometimes do.

In football terms, the court "punted." This might be the proper decision in a physical contest between opposing teams, but a legal battle should not be treated like a game. The court avoided an issue in which the public had great interest—the acknowledgment of God by their elected representatives while in office. It was not the first time the court pulled this stunt, and it would not be the last.

I had worked many extra hours the past year and a half doing my job as a judge while corresponding with my attorneys about my case. I had maintained a busy speaking schedule nearly every weekend and had resolved more than my share of cases in the court system. Although I was disappointed in the failure of the Alabama Supreme Court to do its duty, I was relieved that I could return to a normal life—or so I thought. But before the ACLU struck again as they had promised to do, there was another type of attack—more subtle and more vicious.

12

STAR CHAMBER

The war will come. It's inevitable but it will come."[1] Speaking to approximately twelve hundred people assembled at Bayside Christian Fellowship in Green Bay, Wisconsin, on March 15, 1998, I knew that there was another battle ahead. The Alabama Supreme Court's decision (or non-decision) left me vulnerable to still another attack and perhaps three more years of litigation. I told the audience that the ACLU was stripping our nation of its godly heritage. I expected that the ACLU would be back to harass me, but I did not know when that would happen. All I could do was wait.

I was invited to Wisconsin by Dennis Pape, who had heard a radio interview I had given. This motivated him to become active in spreading the truth about God's law and our nation's relationship to God. He approached several municipalities about posting the Ten Commandments and met with considerable success as several of them adopted resolutions in support of such displays. I met many wonderful people like Dennis as I traveled around the country speaking about the First Amendment. I enjoyed teaching others about the importance of our nation's Constitution and our right to acknowledge publicly the Creator God who was responsible for our rights to life, liberty, and the pursuit of happiness. The activities in Alabama during the previous three years had sparked a national movement.

Some people did not interpret the rise of this movement as a positive thing. Steve Green, legal director of Americans United for Separation of Church and State, insisted that "the promotion of the Ten Commandments is part of a national campaign by the religious right to adorn all public buildings with religious displays."[2] He believed it was his group's responsibility to nip those efforts in the bud. "Otherwise," he said, "they could become a springboard to bring religion to other public places such as the schools."[3]

Indeed, Americans United, the ACLU, and People for the American Way have worked to strip our schools of any knowledge of religious virtue and morality. They ignore the fact that our second president, John Adams, stated that, "Our Constitution was made only for a moral and religious people. It is wholly inadequate to the government of any other."[4] Similarly, President Washington, in his Farewell Address on September 17, 1796, reminded the people that "[o]f all the dispositions and habits which lead to political prosperity, Religion and morality are indispensable supports."[5] Obviously, if religion and morality are so important to the welfare of the nation, they ought to be encouraged rather than shunned in the public schools.

However, groups such as Americans United and the ACLU have attempted to deprive us of these "indispensable supports," and, unfortunately, too many Americans have looked on with indifference. We have been led to believe that the American Civil Liberties Union exists to secure our civil and religious liberties. In reality, their main agenda is to strip those liberties from us. Liberty of conscience and the right to acknowledge God were presumed under the First Amendment.

In November of 1996, I was "asked" to appear before the Judicial Inquiry Commission (JIC) on December 12 to address my "comments to the press regarding [my] intentions not to comply with a court order about prayer in the courtroom."[6] The JIC is a non-judicial body composed of judges, lawyers, and ordinary citizens serving as a disciplinary board for judges who violate the Canons of Judicial Ethics.

I remember the excitement I felt on December 12 as Kayla and I headed to Montgomery, Alabama, where I would appear before the commission and prove my case—or so I thought. I arrived with five briefcases packed with books, articles, and documents which I planned to use to prove beyond all doubt that America was founded on God and that acknowledgment of God was not a violation of the United States Constitution or the Constitution of Alabama.

The JIC's first act when I arrived was to prohibit Kayla from being present. When this happened perhaps I should have realized that this meeting with the JIC was not what I had anticipated. I had expected an opportunity to explain the legal and historical support for my posi-tion, but what I got was an "inquisition." The term *inquisition* means an intense examination, or a severe questioning with little regard for indi-vidual rights.[7] In the Middle Ages, persons suspected of crimes against the Church were interrogated with no right to defend themselves. They were punished with penalties ranging from prayer and fasting to confiscation of property, imprisonment, and even death.

Later, in the fifteenth and sixteenth centuries in England, another form of inquisition appeared. It was known as the Court of the Star Chamber because of the stars painted on the ceiling of the Westminster Palace in London where the court convened.[8] The Star Chamber was used by British monarchs as a "political weapon" against those who opposed the king's orders and edicts. It was also used to enforce unpopular political and ecclesiastical policies. At its height, the Star Chamber operated in a secret and arbitrary manner. It oper-ated without a jury and according to its own procedures and rules rather than those of the Common Law. Until it was abolished in 1641, the Star Chamber was a sinister tool of royal tyranny and a symbol of oppression to Parliament and Puritan opponents of King Charles I.[9]

As I sat at the end of the long table with more than a dozen solemn people staring at me, I realized that this hearing would not be pleasant. A court reporter was there to take down every word. An air of intimidation permeated the room. The questioning was pointed and direct. The JIC wanted to know why I had told the press that I would not obey a court order. I replied that the issue was not about obedience to a court order but acknowledging the sovereignty of God and obedience to the Constitution.

When asked about my opinion on the acknowledgment of God in court, I began to explain the First Amendment by referring to an original *Commentaries on the Constitution of the United States*, written by Joseph Story in 1833. My quotations of earlier Supreme Court justices and cases were met with blank stares. I could discern nothing but contempt in their voices. Nevertheless, I continued to argue my position forcefully for nearly an hour, answering each question. Then, in the middle of an answer, the chairman of the JIC, Braxton Kittrell, interrupted: "We've heard enough."

I was too surprised by such a rude comment to respond. I could not imagine one circuit judge talking to anyone—much less another circuit judge—in such a disrespectful manner. I put my books and documents back in my briefcases and left.

In some ways, the JIC had used its powers both as a "political weapon" and as a weapon to actually suppress "religious faith." In their minds, obedience of a court order was superior to all other concerns, even the suppression of belief in the sovereignty of God. I met this attitude seven years later when I was taken again before the Court of the Judiciary and, later, a specially appointed Alabama Supreme Court.

I told Kayla that we could expect a complaint within days, which would, in effect, relieve me of my duties as a judge. But the Alabama Supreme Court had not yet ruled on my appeal. It would have been an embarrassment for the JIC to act prematurely, so that body obviously decided to wait. After a few weeks, I concluded that they would not proceed.

Nearly a year and a half later, I was astounded to learn that the JIC investigation had never been terminated. In April of 1998, I was informed by a teller at the bank where I carried an account that a subpoena *duces tecum* (order to obtain documents) had been served on the bank by the JIC, demanding all my bank records, which had also included those of my wife. The JIC gave me no notice of this, as required by the Alabama Rules of Civil Procedure. The JIC even served a subpoena on another bank in town where I had never held an account. (So much for keeping the complaint confidential, which the JIC had an obligation to do.)

Later, a television station in Huntsville was served an order to obtain one of my speeches, even though one of the judges on the JIC panel, Judge Randall Cole, had been present for the entire speech. It seemed that everyone but me knew I was being investigated.

Then I learned that the JIC investigators had questioned several lawyers in the jurisdiction over which I presided, asking them what, if anything, I had ever done wrong. Not only was this an improper "fishing" expedition; it was also an attack on the integrity of my court. The attorneys to whom I spoke were told not to discuss the matter with me.

On several occasions my attorney, Stephen Melchior, requested of the JIC any information about the charges for which I was being investigated and what materials the JIC was trying to obtain. Melchior wrote to Rosa Davis, attorney for the JIC:

> When you phoned me months ago to ask questions of
> me regarding Judge Moore, the defense fund, etc., I told you
> at that time that Judge Moore had been above board on
> everything and in all of his dealings, that he has nothing to
> hide, and that if you had any questions you could feel free to

contact me. Instead of directly contacting me, or directly contacting Judge Moore for that matter, you have instead chosen to "investigate" Judge Moore in a clandestine fashion, resulting in my learning that Judge Moore was again being investigated by the Commission from third parties not even associated with the investigation. Not only is this disturbing, it is alarming.[10]

Attorney Davis responded that everything the JIC did was confidential, and even the existence of a complaint could not be disclosed. But the reason for confidentiality under the law is to protect a judge from public disclosure of frivolous complaints, *not* to keep him from knowing he is being investigated or to hide from him the subject matter of that investigation.

The JIC even started seizing records and bank accounts belonging to Dean Young, who originally headed the Judge Moore Defense Fund. But Dean went public, accusing the JIC of harassment. The JIC implied to Dean that I might have received funds from this account improperly. Dean replied, "Judge Moore never has taken a penny. He gets his expenses paid, but he will never take any money."[11] Dean was also angry because his wife's records were being reviewed by the JIC.

Then I learned that Justice Mark Kennedy, an associate justice of the Alabama Supreme Court, was serving on the JIC in violation of an explicit provision of the law. He had made derogatory comments about me during the time when my appeal was pending before the Alabama Supreme Court. On June 19, 1996, even before I appeared before the JIC, the people of Alabama ratified an amendment to the Alabama Constitution which clearly provided that the JIC would consist of nine members and that "[t]he Supreme Court shall appoint one appellant judge *who shall not be a Justice on the Supreme Court*."[12]

Obviously, Justice Kennedy was in breach of the plain letter of the law. Furthermore, in a speech in Washington State, he had accused me of wanting to be the "King of Siam" or a United States senator. This was an improper comment for a justice of the Supreme Court about a party before his court.[13]

I finally had enough. On October 7, 1998, I filed motions in court to stop the JIC from an illegal investigation and to remove Justice Kennedy from sitting on the JIC. Bill Gray, former adviser to Governor James, noted that "for anyone to be charged, tried, or investigated in secret" as the JIC was doing was akin to holding "a Star Chamber proceeding."[14] Chief Justice Perry Hooper later said of the JIC, "The power to intimidate a judge would turn the JIC into some sort of Star Chamber, hidden from the public and private scrutiny of any kind and acting as a kingmaker or kingbreaker—in this case a judge-breaker—in Alabama judicial politics."[15]

Justice Kennedy quietly stepped down from the JIC soon thereafter, claiming that his term had come to an end. Then, without warning, a sister commission to the JIC, the Alabama Ethics Commission (AEC)—which oversees ethics complaints against all public officials—voted 5 to 0 to refer a complaint against me to the attorney general. The complaint charged that I had wrongfully benefited from the defense fund. But James Sumner, the director of the AEC, had acknowledged that "there was no evidence that [Judge Moore] pocketed money other than the bills being paid."[16] According to Sumner, the possible punishment for a conviction was twenty years in prison and a ten-thousand-dollar fine.[17]

At the request of the ACLU, Attorney General Bill Pryor recused from the case. Pryor assigned the matter to District Attorney Van Davis, who conducted a thorough investigation. He concluded that I had not used my office for personal gain, did not have any control over the defense fund, was entitled to state representation because I had been sued in my official capacity, and had voluntarily assumed my own defense.[18]

Davis went even further, stating that the complaint never should have been brought because "it was based solely on information the man [John Lewis, who had filed the complaint] obtained by reading newspaper articles, not by first-hand or actual knowledge as is required by [the State Ethics Code]."[19] I had been cleared of fraudulent charges by Van Davis, a man whom I had never met, but to whom I shall always be grateful. The complaint was determined to be completely frivolous.

Adding insult to injury, Lewis later told the *Birmingham News* that he had filed the complaint against me out of a desire to take revenge on Southern Baptists who had defeated a dog track referendum in Bridgeport where he had served as a mayor twelve years earlier.[20] In the interview, Lewis opined, "I think Judge Moore is probably an honest man who really believes in what he is doing. I just feel like Judge Moore has used his office to express his religious philosophies and I think that's wrong."[21]

Two weeks later, AEC Director Sumner commented: "Had the Commission known Lewis's motive, I think we would have probed a little bit deeper as to his motives so that we would not be used in this situation. . . . We tried to avoid the Commission [from] being used for any political purpose."[22] Curiously, this "ethics" commission had stepped forward to file a frivolous complaint, taking attention away from the JIC, which, in my opinion, had been caught running an illegal investigation.

My family had suffered tremendously through all of this. We were overjoyed to be out of court after nearly five years of nonstop litigation. We had been fighting the ACLU and the established system since 1995. Hundreds of thousands of dollars had been spent to cover attorneys' fees, and we were tired. I had not spent enough time with the family during the past several years, and I looked forward to a more peaceful life after all the court proceedings were over.

The AEC had not done its job. A simple inquiry would have revealed Mr. Lewis's real motives. The JIC, pretending to be a disciplinary board for wayward judges, had been used exactly as the Star Chamber had been used in England—as a political weapon against those who opposed the edicts of those in power. In England, those who opposed the king's edicts were punished by the Star Chamber regardless of the reason for the person's opposition. In Alabama, I was investigated and maligned without regard for my due process rights or the substance behind the allegations. I believe this happened simply because I had stated I would oppose a court order. Little did I know that I would experience similar disrespect for my due process rights from another tribunal seven years later over the same issue.

What really motivated the JIC's actions? In my opinion, the JIC was embarrassed by a circuit court judge who stood for the truth that God governs in the affairs of men. Politicians do not mind campaigning as Sunday school teachers, deacons, and choir directors. But once elected, they often deny the sovereignty of God and feel embarrassed by anyone who acknowledges God. I openly acknowledged God and suffered the consequences: false accusations, charges, public embarrassment, and financial loss. According to one estimation, the legal fees to defend against all the ridiculous charges brought against me amounted to more than twenty-five thousand dollars.

After finally being cleared of all charges, I stated publicly, "I feel like today we have been delivered in His righteousness. . . . I feel that we owe our first thanks to God for seeing us through this battle, and it has been a battle and an ordeal for me and my family."[23]

Shortly after that I was scheduled to speak at a Thanksgiving breakfast in my hometown of Gadsden on November 23, 1999. During my speech, I remembered all the things for which I was thankful. But even more, I was impressed that God has blessed our country so richly, and that Thanksgiving was a time when all Americans should be thankful for our many blessings.

I still had my job as a judge in Etowah County. In spite of all the commotion, I felt God's sustaining strength. I managed to maintain my court dockets. I had the lowest number of cases pending in Etowah County in both the civil and criminal divisions, according to statistics published by the Administrative Office of Courts. The ACLU was quiet for the first time in years. For now, at least, the JIC had been silenced because of my motions pending before the Alabama Supreme Court.

13

RACE FOR CHIEF JUSTICE

I was looking forward to the new year. My term of office would soon be ending, and I would be required to run for reelection. I was eager to kick off my first political race in Etowah County without opposition. Recent victories over the ACLU and those who had pursued false charges against me before the ethics commission of Alabama had increased my popularity.

I was content as a circuit judge. My staff, consisting of secretary Delbra Adams, bailiff Scott Barnett, and court reporter Larry Cross, were outstanding professionals who were dedicated to their jobs. Furthermore, during my next term my retirement pay would become vested—benefits that I could not lose—which was an important consideration for my family.

Our office had also moved into the newly constructed Etowah County Judicial Building. I was able to design my own offices for maximum efficiency. I decorated it in an appropriate manner, including, of course, the redwood plaque of the Ten Commandments that I placed over my bench. My staff and I loved the refreshing change of atmosphere from the old Etowah County Courthouse.

Nearly every day for lunch I met my wife and—school permitting—my children at the Poor House Restaurant in Gadsden. There we enjoyed a special meal from my favorite cook, Johnnie Mae Pinson, who was also a personal friend. She had helped Kayla and me a lot with the children over the years.

Kayla and I were very happy in our home at Gallant. Micah had not yet begun school, but all the other children were performing well in the public school system of Etowah County. Heather had just turned sixteen and was a cheerleader at Etowah High School where I had attended thirty-five years before. Ory and Caleb were involved in sports and loved to hunt and fish in their free time. Micah was looking forward to Christmas, while Kayla and I looked forward to a more peaceful existence after all the legal and political battles we had been through.

However, on November 9, 1999, a *Birmingham News* article announced the beginning of the race for chief justice of the Alabama Supreme Court. Chief Justice Perry O. Hooper was ineligible for reelection because of the age limitation established by the Alabama Constitution.[1] Three candidates had already indicated their intention to run: Associate Justice Harold See, who was already a member of the Supreme Court, Court of Criminal Appeals Judge Pam Baschab, and Jefferson County Presiding Circuit Court Judge Wayne Thorn. All three candidates had previous political experience and were well qualified to run for the position of chief justice.

The same day another article appeared in the *Birmingham News* which noted that a petition drive had been started to recruit me to run for the office of chief justice.[2] The Christian Family Association had circulated a petition and resolution seeking my candidacy. The response was overwhelming.[3] Although many people had asked me to consider higher office, I had never considered the prospect.

I knew a decision to run was hazardous. I had never run a statewide race, and I had absolutely no funds with which to begin. In contrast, the other three candidates were already well funded. Associate Justice Harold See was particularly well financed because he had the backing of the powerful Business Council of Alabama (BCA). His campaign was managed by associates of Karl Rove, whose organization represented George W. Bush in his campaign for president.

I also knew that I would be running at the end of my term as circuit judge. This meant that if I lost the race, I would be out of a job. The other candidates chose, as most judges do, to run in the middle of their terms so they would not risk becoming unemployed if they lost the election. Finally, a loss would automatically prevent me from receiving state retirement benefits because my retirement had not yet become vested.

Still, a win would be a great honor. With the new position would come increased responsibility and more pay. But no amount of money could replace leaving my home and my extended family. An election would mean taking my children from the schools to which they had grown accustomed and beginning new lives in Montgomery, Alabama, where we had virtually no friends or acquaintances.

The implications of the choice drove me to pray for weeks to discern God's will. During the past five years, He had been my shield and my rock, and I did not want to make a decision based on my own ideas. I had to know God's direction for my life.

My mind continued to return to the parable of the talents in Matthew in which Jesus tells the story of a man who traveled to a foreign country, leaving behind his servants with a certain number of talents, each according to his own ability (Matt. 25:14–30). When the master returned, he required them to give back to him the amount he had given each servant, and more. Those who had invested their talents wisely were rewarded. But the servant who hid his talent and did not invest it for his master's good was cast into darkness.

To me the parable had a special meaning. I knew that during the past seven years God had given me a better understanding of our American Constitution and our law. I also had learned that the United

States was founded on principles of the revealed, divine law of God recorded in the Holy Scriptures. Upon that firm foundation, our nation had grown to be the brightest beacon of civil and religious freedom ever known. It is because of that foundation that we know that the freedom of conscience and the right to worship God was not a concession or a privilege, but a right given by God and secured by the First Amendment to the U.S. Constitution.

Today, this is a right that we are losing as federal courts continue to deprive us of that knowledge. I considered it my duty to stand boldly on this truth as a circuit judge. If this were my talent, should I not invest it for the Master? In the end, my duty to acknowledge God and His laws which form the basis of our government and our law motivated me to run for higher office.

On Tuesday, December 7, 1999, I announced my decision to run for chief justice of the Supreme Court of Alabama. Standing in my courtroom in Etowah County with my family by my side and the plaque of the Ten Commandments on the wall behind me, I said, "Etowah County has been home all my life. I was born here. My wife is from here. I went to high school here. . . . I have twenty years in the judicial system. I am familiar with problems facing this nation and I am concerned about the direction our society is headed.[4] . . . My job here in Etowah County is done. Somebody needs to lead the judiciary. This is a tremendous step, and I don't take it lightly. I think I must. It's a duty I must answer."[5]

The decision meant that for the first time in nearly twenty-five years, I might have to leave the home I had worked so hard to build and take my family to Montgomery. I knew that it would be especially difficult for Heather in the middle of her junior year of high school; she had worked hard to become a varsity cheerleader. Nor was it an easy decision for Kayla and the boys. But we were a family, and we would go to Montgomery if this was what God wanted us to do.

I stepped out in faith, knowing that if it was God's will, I would be elected. But if not, I would have to start over again as an attorney. This would be difficult. And yet, if it were not in God's plan for me to run, I prayed to be defeated. The result was in His hands.

Within a week after the campaign kicked off, a near tragedy occurred. On our wedding anniversary, December 14, 1999, Kayla was struck by a car in a hit-and-run incident at Colonial Mall in Gadsden. She sustained serious injuries, but we were thankful to God that her life was spared. The driver of the vehicle that struck her was a seventeen-year-old who was later arrested and prosecuted through the fine work of the Gadsden Police Department.

When I returned to the campaign, I was relieved that the JIC was finally leaving me alone. Perhaps their decision on January 27, 2000, to stop all investigations was motivated in part by the fact that the investigation by the Ethics Commission had resulted in a complete exoneration, with a finding of no wrongdoing. But the JIC also suffered embarrassment when Braxton Kittrell, JIC chairman, was reported to have allegedly taken social trips to Super Bowl resorts with attorneys who practiced before his court. This was the same Braxton Kittrell who, as head of the JIC, had been investigating me for more than three years for unethical conduct. Perhaps the members of the JIC knew that any further investigations would focus attention on them.[6]

After the JIC announcement, the Alabama Supreme Court, on March 31, 2000, dismissed my action against the JIC as moot, thereby avoiding any litigation of their wrongful conduct. But I knew that I would see them again if I were elected to the Supreme Court.

In the meantime, on February 2, 2000, I was surprised to be invited by our presiding judge to join a conference call with Governor Don Siegelman about a judicial pay raise proposal. Collusion between two branches of government to influence a bill pending before the Alabama legislature appeared improper. Judges should avoid the appearance of impropriety and never use their influence for personal gain. Because of my past experience with the JIC, my attorney, Steve Melchior, advised me to record the conference call for my own protection.

During the conference call, Governor Siegelman asked the judges to take newspaper editors to lunch to convince them to write favorable articles about pay raises for judges. I was shocked! Then I learned that the new chairman of the JIC, Randall Cole, was an active participant in the conference call. How could the head of the JIC, the body that investigates judicial ethics, take part in a conference where judges were being asked to use their influence for personal gain?

Specifically, Governor Siegelman told Judge Cole and other judges, "Again, if you could do a couple of things. One, go to your newspaper, talk to the editor, take him to lunch today, try to prepare them to write the right stories should this become law."[7] To my further amazement, several judges agreed to do what Governor Siegelman requested. I immediately reported the matter to the JIC, providing it with the taped conversation.

The governor at first denied the substance of the conversation. But when the recorded conversation became public, he suddenly forgot exactly what had been said. Because of their later actions, it was obvious that neither Governor Siegelman nor Judge Cole ever forgot the embarrassment that resulted from my bringing this conference call to the attention of the public.

These events drew my attention away from the campaign, but after they were resolved, I returned in earnest to concentrating on the race. I spoke to enthusiastic audiences across the state, telling them that God was not finished with our country yet, that the United States was a special nation founded on the laws of God, and not just any God. We were not founded on the faith of Buddha or the Hindu faith or the faith of Islam, but on the faith of Jesus Christ.

While Christianity was not an "established" religion, it was the faith of our forefathers. We had a duty to acknowledge God—the same God who gives us the freedom to worship Him according to the dictates of our consciences, free from government interference. But we seemed to be turning from God as a nation.

The removal of God from our public life corresponded directly with an increase in school violence, homosexuality, and crime. Parents were killing their children, and children were killing their parents. As we drifted from God we were losing our sense of right and wrong. The courts were imposing their own morality, which was actually immorality. My campaign message was simple and direct: We must return God to our public life and restore the moral foundation of our law.

My main opponent in the Republican primary was Justice Harold See, who had obtained endorsements from Chief Justice Hooper, both United States senators, and Attorney General Bill Pryor before I entered the campaign. The Business Council of Alabama and others poured millions of dollars into his campaign coffers. But the people of Alabama knew me and the things I stood for. The polls began to indicate my lead in early May, and even the *Washington Times* reported that I was pulling ahead in the race.[8]

Aware that the race was slipping away, the Harold See campaign turned to questionable advertising to increase his poll numbers, advertising that the JIC later determined to be false advertising. But this tactic did not succeed. In spite of my campaign's lack of money or high-powered support, I won the primary without the need for a runoff.[9] I won with 56 percent of the vote in a race among four strong candidates.[10]

In my response to this great victory, I noted, "Of course we give our first recognition to God."[11] Phillip Jauregui, one of my attorneys and my campaign coordinator, was a newcomer to state politics, but he did an outstanding job of keeping the campaign focused on the issue and not allowing me to be distracted from the message. "Prayer has been the first thing and the last thing we do," Phillip informed the assembled crowd in downtown Gadsden.[12] I told the people, "I do believe God's blessing has been upon us."[13]

The general election seemed to go much smoother and quieter. My opponent, Sharon Yates, a judge on the Court of Civil Appeals, ran a cleaner campaign than my Republican opponents had done. There was also more support from some people who had previously opposed me. Numerous mailouts were sent to voters depicting me with other Republican candidates for the Supreme Court of Alabama. Lynn Stuart, Champ Lyons, Tom Woodall, and Bernard Harwood appeared in a full-color mailout with a message from me:

> Nothing is more important to the future of our State than upholding the moral foundations of the law. When I become Chief Justice of the Alabama Supreme Court, my top priority will be to restore the moral foundation upon which our laws are based. We need justices on the Supreme Court and judges on the Courts of Criminal and Civil Appeals who share these values. You can help by electing men and women who are committed to this task.[14]

I would live to regret such a blanket endorsement of men and women who professed their faith but eventually voted to remove God's law from public view simply because a federal judge ordered them to do so.

When the votes were tallied on the evening of November 7 and into the early morning of November 8, the people had spoken: I was elected to become the twenty-eighth chief justice of the Supreme Court of Alabama, garnering 54 percent of the vote. The headline in the *Gadsden Times* told the rest of the story: "Coattails Affect Races."[15]

All of the Republican candidates for the Supreme Court were victorious. Of nineteen appellate judges, only one Democrat remained on each court. I was credited by the media with affecting the races for statewide judicial candidates,[16] but that was far less important to me than my realization that God had allowed me to win for His glory and not my own.

My comments to those assembled in Gadsden were basically the same as I had made in the primary victory. "Remember the One responsible for it all, and that's God. This campaign is about morality. It's about the loss of morality in our State and Nation."[17]

Soon Christmas was upon us. As our family celebrated, we wondered if this would be the last Christmas in the only home we had ever known. It was sad in some ways, and my children were not particularly happy to be leaving their schools and their friends. We had enrolled them in a school not far from our new home in Deatsville, a small farming community much like the one in Gallant, and only a short drive from the Alabama Judicial Building in Montgomery. Eventually my children would adjust and acquire many new friends. Kayla and I were apprehensive, but there was also an excitement in knowing that I would soon assume the highest judicial position in the state of Alabama.

During the Christmas holidays and into the new year, I was busy moving and closing my office in Gadsden. My secretary, Delbra, remained employed in the clerk's office in Etowah County. My court reporter, Larry Cross, was assigned to a new judge. My bailiff and legal assistant, Scott Barnett, went with me to the Supreme Court and was assigned to the legal division of the Administrative Office of Courts (AOC).

It was not pleasant to say good-bye to those with whom I had worked for many years, but we all knew that things would soon be different for everyone. We had done a good job in Etowah County, and I knew the system had improved to better serve the public during my tenure there. Soon I was moving back and forth to Montgomery to establish my new residence and my new office in the Alabama Judicial Building. I became acquainted with my new staff and agency directors, as well as the associate justices with whom I would work. It was an exciting and busy time as I prepared to take the oath for the office of chief justice of the Supreme Court of Alabama.

14
"So Help Me God"

I t was finally time to take the oath of office as the next chief justice of Alabama. The sky was clear as we arrived at the Alabama Judicial Building in Montgomery on January 15, 2001. An overflow crowd stood among the stately columns that reached to the upper floors above the rotunda. The large courtroom was filled with friends, acquaintances, and political figures from across the state who came to see the swearing in of the man known as the "Ten Commandments Judge." The title had been given to me by the media around the state and across the nation.[1]

I knew that this was about much more than the media would ever realize. I would soon be sworn in as the chief administrator of the justice system of Alabama, and the job would be enormous. The media wondered if I would bring the Ten Commandments to the Supreme Court courtroom. Of course, they were speaking about the small plaque from my Etowah County Courthouse. I knew it would not be of the proper size and quality to adorn the imposing walls of the rotunda, which did not have any decoration.

Unknown to nearly everyone, I had already started designing a much larger display of God's law. As early as a month after I was elected to the position of chief justice, I drew a sketch of a monument depicting the Ten Commandments and contacted a man in Huntsville, Richard Hahnemann, who had some experience with bronze sculpting.

He, along with Steve Melchior, my attorney, were a great help in designing the monument. We knew it would take several months to obtain the granite we planned to use. For now, it was sufficient that the press understand that I would, in fact, bring my handmade plaque to Montgomery in my new job.

Among those in the crowd for my swearing in were my wife Kayla, our four children, my mother, brothers, sisters, and numerous other family members. Friends from Gallant Baptist Church also made the long journey to Montgomery along with others from the Gallant and Gadsden areas. My pastor, Tom Brown, came with several other ministers from Etowah County. Reverend Phillip Ellen of Crosspoint Community Church, who had opened my court in Etowah County many times with prayer, came to close the ceremony with a benediction. Another minister and friend from Montgomery whom I had come to know, Carmon Falcione of "The Gathering" ministry, opened the ceremony with an appeal to God for His blessings.

I was sworn in by the retiring chief justice, Perry Hooper Sr. Many other dignitaries were present for the occasion, including two former governors, another former chief justice, and numerous representatives and senators of the Alabama legislature. Even former Congressman Jim Martin, who had appointed me to West Point, was in attendance. Several other judges and justices of the Alabama appellate courts also observed the ceremony. I was especially pleased that my old staff— George Hundley, Delbra Adams, Larry Cross, and Scott Barnett—were able to attend, along with their families.

It was an exciting and impressive occasion. My beautiful wife stood proudly holding the three family Bibles on which I placed my left hand as I raised my right hand to take the oath of office. I was a little nervous as I repeated the oath administered by Chief Justice Hooper. Slowly and deliberately, I again pledged to do my duty to support the Constitution of the United States and the Constitution of Alabama and to "faithfully and honestly discharge the duties of the office of Chief Justice of the State of Alabama, to the best of my ability." Then I paused and concluded, "So help me God!"[2]

I had taken similar oaths on several other occasions. As a new cadet at West Point in 1965 and upon graduation four years later as a second lieutenant in the United States Army, I swore to support and defend the Constitution of the United States, "so help me God." In Vietnam I was called to fulfill that oath. When I became an attorney in 1977, and again as an assistant district attorney shortly after that, I took the oath required by the Alabama Constitution to support both the Constitution of the United States and the Constitution of Alabama, "so help me God." After my appointment as a circuit judge in Etowah County, I was administered a similar oath by the county circuit clerk, Billy Yates. Then in 1994 after my successful election to that position, Governor Fob James administered my oath, "so help me God."

But this occasion was something special. Over the last ten years I had come to realize the real meaning of the First Amendment and its relationship to the God on whom the oath was based. My mind had been opened to the spiritual war occurring in our state and our nation that was slowly removing the knowledge of that relationship between God and law.

I pledged to support not only the U.S. Constitution, but the Alabama Constitution as well, which provided in its preamble that the state "establish[ed] justice" "invoking the favor and guidance of Almighty God." The connection between God and our law could not be more clear. As chief administrator of the Alabama justice system,[3] I had a statutory duty to recognize the basis of that justice system.

In fact, I was charged with "tak[ing] affirmative and appropriate action to correct or alleviate any condition or situation adversely affecting the administration of justice in the state," and "[t]o take any such other, further additional action as may be necessary for the orderly administration of justice within the state, whether or not enumerated in this section or elsewhere."[4] I believed that the removal of the knowledge of God from our law was "adversely affecting the administration of justice," and I wanted to do my part, my duty, to correct that situation by properly acknowledging God as the foundation of our justice system.

As chief justice I had another title—lessee of the Alabama Judicial Building. This meant that I was in charge of designating office and parking spaces and decorating the building.[5] None of the other officers in Alabama government was assigned such responsibilities for the Alabama Judicial Building.

The judicial building in which I took the oath housed all the appellate courts of Alabama. The building, only ten years old, contained no recognition of the foundation of our justice system. Although there were historical artifacts in the building, nothing else had ever been placed in the building to acknowledge the faith and law on which our entire system rested. I was determined to acknowledge God as the moral foundation of our law as I had pledged to do during my campaign. This included setting before the public appropriate displays acknowledging the source of our justice system. I resolved that nothing would prevent me from performing this duty.

I knew that the Constitution of the United States did not restrict acknowledgments of God. The purpose of the First Amendment Establishment Clause was to prevent Congress from interfering in any way with the worship of God by the states. Not only in Alabama, but in every other state, the declaration of a belief in God could be found in the state constitution, and the First Amendment secured that freedom. I also knew that all three branches of the federal government recognized God, so it would be hypocrisy for the federal government to prohibit such practices by the states.

The essence of my oath was to "faithfully" and "honestly" discharge the duties of my office, "so help me God." A belief in God was historically the faith on which all oaths were based. It is for that reason that the Alabama Constitution requires all oaths taken by officers of the state government to end with the words, "so help me God." Although it has been deemed unconstitutional for a state to require compliance with an oath invoking the help of God, that fact certainly did not negate the meaning for those who chose to take such an oath.

The Alabama Rules of Criminal Procedure require grand jurors and jurors in criminal cases to take oaths ending in "so help me God."[6] The history of such requirements goes back to at least the thirteenth century. In 1256, Henry de Bracton in *On the Laws and Customs of England* wrote that jurors of townships took an oath after this fashion: "Hear this, ye justices, that we will speak the truth about what is asked of us on the King's behalf, nor will we for any reason fail to tell the truth, so help us God."[7] According to de Bracton, the justices responded by stating,

> And therefore we tell you that on the faith that binds
> you to God and by the oath that you have taken you are to
> let us know the truth thereof, nor are you to fail in saying
> whether or not he is guilty of what is alleged against him . . .
> through fear or love or hate but with God only before your
> eyes, nor are you to oppress him if he be innocent of the said
> offense.[8]

In other words, a juror was sworn to his faith in God as the basis for ruling in truth on the guilt or innocence of the defendant in a criminal case.

That concept was well understood by George Washington, who, in the Farewell Address on September 17, 1796, commented, "Let it simply be asked, where is the security for property, for reputation, for life, if the sense of religious obligation *desert* the oaths which are the instruments of investigation in courts of justice?"[9]

With regard to the testimony of witnesses, John Jay, the first chief justice of the United States Supreme Court, in his charge to a grand jury in Vermont on June 25, 1792, stated, "[T]his testimony [of witnesses] is given under those solemn obligations which an appeal to the God of truth impose; and if oaths should cease to be held sacred, our dearest and most valuable Rights would become insecure."[10]

On October 19, 1789, Chief Justice Jay took an oath similar to the one I was administered by Chief Justice Hooper. His oath ended with the words "so help me God," as required by the Judiciary Act of 1789 under which our first federal judiciary was organized.[11]

Although not specifically required by the Constitution, our nation's first president under the new federal Constitution, when administered his oath on April 30, 1789, on the balcony of Federal Hall in New York City, voluntarily ended his oath with "so help me God."[12] His oath conformed in virtually every respect to the oath of British monarchs who laid their hand "upon the holy gospels" and said, "The things which I have here before promised I will perform and keep, so help me God."[13]

Both John Jay and George Washington realized that a belief in God was the foundation of all oaths, and that without such a belief, people could not be expected to tell the truth because they had no fear of a future state of rewards and punishments. Blackstone in his *Commentaries* explained oaths this way:

> The belief of a future state of rewards and punishments,
> the entertaining just ideas of the moral attributes of the
> Supreme Being, and a firm persuasion that he superintends
> and will finally compensate every action in human life all

which are clearly revealed in the doctrines, and forcibly inculcated by the precepts, of our saviour Christ. These are the grand foundation of all judicial oaths; which call God to witness the truth of those facts, which perhaps may be only known to him and the party attesting: all moral evidence therefore, all confidence in human veracity, must be weakened by apostasy, and overthrown by total infidelity.[14]

Blackstone was restating a truth known to his generation and those that preceded him: People are bound to the truth by a fear and respect for the Supreme Being who will ultimately compensate them for their adherence to the truth, which in many cases is only known by God and the person giving testimony. Without such fear, people out of their own self-interest or personal motivations will not be motivated to tell the truth.

After the oath had been completed, a thunderous applause filled the courtroom. It was now my turn to address the crowd for the first time as chief justice. I began by quoting the beginning of President Washington's first inaugural address:

Such being the impressions under which I have, in obedience to the public summons, repaired to the present station, it would be peculiarly improper to omit, in this first official act my fervent supplications to that Almighty Being, who rules over the universe, who presides in the council of nations, and whose providential aides can supply every human defect.[15]

Like Washington, I wanted my first act to be a recognition of the God who provides all good things in civil government, as well as in our personal lives.

I continued, "We need today, as they did then, God's blessings."[16] After several other observations, I addressed the judiciary specifically: "Judges are bound by the Constitution as the law of the land and that Constitution doesn't prohibit the acknowledgment of God. I hope in my tenure as Chief Justice I will bring back an understanding of that Constitution which remains law. . . . I ask that you join with me to secure the blessings of liberty, and that once again we'll be 'One Nation under God, with liberty and justice for all.'"[17]

After the day and its celebrations were over, I soon began the work of the chief justice—reading briefs, writing opinions, and overseeing the lower courts. It was overwhelming at first, but I had an outstanding group of young law clerks who worked diligently researching cases and preparing memoranda for my review. Win Johnson, my senior staff attorney, was responsible for supervising the legal staff.

The Ten Commandments plaque from my office in Gadsden was displayed outside the door to my chambers for the time being. Here it remained while the larger monument was being designed. The granite, ordered from Vermont, was delayed when the first stone cracked and had to be returned. Weeks turned into months. Many people wondered if I was satisfied with leaving the plaque in its current location—an arrangement the ACLU indicated was acceptable to them.

This arrangement was not acceptable to me, but there was still much to be completed on the monument I had planned. Everything had to be just right. The size, color, texture, and design had to complement the stately design of the rotunda. What was more important, it had to convey the message that this nation was founded on a sovereign God and His divine, revealed law.

Hahnemann, Melchior, and I worked together to select various quotations from founding fathers such as Washington, Madison, and Jefferson, as well as Chief Justice Jay and Associate Supreme Court Justice James Wilson. I also decided to use a reference from George

Mason, the "father of the Bill of Rights," and Sir William Blackstone, on whom American lawyers had depended for an understanding of the Common Law. All the quotations recognized God as the source of law and government. Melchior and Hahnemann helped in the placement and design so that the message was clear that legally, logically, and historically we were truly "one nation under God, with liberty and justice for all."

A major concern of mine was the proper location for the monument to prevent damage to the judicial building. When the weight was determined to be approximately two and one-half tons, I knew that it had to be located on a portion of the floor with sufficient support. We consulted with engineers and blueprints of the building to ensure the monument's proper placement.

Clark Memorial of Birmingham was selected to letter and inscribe the monument exactly as we directed. Pierre Tourney and his son Pierre Jr. did an outstanding and professional job.

Finally, the monument was ready and installation was scheduled for 6:30 p.m., July 31, 2001. I wanted to cause minimum disruption of the workday and prevent injury to bystanders, so installation was scheduled to begin immediately after the close of business. The marshall's office was notified, along with the Administrative Office of Courts.

As I sat in my office alone waiting for the monument to be delivered, I was suddenly overwhelmed by feelings of doubt and fear that I would not be able to complete the mission I had long envisioned. Things had gone very smoothly in my new job, and I had been commended in the press and by my associates on the Alabama Supreme Court. I knew that this monument would be difficult for them to understand. And I wondered if I could stand the pressure of being sued and how my fellow justices would react to such a situation. Would they be supportive, or would they turn on me?

The minutes seemed to drag by. I recalled how Jesus had turned to His Father during His hour of temptation. I knew that I should follow His example, so I asked God for strength and wisdom to do His will. After all, I knew that I would not be in this job except for Him. He had never forsaken me, and I had prayed not to be elected unless God intended me to do exactly what I was doing. After I prayed this prayer, the fear and doubt was removed just as quickly as it had descended upon me, and my resolve was restored.

The monument did not arrive at the judicial building until about 9:30 p.m. We were forced to work through the night, positioning it in exactly the right location. The next morning, with the monument covered by a red veil, the news media arrived. Tom Parker, head of the legal division of the Administrative Office of Courts, opened the ceremony with prayer and then introduced Richard Hahnemann. Silence fell over the crowd as all eyes turned toward him and the monument. When he removed the veil, I began my remarks:

> By the authority vested in me by the Constitution of the State of Alabama as Chief Justice of the Alabama Supreme Court, as administrative head of the judicial system of this state, by the authority vested in me by Section 41-10-275 as Chief Justice, as the authorized judicial representative of the Unified Judicial System, and finally by the authority vested in the Chief Justice as the authorized representative under the lease of this building in which you stand, I'm pleased to present this monument depicting the moral foundation of our law and hereby authorize it to be placed in the rotunda of the Alabama Judicial Building.
>
> It is altogether fitting and proper that we should do this. By placement of this monument in the rotunda housing the Alabama Supreme Court, the Alabama Court of Criminal

Appeals, the Alabama Court of Civil Appeals, the Alabama State Law Library, and the Alabama Administrative Office of Courts, this monument will serve to remind the appellate courts and judges of the circuit and district courts of this state, the members of the bar who appear before them, as well as the people who visit the Alabama Judicial Building, of the truth stated in the preamble of the Alabama Constitution, that in order to establish justice, we must invoke "the favor and guidance of Almighty God."

"The institutions of our society are founded on the belief that there is an authority higher than the authority of the State, that there is a moral law which the State is powerless to alter, and that the individual possesses rights conferred by the Creator which government must respect. The Declaration of Independence stated the now familiar theme, 'We hold these truths to be self-evident, that all men are created equal, that they're endowed by their Creator with certain inalienable rights; that among these are life, liberty, and the pursuit of happiness.' And the body of the Constitution as well as the Bill of Rights enshrined these principles."

Some of you might think the words that I just spoke are my words, carefully structured to fit my own ends; or perhaps a quote from a past long ago, but certainly not true or relevant to our law today. On the contrary, those words are not my words, they're not an ancient quote irrelevant to law. They're the words of Justice William O. Douglas in 1961 in the case of *McGowan v. Maryland.*[18]

But today, a mere forty years later, many judges and other government officials across our land deny that there's a higher law. They forbid teaching your children that they're created in the image of Almighty God, and they purport all the while that it is government and not God who gave us our rights. Not only have they turned away from those absolute standards which form the basis of our morality and the moral foundation of our law, but they have divorced the Constitution and the Bill of Rights from these principles. As they have sown the wind, so we have reaped the whirlwind, in our homes, in our schools and in our workplaces.

When I ran for the office of Chief Justice of the Alabama Supreme Court, I made a pledge to restore the moral foundation of law. It is axiomatic that to restore morality, we must first recognize the source of that morality. From our earliest history in 1776, when we were first pleased to be called the United States of America, our forefathers recognized the sovereignty of God.

As late as 1954, the United States Congress placed in our Pledge of Allegiance the words "under God," and said "[t]he inclusion of God in our Pledge, therefore, would further acknowledge the dependence of our people and our government upon the moral directions of the Creator."[19] Judges, legislators, and executive officers around our Country have, since our Nation's birth, consistently pledged under oath, "so help me God," to uphold the Constitution.

Immediately after my election in November of 2000, I contacted Mr. Richard Hahnemann, an accomplished sculptor, to assist me in the construction and design of this monument. Based upon my specifications, he worked, together with myself and my legal assistant and attorney, Mr. Stephen Melchior, for the past eight months to complete this project.

I would like to point out that no tax funds were used in the construction or installation, which was accomplished

Mother, Evelyn Stewart Moore
(approx. 1945)
        and Father, Roy Baxter Moore
    (Sgt., U.S. Army, WWII, 1943)

Roy Stewart Moore
born February 11, 1947

Jerry, Mama, me, and Dad
1950 (l-r)

*First grade,
Six years old*

*Easter 1959 with family—
(clockwise) Mama, Dad, Jerry, Nancy,
Joey, and me (sister Toni not yet born)*

*President,
Etowah HS
Student
Council,
1964–65
(top center)*

Gadsden Times

United States Military
Academy Gymnastics
Squad (second row,
fourth from the left),
December 1967

On pommel horse

USMA cadet, 1969

Change of command, Da Nang, Vietnam, 188th M.P. Company, 1971

Boxing in Da Nang, Vietnam, 1972 (left)

Captain, U.S. Army, Military Police Corps, June 1974

Oath of office for deputy district attorney of Etowah County, 1977, with (l-r) former U.S. Congressman Albert Rains, Judge Hobdy Rains, and District Attorney W. W. Rayburn

Outback, on "Patton," Queensland, Australia, June 1984

*Married to
Kayla Kisor,
December 14, 1985*

*Oath of
office for
circuit judge,
given by
Governor
Fob James,
January 17,
1995*

Announcing decision to run for chief justice, December 7, 1999

Oath of office for chief justice, given by Chief Justice Perry Hooper Sr., with mother, wife, and children looking on, January 15, 2001

Family with the Ten Commandments monument, 2001

With Rich Hobson (second from left) and attorneys Phillip Jauregui, Steve
Melchior, John Eidsmoe, and Herb Titus (l-r)

Leroy Pierce (left), former marshal of the Alabama Supreme Court, and Willie James, first black marshal, appointed by Chief Justice Moore, August 15, 2001

Supreme Court of Alabama, 2001–2003

Kevin Glackmeyer / Courtesy of Coral Ridge Ministries

Themis, Greek goddess of justice outside federal courthouse in Montgomery

Leaving federal trial with wife Kayla, Art Baylor (left), and Leonard Holifield

AP / Wide World Photos

Mrs. Karen Kennedy handcuffed and arrested August 20, 2003

Partitions placed around monument by associate justices, August 21, 2003

Drew Dill

AP / Wide World Photos

Addressing media and crowd outside Judicial Building re: partitions around monument

Monument moved to storage room in Judicial Building, August 27, 2003

Dr. James Dobson at a rally outside Alabama Judicial Building, August 28, 2003

Announcing Constitution Restoration Act with (l-r) Rep. Robert Aderholt, Sen. Richard Shelby, Dr. Alan Keyes, and Sen. Sam Brownback, February 13, 2004

Testifying about religious liberty before United States Senate Judiciary Subcommittee, June 8, 2004

Foundation for Moral Law, Montgomery, Alabama, 2004

Ben DuPré

A much-needed family vacation after removal from office, March 2004

last evening so as not to conflict with this workplace. I would like to recognize Clark Memorial of Birmingham, Mr. Pierre Tourney Sr., and Mr. Pierre Tourney Jr., for their help in the construction, design and installation, as well as the transportation of this monument to this building.

And what an appropriate date this is. For it was on August 1st of 1776, exactly 225 years ago today, that Samuel Adams, the father of the American Revolution, stood before a rather large crowd at the Philadelphia Statehouse. And on its steps, he delivered a speech prior to the formal signing of the Declaration of Independence on August 2nd of 1776. He began by stating, "We have explored the temple of royalty and found that the idol that we have bowed down to has eyes which see not, ears that hear not our prayers, and a heart like the nether millstone."

Today a cry has gone out across our land for the acknowledgment of that God upon whom this Nation and our laws were founded and for those simple truths which our forefathers found to be self-evident; but once again, we find that those cries have fallen upon eyes that see not, ears that hear not our prayers, and hearts much like that nether millstone.

Samuel Adams concluded his remarks by saying, "We have this day restored the Sovereign, to whom alone all men ought to be obedient. He reigns in Heaven and with a propitious eye beholds his subjects assuming that freedom of thought and dignity of self-direction which he bestowed upon them. From the rising to the setting sun, may His kingdom come."[20] And may this day mark the restoration of the moral foundation of law to our people and the return to the knowledge of God in our land.

This monument, ladies and gentlemen, tells a story. If you look to the front, you'll see on the inset, "The Laws of Nature and of Nature's God." It was on those laws, the will of the Maker, upon which the Declaration of Independence was premised and upon which the Constitution was predicated.

James Madison, for example, the chief architect of the Constitution, said we were entitled to have a constitution because of the transcendent law of nature and of nature's God, which declares that the safety and happiness of society are the objects at which all political institutions aim and to which all such institutions must be sacrificed.

They knew the law. The law was clearly written by Sir William Blackstone, which was the law of this Country for many, many decades. He said, "This law of nature, being co-eval (originating together) with mankind and dictated by God himself, is, of course, superior in obligations to any other. It is binding over all the globe in all countries and at all times, and no humans laws are of any validity if contrary to this."[21] This law of nature and the law of revelation pin all human laws on these two foundations.

On each side of this monument, you'll see quotes from various presidents. For example, George Washington, on the back, said, "Let it simply be asked, where is the security for property, for reputation, for life, if the sense of religious obligation desert the oaths which are the instruments of investigation in our courts of justice."

The first Chief Justice, John Jay, also with President Washington, said, "If oaths should cease to be held sacred, our dearest and most valuable rights would become insecure."

On the right side as you face it, you'll see the Constitution and the Preamble of Alabama, which says that we must invoke the favor and guidance of Almighty God; but you'll also see the National Anthem. Oh, you won't see the first stanza, "Oh, say can you see"—you know it very well—"by the dawn's early light." You'll see the verse we neglect today: "Thus be it ever when freemen shall stand between their loved home and the war's desolation, blest with vict'ry and peace. May the heaven rescued land praise the power that has made and preserved us as a nation. And conquer we must when our cause it is just. And this be our motto—in God is our trust. And the star-spangled banner in triumph shall wave over the land of the free and the home of the brave."

Indeed, in 1956, the United States Congress, by act of Congress, by law today, made "In God We Trust"—our National motto. "So help me God," by which we pledge to uphold the Constitution, has been around since 1789, when the Judiciary Act established that as the basis of our oath.

You'll see quotes from that famous third President of the United States, Thomas Jefferson. He said, "Can the liberties of a nation be thought secure when we have removed their only firm basis, a conviction in the minds of the people that these liberties are the gift of God, that they're not to be violated but with His wrath? Indeed, I tremble for my Country when I reflect that God is just and that His justice cannot sleep forever."

Surrounding this monument, you see every ounce of support for the acknowledgment of the sovereignty of that God and those absolute standards upon which our laws are based. Oh, *this isn't surrounding the plaque with history, historical documents. All history supports the acknowledgment of God. You'll*

*find no documents surrounding the Ten Commandments because
they stand alone as an acknowledgment of that God that's contained in our Pledge, contained in our motto, and contained in
our oath.*[22]

Here I took a first step in a long journey by acknowledging God as
the moral foundation of our law. I knew that surrounding the Ten
Commandments with historical documents in order to "secularize" the
display had been something invented by the federal courts to reduce
the display to mere history, rather than the present reality of a living
God. It was a subtle way of denying the truth, and I would not be a
party to it. God had answered my prayers by giving me the courage and
strength to complete the installation as I had planned. I knew the message did not suit some of the intellectuals who worked in the judicial
building and some of the representatives of the media who were not
accustomed to such a bold and public acknowledgment of the Creator
God.

My first act was to meet with the other justices of the Alabama
Supreme Court and answer their questions. After explaining to them
that they had not been notified to protect them from any potential
lawsuit and because I considered it my duty as chief justice to acknowledge God as the moral source of our law, most of them seemed resigned
to leave the monument alone.

Nevertheless, two justices chose to speak out against what I had
done. One of them commented, "While I believe in God, I oppose the
movement to govern in the name of God."[23] Another justice stated
that while he shared many of my beliefs, he "would not try to subject
them on other people."[24] But I did not claim to be governing in the
name of God, nor was I attempting to impose my beliefs on others; I
was simply acknowledging God's providence, just as the Alabama
Constitution does.

In running for public office, candidates have no problem with trumpeting their church membership and Christian affiliation, but only because it is politically beneficial to do so. My acknowledgment of God had nothing to do with politics. The real problem was that some of my colleagues felt shame and embarrassment over the public acknowledgment of God.

In the midst of the growing controversy, tragedy again struck our family when Kayla's dad, Mack, passed away on August 7, 2001. Mack had been a mentor to my boys in learning to play football. Their "Paw-Paw" would be missed. After the funeral, it was even more difficult to return to court business, but I soon found myself extremely busy.

15

OUR MORAL
FOUNDATION

From the moment I took office as chief justice of the Alabama Supreme Court and even before the monument of the Ten Commandments was installed, I faced political challenges I had not anticipated.

Within a month of taking my oath of office, the proposed judicial budget for the next fiscal year was reduced by more than five million dollars. Still upset at having been caught playing politics with judicial pay raises, Governor Siegelman was embarrassed publicly by recorded conversations showing his efforts to use judges to influence newspaper editors. I had made the recorded conversations public, and Siegelman had not forgotten!

I responded immediately by calling his budget cuts unfair, noting that "[t]he Governor's proposed budget cuts are unprecedented in their impact and their unequal treatment of the judicial branch within this State."[1] Of course, Siegelman claimed budget shortages, but our records and calculations at the Administrative Office of Courts revealed that the executive branch would actually receive an increase and the legislative branch would receive the same amount of funding it had the year before. The proposed budget even showed an increase in prison and mental health programs.[2] Furthermore, the executive and legislative branches continued to receive merit raises for their employees while the judicial branch suffered layoffs of personnel and no merit raises.

John Giles, a former aide to Governor Guy Hunt and Governor Fob James, observed, "The best way to accuse someone of mismanagement is to cut their funds short. Government services are then handicapped and a chain reaction begins with poor services, resulting in escalation of public criticism."[3]

The governor's office was quick to say that the judicial pay raises were the problem, but these were the same judicial pay raises Siegelman had supported and had used politically with judges to get their support before his election. But Siegelman knew that the issue would resonate well with the press and at the same time undercut my support with the other judges, weakening my ability to oppose his arbitrary and punitive measures.

But the attack by the governor on the judicial branch was minor compared to his efforts to rewrite the entire Alabama Constitution, which I had just been sworn to uphold and support. Of course, he had also taken an oath of allegiance to that constitution. I am sure my comment to the press did not please the governor and others who were trying to destroy the constitution: "It has kept our taxes reasonable. It has kept things like the lottery out of the State. It has held down special interests. We need to look closely at why people want to change it."[4]

The truth is that more taxes was exactly why proponents of a new constitution wanted to dispose of the old one. In an attempt to confuse the issues, proponents used the same old fictions designed to motivate people to support their cause. The constitution was declared to be a racist document. But supporters of change failed to mention that the first black associate justice of the Alabama Supreme Court, Oscar Adams—a man I admired for his courage and conviction—had written an opinion that stopped a similar attempt to undermine the Alabama Constitution in 1983.[5]

The people of Alabama saw through the ploy of the "reformers" and defeated their proposed scheme in a referendum election. The Alabama Constitution was preserved—at least for the time being.

In early 2001, State Senator Charles Steele introduced a bill (S.B. 257) to allow video poker in the state. A state House of Representatives resolution (No. 251) requested an opinion of the justices of the Alabama Supreme Court on whether the senate proposal was actually a revenue-raising measure, and if it should originate in the house.

In April of 2001, the Alabama Supreme Court released an advisory opinion that I wrote, with three justices concurring, which declared video poker machines to be unconstitutional under the anti-lottery provision of the Alabama Constitution.[6] The opinion overturned a 1997 state supreme court opinion which determined that such games were legal if approved by the legislature.[7] "It is imperative," I emphasized, "for [the Supreme Court] to declare acts unconstitutional when the Legislature transgresses its constitutional authority."[8] The Alabama Supreme Court had concluded that this was one such occasion: "We cannot be so derelict in our duties as to ignore the fact that [this video poker bill] is unconstitutional, when the safety and welfare of the public are at stake, but we must support and defend the Constitution we are sworn to uphold."[9]

The Alabama Christian Coalition called the advisory opinion "earthshaking."[10] Indeed, it spurred district attorneys throughout the state to begin closing down video gambling arcades.[11] The Alabama gambling lobby was infuriated, but the Alabama Constitution had again been vindicated. Video poker gambling was not allowed to undermine the morality and virtue of Alabama's citizens. The moral foundation of our state law was defended by recognizing the prohibition against games of chance contained in the Alabama Constitution.

The Alabama Constitution, like the United States Constitution, does not dictate our morality. Prohibitions against sodomy, bestiality, adultery, incest, pornography, stealing, murder, rape, and so forth, are generally found in the criminal laws or civil laws of the state, reflecting Common Law concepts that originated in the Holy Scriptures. But as we distance ourselves from God, judges tend to disregard historic precedents about moral virtue in an effort to impose their own values and immoral beliefs on society. When they do this, they usurp the role of the legislative branch and undermine the moral foundation of our law.

I was determined to follow the law and not to impose new, "politically correct" social policies in my written opinions. But I soon found this to be more difficult than I had anticipated.

In February of 2002, a case came before the court that involved child custody. The mother was an admitted homosexual who lived with her female companion and with whom she had formed a domestic partnership under the laws of the state of California. The trial court had awarded custody of the children to the father, but that decision had been reversed by the Alabama Court of Civil Appeals, which found that "no evidence indicated the mother's homosexual relationship . . . would have a detrimental effect on the well-being of the children."[12]

In fact, the opposite was the case. *The detrimental effect of homosexual conduct was confirmed by Alabama law.* As late as 1975, the appellate court of Alabama had "no hesitancy whatsoever" in concluding that "sexual relations between persons of the same sex," however denominated, "involves moral turpitude."[13] That court went on to define moral turpitude as: "[A]n inherent quality of baseness, vileness, [and] depravity" and "implies something immoral itself, regardless of the fact whether it is punishable by law."[14]

Sir Edward Coke, the dean of English jurisprudence, called homosexuality "a detestable, and abominable sin, amongst Christians not to be named, committed by carnal knowledge against the ordinance of the Creator, and order of nature, by mankind with mankind, or with brute beast, or by womankind with brute beast."[15]

The Alabama Supreme Court ultimately reversed the Court of Civil Appeals and restored custody to the father, but it did not address the issue of homosexuality. I decided to address the issue in a concurring opinion in order to make clear the law in Alabama.

> Homosexual conduct is, and has been, considered abhorrent, immoral, detestable, a crime against nature, and a violation of the laws of Nature and Nature's God upon which this Nation and our laws are predicated. Such conduct violates both the criminal and civil laws of this State and is destructive to a basic building block of society—the family. The law of Alabama is clear not only in its condemning such conduct, but the courts of this State have consistently held that exposing a child to such behavior has a destructive and seriously detrimental effect on the children.[16]

The Alabama Supreme Court had avoided precedent when it came to a moral standard, but I believed it was my duty to uphold the moral foundation of law. The problem with some judges today is that they rely on precedent until such precedents conflict with socially immoral behavior that is now tolerated or accepted by some people in our society. This selective adherence to precedent is not only hypocritical, but also unreliable because it forsakes the law in the name of toleration, avoiding the criticism that would descend on the courts if they properly applied the law.

Those angered by the opinion confused the sin with the sinner. I never stated—nor would I state—that homosexual *people* are evil, detestable, or reprehensible. My comments referring to homosexual *con-*

duct as immoral, vile, and abhorrent quoted from a myriad of legal precedents stating a truth that has been recognized for centuries. In fact, my Christian belief is that we should love all people "for all have sinned, and come short of the glory of God" (Rom. 3:23). But Scripture also teaches that we should "let love be without dissimilation [hypocrisy]. Abhor that which is evil; cleave to that which is good" (Rom. 12:9). In other words, to tolerate a person's sin does not demonstrate true love. Have we reached the point in our society where we must avoid the truth and, in a fit of political correctness, permit the destruction of our law?

The media had a field day with my strong judicial opinion in this case.[17] A *Birmingham News* editorial complained that I had allowed my personal beliefs to interfere with judicial rulings.[18] An organization, Equality Begins at Home, called for my resignation, and others pursued a complaint to the Judicial Inquiry Commission about my writing.[19]

Those who commit homosexual acts do not have a monopoly on immoral behavior. In another custody case, *Ex parte Pankey*,[20] the other justices of the Alabama Supreme Court again avoided the moral issue involved when it declined to hear a Court of Civil Appeals decision that favored a parent who had committed adultery by requiring the non-adulterous parent to show how the admitted adultery of his spouse had a "detrimental effect" on the child. The mother had confessed living with a man who was not her husband while she was still married and the child was in her care.

In my research, I discovered that the "marriage relationship" had been declared by both the United States Supreme Court and the Alabama Supreme Court to be vital and sacred to our society. In *Sturgis v. Crowninshield*,[21] the United States Supreme Court called marriage "the most solemn and sacred of all" institutions. In 1870, the Alabama Supreme Court stated, "The present age is wonderfully demoralized on the subject of marriage and divorce. It seems to be forgotten that marriage is a divine institution; therefore, [it] imposes upon parties higher moral and religious obligations than those imposed by a mere human institution or government."[22]

In the *Pankey* case, I dissented from the Alabama Supreme Court's decision not to hear the case, writing, "The moral and *legal* condemnation of adultery is historic. When lower courts embrace adultery as an insignificant act without moral consequence they may be embracing a current cultural trend, but by doing so they are disregarding the law their judges are sworn to uphold."[23]

I went on to explain the serious consequences that would result from failing to correct the error of the Court of Civil Appeals in its award of custody of the child to the adulterous parent. "To destroy the conclusive presumption of relative unfitness to custody of a minor child that has historically attached to a parent who has committed adultery is to disregard a moral foundation of our law."[24]

In essence, the justices of the Alabama Supreme Court had avoided the moral issue and had allowed an opinion of the Court of Civil Appeals to remain precedent for the lower courts in years to come. Once again, I saw the moral law being undermined by activist judges on lower courts. Those responsible for upholding the law at the higher court were avoiding their responsibility rather than addressing a "sensitive" issue like adultery.

But the Alabama Supreme Court did step forward to do the right thing in one important case that had been pending in the court system for approximately twelve years. It was known as the "equity funding" lawsuit. An amendment to the Alabama Constitution[25] states clearly that no child has a constitutional right to a public education at taxpayer expense; however, it is the job of the state legislature to adequately fund public education as funds are available. All children enjoy equal access to the state public education system. This amendment states further that it is the policy and duty of the state to promote education.

The right of education has historically belonged to parents. When the parents allow a schoolmaster, a tutor, or the public education system to perform their duty, such educators do so *in loco parentis*, or "in the place of the parent." In this manner, the parents always retain control of their child's education because they do not surrender the right to educate their child; they simply delegate part of their responsibility to a qualified person or institution.

In 1991, a lone Alabama circuit judge, who later campaigned for the Alabama Supreme Court as the "Education Judge," decided to declare the entire education amendment unconstitutional under the United States Constitution. He did so in order to shift the "right" of education from parents to children to permit the state to be ultimately responsible for the education of all children. The judge further concluded that because there is a state right to public education, such education must be "equitably funded" for every child. In his campaign literature, the judge claimed to be a "tough judge" because he had commanded the state legislature to increase taxes in order to comply with the "constitutional mandate" of equity funding in education.

For more than a decade this case was litigated in the state court system as the Alabama Supreme Court permitted this circuit judge to assume the role of "education czar" and to perform the duty of determining what constituted appropriate funding for public education in Alabama. In October of 2001, the Alabama State Board of Education submitted a $1.7 billion tax plan, undisclosed to the public, to the circuit court for approval.

In May of 2002, the Alabama Supreme Court dismissed the case and ended the "equity funding" litigation on the ground that the Montgomery circuit court had interfered with a duty that clearly belonged to the legislature.[26] The $1.7 billion tax plan was stopped. I agreed with the majority of the Alabama Supreme Court that the repair, renovation, improvement, and/or overhaul of the education system of

Alabama belonged to the legislature, state and local boards of education, and, of course, to the people—but never to the courts.

Nobody disagrees with the proposition that every child should have equal access to a public school system. But the creation of a government "right" in the child ultimately results in more government control and a loss of parents' control over their own children. Furthermore, increased government control is exercised not only over the funding of education (guaranteed to result in increased taxes), but also over the quality and substance of education. This would place home schooling and private schooling in jeopardy.

I urged the Alabama Supreme Court to go further and declare that this was a matter that never should have been brought before the trial court and that the trial court had no jurisdiction to hear the case, but the court declined.

When judges put on their social engineering hats and go beyond the law to correct perceived inequities, they assume the role of the state legislature and violate the basic doctrine of separation of powers. This doctrine provides that each branch of government—the legislative, executive, and judicial—has a particular function. No branch should interfere with the responsibility of another. The legislative branch makes the law; the executive branch enforces the law; and the judicial branch interprets the law. Courts and judges have a duty to interpret the law and to prevent arbitrary and dangerous departures from the law.

Separation of powers is a basic principle of both the United States Constitution and the Alabama Constitution. President George Washington warned us in his Farewell Address that

> It is important, likewise, that the habits of thinking in a
> free country should inspire caution in those entrusted with
> its administration, to confine themselves within their respec-

tive Constitutional spheres; avoiding in the exercise of the Powers of one department to encroach upon another. The spirit of encroachment tends to consolidate the powers of all the departments in one, and thus to create whatever form of government, a real despotism. . . . If in the opinion of the People, the distribution or modification of the Constitutional powers be in any particular wrong, let it be corrected by an amendment in the way which the Constitution designates. But let there be no change by usurpation; for though this, in one instance, may be the instrument of good, it is the customary weapon by which free governments are destroyed.[27]

Many attractive reasons exist to usurp (wrongfully seize) the powers of another branch of government, especially when you wear a black robe, but it is always improper to do so. The judicial branch has no authority to assume the lawmaking mantle that belongs to the legislature even when it seems to be convenient to allow judges to do so because it will make things better. Such a misuse of power will always result in a permanent "evil," by leading to further usurpations. Consequently, I concluded in my judicial opinion that the genuine desire for a quality education does not give a judge the right to impose his will on the state legislature or the people. While all of us are concerned for the education of our children, it is the legislature's role—not the courts'—to fund the public education system. Any state court that goes beyond its authority infringes on the jurisdiction of another branch of government and subverts the foundation of our constitutional system of government.

Finally the "equity funding" lawsuit came to an end. A dozen years of costly litigation had proven fruitless to those who tried to use the judicial system for political ends. A wrong was righted, and the trial court was admonished to leave the job of policy making to the legislature. Judicial activism was halted—at least for the moment.

But it was clear that the modern judicial trend of legislating from the bench was not restricted to judges on the trial court. Some people on the court on which I served were prone to the same folly. Such was the case in 1989 when the Alabama Supreme Court "created" a duty of post-minority support—a parent supporting a child after the age of eighteen—in the case of *Ex parte Bayliss*.[28]

The case resulted in children of divorced parents having a right to a paid college education, whereas children of parents who remained married did not. Writing for the court, Justice Gorman Houston acknowledged that post-minority support was a "new" rule, stating that "we are merely refusing to limit the word 'children' to minor children because of what we perceive to be just and reasonable in 1989."[29] This is exactly what the Massachusetts Supreme Court did in 2003 with the word *marriage* in order to justify same-sex marriage.[30]

Chief Justice John Marshall, in *Marbury v. Madison*,[31] long ago stated that "the province and duty of the judicial department [is] to say what the law is," not what it should be. Making law is the exclusive province of the legislature, not the courts.[32]

In June of 2002, I pointed out this abuse of judicial power in a case known as *Ex parte Tabor*.[33] But my criticism of the court's ruling in *Bayliss* was not limited to the fact that it ignored legal precedent, or even that it breached the separation of powers doctrine, but that it had improperly intruded on the jurisdiction of the family and the relationship between parents and their children.

In his writing, Justice Houston justified the court's intrusion by quoting the story of King Solomon, concluding that Solomon was noted for his wisdom in a "child custody case."[34] But King Solomon was not faced with a custody issue between two parents; he was dealing with a kidnapping case. Through his wisdom, Solomon did not interfere with the relationship between a parent and her child; he reaffirmed their relationship.

Some people complained that my repeated references to the Bible and the moral underpinnings of our laws in my legal opinions represented an improper mixing of religion and government. But just as the time for the start of the federal trial over the Ten Commandments monument was drawing close, a case came before the Alabama Supreme Court that highlighted the line of demarcation between the true "separation of church and state."

In *Yates v. El Bethel Primitive Baptist Church,*[35] allegations of misconduct against a church's pastor placed the pastor at odds with the church's board of elders. The congregation eventually held an election and voted to elect a new board of elders that supported the pastor. But the ousted board members complained that the voting procedures had violated the church's disciplines. Instead of using the Primitive Baptist church's appeal process for resolving intra-church disputes, the ousted board members filed a lawsuit in an Alabama circuit court, seeking to have the court enforce church law in their controversy with the church's pastor.

Incredibly, the circuit judge agreed to hear the case. Then he set aside the church election, ruling that the election was not proper under the church's laws. To my dismay, the Alabama Supreme Court also assumed jurisdiction on appeal and affirmed the circuit court's intrusion into the church's affairs.

I wrote a lengthy opinion about the proper (and separate) roles of civil government and church government. I insisted that neither the circuit court nor the Alabama Supreme Court had any authority to get involved in such a church dispute. I wrote:

> By interfering with and interrupting the procedure of the
> National Primitive Baptist Convention, a circuit court of
> this State has adjudicated a purely ecclesiastical dispute that

should have been settled by the church's denominational process. As our courts have long recognized, a valid line separates the jurisdictional spheres of state and church, and this line may not be crossed without violating the integrity of the governments of each of those spheres. *Watson v. Jones.*[36] In recent times, we have commonly referred to this line as the separation of church and state. While the separation of church and state is a familiar phrase in today's society, it is one whose meaning has been obscured through overuse and repeated misapplication.[37]

No court in the land may involve itself in a case unless it first has jurisdiction over both of the parties to the case and over the subject matter of the dispute. In a case such as this, the Alabama courts had no jurisdiction because the dispute was one solely for the El Bethel church and its denomination's governing bodies to decide—not Alabama's courts.

> The church—as an institution—does not have authority over the affairs of civil government, and the state—as an institution—does not have authority over the affairs of church government because the state has concern for the things of this world while the church has concern for the soul of man in the next. Although civil government has the authority to enforce its laws with physical punishment and/or a monetary fine, a church cannot enforce criminal sanctions. Acknowledgment of this separation comes from a recognition that God is the source of all power.[38]

God had separated the two jurisdictional "spheres," I explained, and it was not for our court or any other to breach the gap. I concluded forcefully that the Alabama Supreme Court was making a mistake in governing the internal affairs of a church, and that a true acknowledgment of God and His sovereignty would provide a check on the power of the state in matters of faith and worship. A state court's interference in the governance of a church violates the jurisdictional principle of separation of church and state.

> Jurisdictional separation of the *institutions* of church and state finds its origin in the history of the nation of Israel as found in the Old Testament. Throughout English and American history, a high regard for that separation has been manifest in numerous Supreme Court, federal court, and state court opinions. Those who today misunderstand the true meaning of the phrase "separation of church and state" wrongfully believe that it precludes the recognition of a sovereign God who is "lord both of body and mind" who "chose not to propagate it by coercions on either, as was his Almighty power to do." Thomas Jefferson, "Bill for Establishing Religious Freedom," *Writings*, 346. To preclude the acknowledgment of Almighty God leads to two destructive errors: First, it denies the very source of the doctrine of separation of church and state; and second, it leads those who misunderstand that jurisdictional separation to wrongfully intrude the powers of the state into matters of faith and worship. To do so is error.[39]

My *El Bethel* opinion later caught the attention of Judge Thompson in the federal trial, and I had the opportunity to discuss it with him on the witness stand. Unfortunately, he did not heed the proper explanation of the true separation of church and state that I had provided in the opinion. Nevertheless, I was thankful that the Lord gave me the opportunity as chief justice to explain in a judicial opinion the proper jurisdictional boundaries of the state and the church and to acknowledge Him as sovereign over both. Although the words *separation of church and state* are not found in the Constitution, the concept is implicit in the First Amendment and the law, which we all must uphold.

My support for the U.S. Constitution and efforts to preserve the moral foundation of law in my written opinions created a great deal of opposition among special interest groups. In a guest commentary printed in newspapers around the state, the head of the Alabama Christian Coalition, John Giles, again made some astute observations.[40]

With regard to my advisory opinion that stated video gambling was unconstitutional under the Alabama Constitution, Giles said, "This drew great criticism from the gambling interest and verbal assaults from those legislators carrying water on behalf of the gambling lobby."[41]

Regarding my opinion on homosexual custody, Giles noted that "gay and lesbian activist groups blasted the judge, demanded that he be removed from office, and even filed a formal complaint with the JIC."[42]

Giles summarized his column by stating that I had been attacked by "the gambling interest, gay and lesbian activist groups, the American Civil Liberties Union, and now Governor Siegelman. What an interesting alliance."[43]

I angered several special-interest groups in my first year and a half on the job. The gambling lobby was set back, and their momentum was stalled. A twelve-year lawsuit over "equity funding" in public education was stopped, and the separation of powers was reinvigorated. The agenda of the gay and lesbian alliance was exposed. The ACLU was unsuccessful in its opposition to the Ten Commandments. And some on my own court were resentful of my willingness to address moral issues in my legal opinions.

I was aware that opposing such powerful foes was dangerous, so I had to be careful. But I believe that when judges begin to make "new" law according to their own whims and feelings, they cease being judges or justices and become super-legislators with the power to make law at the stroke of a pen. This love of power may be natural to man's nature, but it is not desirable. Judges must always rule according to the law. Because of this, I went to great lengths to document the moral foundation of our law and history in my legal opinions. I always tried to rule in accordance with the law. My judicial opinions served as a constant reminder of the meaning and purpose of a moral foundation.

But there was one issue on which these groups could unite in their opposition: the display of God's law. I kept in mind the story of Daniel, who had been placed in a high position in government. His enemies could find no occasion for fault in Daniel "except" the law of his God. I knew what had happened to Daniel could happen to me (see Dan. 6:15–16). Soon these groups were joined by others who began to turn their attention to the monument that I had installed to honor God's law. This attention led me to face some monumental challenges. But I knew that the same God who had been with Daniel would be with me.

16

MONUMENTAL
CHALLENGES

Within a week of the installation of the Ten Commandments monument in the Alabama Judicial Building, the ACLU began to threaten a lawsuit. Joel Sogol of the ACLU said civil action was likely: "I would be very surprised if at some point in time there was not some type of lawsuit filed to challenge the constitutionality of that display."[1] Sogol went on to say that he had heard from several persons who were willing to be plaintiffs in such a suit.[2] I anticipated a lawsuit at any point, and probably one brought in federal court.

In spite of this likely possibility, there was a great outpouring of support as Christians from across the state and nation began to call and write. Wendy Aldridge, my secretary, and Mary Ann Rhodes, my receptionist, and the rest of my staff were busy answering the telephone and referring calls to my counsel. Wendy and Mary Ann were wonderful workers and always performed their duties in an exceptional manner.

Some others who supported the display were unsure if I should have been involved with putting the monument in the judicial building. The pastor of one Montgomery church voiced such concerns, saying, "The Ten Commandments should be prominently displayed in public buildings, [but] I guess I am having problems with the way he's doing things and not what he's doing."[3]

Naturally the ACLU and the Southern Poverty Law Center (SPLC), which also eventually brought suit against me, were happy to play on such confusion. They claimed that I had "sneaked in" the monument in the middle of the night. Yet, as I have previously explained, the monument was not "sneaked in." It was scheduled to be delivered after work hours and was delivered three hours late by Clark Memorial because of loading and transportation problems.

Placing a monument weighing two and one-half tons in the State Judicial Building in downtown Montgomery within two blocks of the state capitol under lights using large trucks and equipment is somewhat like "sneaking" an elephant into the White House: It simply cannot be done! Many people who worked at the judicial building were aware of the installation, and they assisted in the operation.

The other justices on the Supreme Court had not been notified because as chief justice I was the custodian of the building. Moreover, their prior knowledge would have disqualified them from deciding any possible legal challenge to the monument, and would have subjected them to being sued as well.[4]

In my opinion, the ACLU and SPLC are built upon one basic principle—deception. The ACLU is neither "American" in its mission (removal of God from our country) nor does it stand for "liberty" when it denies the very source of our liberty. Likewise, the SPLC is in no sense "poor," since it has millions of dollars in assets at its disposal which it uses to deny our inalienable right to the public worship of God, nor does it stand up for the law. Rather, it works to undermine the historic law of our country.

The SPLC pretends to fight "hate groups" like the KKK which have long ago been discredited. They do so for fund-raising purposes. In the process they foster hatred and division to keep their own pockets lined. Their aversion to an acknowledgment of God is understandable since God is a God of love and not hate, unifying and not dividing His church, and establishing moral standards, not destroying them.

Truth is certainly not the objective of these groups. Annie Laurie Gaylor, a member of the Freedom from Religion Foundation, an organization that the ACLU often represents, stated that I was mistaken about the nation being founded on a belief in God. She stated, "He acts as if he's never read the U.S. Constitution. It's Godless. There is no reference to a deity in it."[5] Perhaps Ms. Gaylor should read James Madison, the chief architect of the Constitution, who stated in *Federalist 37* that the Constitution was written as if by the finger of God.[6]

Nor would she agree with Benjamin Franklin who, in his discussion of the Constitution in April of 1788 in the Philadelphia *Federal Gazette*, stated that he had "so much Faith in the general Government of the world by *Providence* that [he could] hardly conceive a Transaction [the U.S. Constitution] of such momentous Importance to the Welfare of Millions now existing, and to exist in the Posterity of a great Nation, should be suffered to pass without being in some degree influenc'd, guided and governed by that omnipotent, omnipresent and beneficent Ruler in whom all inferior Spirits live, and move, and have their Being."[7]

Ms. Gaylor also overlooked the fact that the Constitution is dated "the Seventeenth Day of September in the Year of our Lord one thousand seven hundred and Eighty-seven and of the Independence of the United States of America the twelfth." Both the date and the reference to the day our nation became independent is a reference to God. The "Year of our Lord" dates the Constitution from the birth of Christ. In fact, this showed that the founders chose to date the Constitution according to the Gregorian calendar.

Even though this calendar was established by Pope Gregory XIII more than two hundred years before the Constitution was written, it had not been adopted by England or the American colonies until 1752, a mere thirty-five years before the Constitutional Convention. America chose to date its governing document based on the Gregorian calendar rather than the pagan Roman calendar because America was founded as a godly nation. According to the Declaration of Independence, without God we never would have become a nation.[8]

My purpose and intent was clear in the placement of the monument. I said, "I placed it there . . . to show the moral foundation of law and the legal basis upon which our Country is founded, reflected clearly in the Declaration of Independence and the Constitution of the United States."[9]

The first challenge to the monument, however, did not come from the ACLU, Southern Poverty, or even the Freedom from Religion Foundation; it came from a group of black legislators who tried to force me to put a display of Dr. Martin Luther King's "I Have a Dream" speech beside the monument of the Ten Commandments. Led by State Representative Alvin Holmes and State Senator Charles Steele, a handful of black lawmakers attempted to force their way into the Alabama Judicial Building on August 28, 2001. Holmes and Steele, holding a cardboard display of King's speech, tried "to push their way past a State Capitol Police Officer in the lobby of the Judicial Building."[10] The media reported that the group "noisily but peacefully forced their way through two outer glass doors into the foyer of the Judicial Building."[11]

I was away for lunch and had not left any instructions on how to deal with such an unexpected breach of security. But building security officers and Marshal Willie James took appropriate action to secure the premises from forced entry. Senator Steele stated later that they felt like "[w]e're here in 1955 like the bus boycott. We feel like we do not have any say in these matters."[12]

Regardless of their feelings, the legislature or its members had no legal right to say what should decorate the judicial building, just as the chief justice of the Supreme Court did not have the authority to place a display in the state capitol or in the building that housed the Alabama legislature. I was the lessee of the judicial building which housed the appellate courts of the state. As chief administrator of the justice system and the building lessee, I was responsible for displays and decorations in the judicial building. Under the doctrine of separation of powers, these responsibilities did not fall to the legislative or executive branches of Alabama government.

Besides, the judicial building already had a civil rights display in the lower rotunda. Alvin Holmes and Charles Steele were trying to create the appearance of a racial incident. Holmes remarked, "Back in 1963 Governor George Wallace stood in the schoolhouse door to prevent two blacks from entering the University of Alabama and now in 2001 Judge Roy Moore sent his storm troopers to block us from this building."[13] But this was not 1963, and it had nothing to do with discrimination.

Marshal Willie James was the first black marshal of the Alabama Supreme Court, and I had appointed him to that position several months before. It was Marshal James who ordered the doors locked to prevent these legislators from forcing their way into the judicial building, which they clearly had no right to do. This was not a racial incident, but an improper and undignified attempt to protest the monument of the Ten Commandments. Marshal James was in charge during my absence and acted in accord with the duties of his office to prevent a breach of security. I later commended him for his actions, which prevented possible damage to the building or injury to people.

A statement was released by my office stating that "Chief Justice Roy Moore has the greatest respect for Martin Luther King and Dr. King's view that God's law forms a basis for the law of man."[14] To place a monument recognizing the accomplishments of one man beside the monument to God's law would not have been consistent with Dr. King's theology. This would have destroyed the original message of the monument—that our government began by recognizing the power and sovereignty of Almighty God.

After meeting with the Black Caucus and failing to reach an agreement, I decided to take appropriate action to recognize not only Dr. Martin Luther King, but also another well-known black leader, Frederick Douglass, both of whom had recognized God's law as our moral foundation. Using no taxpayer funds, I designed and purchased a granite plaque entitled the "Moral Foundation of Law." This plaque quoted Dr. King: "A just law is a man-made code that squares with the moral law or the law of God. An unjust law is a code that is out of harmony with the moral law."[15]

The quotation from Frederick Douglass was equally powerful in affirming the preeminence of God's laws. As a former slave and staunch abolitionist, Douglass knew that without God man is reduced to slavery. His quote read: "The first work of slavery is to mar and deface those characteristics of its victims which distinguish man from things and persons from property. Its first aim is to destroy all sense of high moral and religious responsibility. It reduces man to a mere machine. It cuts him off from his Maker, it hides from him the laws of God."[16]

David Williams, a former black commissioner of Etowah County whom I brought with me to the Supreme Court, was the court spokesman on this matter. He explained to the press that "both quotations talk about the laws of God and were selected by the Chief Justice because they tie in with the Ten Commandments monument."[17]

I was pleased to see a quote from Martin Luther King hanging in the Supreme Court Building. At the time Dr. King made the statement on the plaque, he was being held in the Birmingham jail simply for standing for the right of equality for all people. It was a right that he called the American dream, a right given by the Creator God, and a right which he would not surrender. His words written from the Birmingham jail still hang prominently in the building that houses the highest courts of Alabama. I am sure Dr. King would have been proud.

But did that satisfy Representative Holmes? Not quite. It seemed he was more interested in creating a scene and in getting his name in the newspaper by dividing the people of Alabama over a fictitious racial problem. Holmes remarked, "It's not bad. That's a good quote from Dr. King, and a good quote from Frederick Douglass, but my recommendation to the Black Caucus is that we're going to reject this."[18]

Following the lead of Representative Holmes, Bill Teague, an atheist, proposed that a seven-foot sculpture of an atom, representing atheism, be installed in the rotunda. After several requests, I politely refused his offer, stating that it was not "in conformity with the purpose or theme of the foundation of American law or government."[19]

Things seemed to die down after that. The Black Caucus apparently realized the ridiculous position they had taken. To reject a plaque honoring the contribution of great black leaders who acknowledged God's law would be political hypocrisy.

Less than two weeks after the confrontation at the Alabama Judicial Building, our nation was brought to a standstill as the twin towers of the World Trade Center came crashing down from an attack by Muslim terrorists. In one brief moment, our nation suffered a terrible loss of life and security, much the same as it had in the bombing of Pearl Harbor. Congress gathered on the steps of the United States Capitol to seek God's blessings, singing "God Bless America." The president joined in prayer with religious leaders from across our nation to seek God's guidance in this time of great peril and heartache. Americans everywhere fell to their knees in prayer for our country.

Only six weeks after installing the monument of the Ten Commandments to acknowledge the sovereignty of God, I was seeing men and women, young and old, in every state turning to seek His guidance. No longer were we honoring God with ceremonial prayer and meaningless utterances as we had for so many years. People were turning to our true strength in a sincere way. A marvelous work was being performed as God worked in the face of tragedy to bring Americans back to Him.

At the edge of "Ground Zero" in New York City stands a little chapel constructed in 1766. Our first president and Congress under the Constitution assembled at St. Paul's Chapel on April 30, 1789, immediately following President Washington's inaugural address at Federal Hall in lower Manhattan. Above the altar is a scene entitled "Glory" which depicts the Lord's delivery of two tablets of law to Moses on Mt. Sinai. The inscription above is the Hebrew word *YHWH*, the name of God. The altar piece was designed by Colonel Pierre L'Enfant and delivered to St. Paul's Chapel in 1788, the year before Washington's inauguration.

St. Paul's Chapel has withstood fire, storm, and great tragedy throughout history. God's hand of protection has always been on that consecrated place. In September of 1776, when the entire city of New York was burned and Trinity Church, the much larger church nearby, was destroyed, St. Paul's Chapel remained. When the twin towers of the World Trade Center fell and buildings on all sides were damaged, St. Paul's Chapel was miraculously left untouched. Not one pane of glass or piece of stone was damaged. St. Paul's was used as a station for ministering to the needs of firemen, policemen, rescue workers, doctors, and medical personnel who treated victims of that catastrophe.

Even in the midst of great tragedy in September of 2001, God was sending us a message of love and restoration. The prophet Isaiah spoke of a day of "great slaughter, when the towers fall" (Isa. 30:25) and of a breach in a "high wall, whose breaking cometh suddenly at an instant" (Isa. 30:13). But in the midst of such tragedy, God said, "In returning and rest shall ye be saved; in quietness and in confidence shall be your strength" (Isa. 30:15). Today as in earlier times, we should realize that our true strength and security are in God. We need to return to that source.

After our country had survived another great loss of American life in World War II, President Dwight D. Eisenhower and the United States Congress in 1954 put "under God" in the Pledge of Allegiance so "we shall constantly strengthen those spiritual weapons which forever will be our Country's most powerful resource, in peace or in war."[20] After September 11, 2001, I believed America was again turning back to God and that opposition to the monument would diminish. But I was wrong!

On October 30, 2001, the ACLU filed suit to have the monument removed, and we were served notice of the suit the very next day (Halloween). It seemed appropriate that three organizations—the ACLU, Americans United for Separation of Church and State, and the Southern Poverty Law Center, all dedicated to removing God from the public square—served notice of their intent on the day that many people celebrate witches, devils, and evil spirits. The case was assigned to Judge Myron Thompson in the federal district court.

My attorneys, Steve Melchior and Herb Titus, were appointed assistant attorneys general at my request. Even though I was entitled to state representation because I had been sued in my official capacity, I chose to have my attorneys paid by private donations to avoid unnecessary criticism. Phillip Jauregui, my personal attorney with whom I had worked for several years, also assisted in my defense. All of my attorneys were exceptional lawyers and dedicated Christians who were well versed in the First Amendment, constitutional law, and the laws of nature and nature's God. Each had unique qualifications that enabled them to form a very effective team. We began our conferences with prayer and always sought divine guidance in making decisions.

Herb Titus is a constitutional law expert. A former dean of Regent Law School, Herb is not only a legal scholar, but also a biblical scholar.

Until his conversion, Herb was a practicing ACLU cooperative attorney. Today he advises Christians across the country about the divine nature of law and government. He is a man of impeccable character and courage and an outstanding scholar of constitutional jurisprudence.

Steve Melchior is a practicing attorney in Cheyenne, Wyoming. As a former deputy state attorney general, Steve is familiar with legal procedure and discovery techniques and had represented others in defense of Christian principles in court disputes. He is also a very sharp advocate, effective in argument before the court; he thinks quickly and is not intimidated by anyone.

Phillip Jauregui, the youngest lawyer on my team, is an excellent spokesman and quick analyst who always added positively to the debate. Phillip was always there to ensure that we sought God's guidance and wisdom in our decisions.

I was also privileged to have at my service three young attorneys who served as law clerks for me at the Alabama Supreme Court—Drew Dill, Ben DuPré, and Greg Jones. All are outstanding scholars dedicated to the restoration of our moral law. While Drew concentrated mainly on cases before the Alabama Supreme Court, Ben and Greg—in addition to performing their regular law clerk duties—also worked on briefs, memoranda, and discovery in the monument case.

Devoting numerous hours of research, writing, and travel to and from Alabama at great personal expense and sacrifice, my attorneys worked diligently through the following months. I knew that God had assembled a special team who would not fail to present the truth to the court.

The battle proceeded slowly at first. While I continued my duties as chief justice during the week, I often spoke during my spare time to many audiences across the country. On one such occasion before a crowd of about three thousand people at McKenzie arena in Chattanooga, Tennessee, I said that it was time "to take back our land."[21] I continued, saying that "since September 11, we have been at war. I submit to you that there is another war raging—a war between good and evil, between right and wrong."[22] Then I added, "For over forty years, we have wandered in the wilderness like the children of Israel. In homes and schools across our land it is time for Christians to take a stand."[23]

I knew that it was time to stand for the truth, not to back down. Over the past five decades, prayer has been taken from our schools, innocent children have been slaughtered in the name of "choice" and the "right of privacy," religious symbols have been stripped from our public places, and our moral foundation has been torn asunder with cries of "intolerance" and "pluralism," while many Christians have remained silent.

Would we continue to be "one nation under God?" My thoughts were expressed in a poem I wrote in July 1998 at the end of the second court case over this issue. This poem was an accurate depiction of the battle ahead.

OUR AMERICAN BIRTHRIGHT
One Nation under God was their cry and declaration,
Upon the law of Nature's God they built a mighty Nation.
For unlike mankind before them who had walked this earthen
        sod,
These men would never question the Sovereignty of God.

That all men were "created" was a truth "self-evident,"
To secure the rights God gave us was the role of government.
And if any form of government became destructive of this end,
It was their right, indeed their duty, a new one to begin.

So with a firm reliance on Divine Providence for protection,
They pledged their sacred honor and sought His wise direction.

They lifted up an appeal to God for all the world to see,
And vowed their independence forever to be free.

I'm glad they're not here with us to see the mess we're in,
How we've given up our righteousness for a life of indulgent sin.
For when abortion isn't murder and sodomy is deemed a right,
Then evil is now called good and darkness is now called light.

While truth and law were founded on the God of all creation,
Man now, through law, denies the truth and calls it "separation."
No longer does man see a need for God when he's in full control,
For the only truth self-evident is in the latest poll.

But with man as his own master we fail to count the cost,
Our precious freedoms vanish and our liberty is lost.
Children are told they can't pray in school and they teach them
    evolution,
When will they see the fear of God is the only true solution?

Our schools have become a battleground while all across the
    land,
Christians shrug their shoulders afraid to take a stand.
And from the grave their voices cry, the victory has already been
    won.
Just glorify the Father as did His only Son.

And when your work on earth is done, and you've traveled where
    we've trod,
You'll leave the land we left to you, *One Nation Under God!*[24]

17

THE FEDERAL COURT TRIAL

Nearly a year passed from the filing of the lawsuit against me on October 30, 2001, until the date the case was set for trial on October 15, 2002. During that time an endless series of motions and other legal documents flowed between the attorneys and the court. As in any case, the parties and potential witnesses were questioned by attorneys (depositions), and my counsel were kept busy attending conferences and other matters in preparation for the trial.

With so much paperwork passing between attorneys on both sides, it was only natural that mistakes would occur. On July 16, 2002, a letter written by Morris Dees of the Southern Poverty Law Center to Ayesha Khan, legal director of Americans United for Separation of Church and State, was mistakenly sent to my attorney, Steve Melchior. In the letter, Dees revealed exactly what he intended to accomplish at the trial:

> I also know that I am a trial lawyer and believe one of my strengths is in telling a story, at least that is what I am told. A judge is nothing more than a jury when it comes to the facts. You might remember that, from the start, I was laying our trial theme, i.e., how this was the act of a lone reli-

gious nut in partnership with a fanatical church. This is the story that will make this case so dirty that no appeals court will reverse Thompson [the trial judge] to make new law. Moore's purposes and intent and effect of the TCM [Ten Commandments Monument] are easy to prove.[1]

Clearly there was a plan by the plaintiffs' attorney to paint a false picture to the court so "no appeals court" would "reverse Thompson." But the real concern was that Dees implied that he knew *three months before the trial* how Judge Thompson would rule. My attorneys immediately filed the letter with the court, and Dees quickly filed a motion to remove the letter from the record.[2]

John Giles, president of the Christian Coalition of Alabama, criticized Dees for "degrading" me and for attacking Coral Ridge Ministries as a fanatical church, and Dr. D. James Kennedy, whom he said had "the highest degree of credibility among evangelicals."[3]

On the basis of unfavorable pretrial rulings by the district court and the letter indicating a possible predisposition against us, my attorneys filed a motion on October 1, 2002, asking that Judge Thompson step down from presiding over the lawsuit. In the motion, I stated, "I am convinced that Judge Thompson has a pervasive and personal bias and prejudice against me in favor of the plaintiffs, that Judge Thompson's impartiality might reasonably be questioned, and that there exists an appearance of impropriety in this case warranting Judge Thompson's recusal."[4] Our motion was denied, and the trial was set for October 15, 2002.

Our strategy in defending the monument at trial was twofold: (1) we would be absolutely faithful to the words and intent of the First Amendment (not as misinterpreted by federal judges), and (2) we would make the federal courts face the fact that the Constitution does not prohibit the acknowledgment of God and His sovereignty. Our other option was to "play the game" and argue that the monument does not violate this or that "test" invented by the Supreme Court to replace the words of the First Amendment. However, arguing according to these tests would have required us to cover up the fact that the monument clearly acknowledged and focused upon a sovereign God and His higher law. Unfortunately, many lawyers—even many Christian lawyers—have such a desire to win at all costs that they will sacrifice the principles of the Constitution and will try to make the "winning" argument, even if it means diluting an acknowledgment of God by making the Ten Commandments into an outdated relic of history that has lost all "religious" significance. This is usually the approach you have to take to appease the federal judges and convince them that you are not really talking about God or anything "religious." But a win on such a basis is actually a loss because each decision that is based on these invented judicial tests takes us further and further down the path of being ruled by judges rather than the Constitution. I refused to take this "pragmatic" approach, and that is why I chose the lawyers that I did: I knew they would be faithful to the Constitution and to their God.

Federal judges are not accustomed to being presented with arguments based on the text of the Constitution, but that is just what we would give them. The First Amendment says that "Congress shall make no law respecting an establishment of religion, or prohibiting the free exercise thereof . . . ." We would tell the federal courts that I was not *Congress* making a *law* (judges can't make law), that the monument was not an *establishment* of anything, and most importantly that the monument (and any acknowledgment of God) was not *religion,* as defined by the founding fathers and even the Supreme Court. This last point was especially important because if the judges could not define the word *religion,* they could not legitimately say that I had "established" it. The Ten Commandments monument did not violate any part of the First Amendment. It would now be up to the federal courts to decide whether to be faithful to the Constitution and the rule of law, or to choose the rule of other federal judges.

On the first day of the trial, Kayla and I proceeded to court accompanied by my security guard, Leonard Holifield. Leonard was a personal friend whom I had met years before in Gadsden when he was a karate instructor for my three boys. A former military non-commissioned officer who served in Desert Storm, Leonard instructed troops of the 82nd and 101st airborne units in combat and was highly skilled as a security officer. Together with Art Baylor, a former Montgomery police officer and good friend, we worked our way through the photographers and cameramen who lined the courtyard outside the entrance of the federal courthouse. As the rain fell under cloudy skies, it was a gloomy day, but I was excited to have an opportunity to finally present my case in court.

As we entered the courtroom, the benches and even the area that a jury normally occupied were filled with spectators, including several groups of schoolchildren. A number of attorneys also filled the room. The SPLC was represented by four attorneys, the ACLU had two, and Ayesha Khan was present for Americans United for Separation of Church and State (AUSCS). I had three attorneys representing me.

The three plaintiffs who had brought the suit were also attorneys: Stephen Glassroth, a criminal defense lawyer in Montgomery; Beverly Howard, an attorney who worked in the juvenile justice system; and Melinda Maddox, a cooperating attorney with the ACLU of Alabama.[5] They were called as the first witnesses in the case.

The first witness, Glassroth, not only exhibited his resentment for what I had done in displaying the Ten Commandments, but also demonstrated contempt for the way the district court opened the proceedings with "God Save the United States and this Honorable Court." But when questioned about this obvious acknowledgment of God by the district court, he said, "Things have become so routinized that they don't get on my radar screen."[6] His "radar screen" apparently detected any references to God as some intrusion into his territory.

Glassroth further testified that it also bothered him that Congress had placed the word *God* on our money.[7] When asked if he believed in God, Glassroth replied, "I can't say I am a believer in God. I question whether there would be a God."[8] Glassroth claimed that his main problem was that he thought the monument expressed a preference by the Alabama judicial department for a particular religious belief. He said that it offended him and made him angry.[9]

Beverly Howard testified that from the age of six until she graduated from high school she had lived in foster homes where she was required to attend church on Sunday mornings and evenings as well as Wednesday evenings.[10] Howard testified that she was shocked that every quote on the monument had "God" in it. She claimed that these "God" quotes made her feel like an "outsider."[11] She said, "I went back to feelings of growing up and being made to go to church."[12] She also said she was offended by the words "under God" in the Pledge of Allegiance.[13]

Melinda Maddox, a member of the ACLU's legal committee, testified that she had decided to *"carry the banner of the ACLU* after seeing pictures of the monument in the newspaper."[14] She stated that she felt the same as the other two plaintiffs about the nation's motto, "in God we trust" on our money, and "under God" in the Pledge of Allegiance.[15] With regard to the acknowledgment of God in the preamble to the Alabama Constitution, Maddox stated that she would also like to take out references to God in the Alabama Constitution.[16] Maddox further testified that she was offended by the words "one nation under God," "in God we trust," and "so help me God," just as much as she was by the monument.[17]

After one full day of testimony it was clear that the three lawyers who had filed suit against me had done so simply because they were "offended" by the use of the word *God* in anything. Their reasons were shallow and without merit and could just as easily have been applied to Judge Thompson, who opened his court with "God save the United States and this Honorable Court" and had his bailiff administer the oath to the plaintiffs, "so help me God." I thought that surely the judge would understand how ridiculous their logic was.

Herb Titus, my attorney, said it best: "The plaintiffs are part of a movement that feels God must be censored from the public square. Individual rights come from God. If they take God out of the equation, the all-powerful state is all that remains."[18] Today, too many people in the legal establishment have been led to believe that the state is all-powerful and that rights come from the state and not from God. But the Declaration of Independence states that man was created by God and "endowed by their Creator with certain unalienable rights" and that the role of government is to secure these rights. The Declaration of Independence is our organic law; for attorneys to deny the existence of God, they must deny the very law which they are sworn to uphold.

But too many people today do not know our organic law or the history from which it originated. Answers by Melinda Maddox, an attorney, to questions by my attorney Steve Melchior provide a prime example of this.

Q: Do you recognize the name James Madison?

A: Yes.

Q: Who would that be?

A: He was one of the founders of the country, I believe.

Q: Do you know whether he held any political office?

A: I believe he did.

Q: Do you know which one?

A: No, I don't.[19]

When a lawyer does not even know that James Madison was president of the United States, I doubt that she would know that he was the chief architect of the Constitution that she was sworn as a lawyer to uphold, or that Madison proposed the First Amendment on which she had brought suit.

I wonder if Mrs. Maddox would have been "offended" at Madison's acknowledgment of God in his *Memorial and Remonstrance Against Religious Assessments* when he said, "It is the duty of every man to render to the Creator such homage, and such homage only, as he believes to be acceptable to Him. This duty is *precedent* both in order of time and degree of obligation to the claims of Civil Society. Before any man can be considered as a member of Civil Society, he must be considered as a subject of the Governor of the Universe," and could only be a member of civil society with a "saving of his allegiance to the Universal Sovereign."[20]

Maddox said that when she first found out about the monument, "[m]y first reaction was that I was embarrassed to be a lawyer in Alabama."[21] Would Maddox have been embarrassed by Madison's reference to God as the "Governor of the Universe," "Universal Sovereign," "Creator," and "Supreme Lawgiver of the Universe," all in the same document (the *Memorial and Remonstrance*)?[22] Too many lawyers have the same problem; they are "embarrassed" to acknowledge God.

As I left the courthouse that day, I was even more anxious to return the next day. Steve Melchior had identified a large fountain-bust display in the front courtyard of the newly constructed courthouse as that of the Greek goddess of justice, Themis. A poster inside the building explained that the display of Themis had cost taxpayers thousands of dollars.

I was struck immediately with the hypocrisy of the district court. The monument of the Ten Commandments had cost the taxpayers nothing because it was constructed and purchased with private funds. According to the Alabama Constitution, the justice system of the state of Alabama was established "invoking the favor and guidance of Almighty God." I was on trial simply for acknowledging this God, and yet the Federal Judicial Building in which I was being tried had a display acknowledging a Greek goddess of justice. How could my acknowledgment be wrong and the other one be acceptable?

I hoped the media would note the hypocrisy represented by the bust of Themis outside the federal courthouse. I insisted that Melchior introduce into evidence the poster describing the display. When court resumed, Dr. Rich Hobson, administrative director of courts, was questioned briefly, then I was called to testify. I would not be intimidated when asked by Morris Dees if I was surprised that people had strong feelings about the monument. I replied that feelings do not determine whether something is or is not constitutional.

> If someone were to feel very strongly about a Greek goddess out in the front of this United States Courthouse, I would imagine they would kneel; but does that make it unconstitutional? But there's a Greek goddess [out front] and I think it does not represent our form of government, and I think people can feel very strongly about that. But it doesn't make it constitutional or not constitutional. What makes it constitutional or not constitutional is whether or not it's the establishment of a religion under the First Amendment.[23]

Soon I had the court's interest, and Judge Thompson began to ask me several questions of his own.

Thompson: You said that the First Amendment does not prohibit the acknowledgment of God. My question is: Acknowledgment by whom or what?

Moore: By anyone, to include a government official.

Thompson: So would you agree, then, that the First Amendment does not prohibit the acknowledgment of God by the State? By state government?

Moore: Right.[24]

When my attorney resumed questioning, time seemed to pass quickly. In response to questions, I recited passages from Madison, Jefferson, Story, Washington, and many others. References to noted philosophical and political thinkers such as Locke, Blackstone, de Bracton, and others also piqued Judge Thompson's interest as he attempted to understand my viewpoint.

"I really want to understand," Thompson stated at one point. "It's beginning to gel. I think I'm beginning to understand where he's coming from, what he's doing, and why he's doing it."[25]

During the third day of trial I was again on the stand, and Judge Thompson expressed his understanding of my position. To the amazement of the attorneys, in the middle of a round of questions that I was answering from Mr. Melchior, Judge Thompson turned his chair toward me and interrupted:

Thompson: Actually, you're touching on a question I was going to ask you.

Moore: Okay.

Thompson: I noticed in the opinion that you entered in the El Bethel case [Yates v. El Bethel Primitive Baptist Church[26]], you quote from Jefferson saying that "A separation of church and state existed because Almighty God was sovereign over both institutions."

Moore: Right.

Thompson: And that to prohibit that recognition would be to disregard both and respect neither.

Moore: Yes.

Thompson: And you say that "Madison explicitly recognized that maintaining a separation in no way meant to separate from civil government a belief in the sovereignty of God; indeed, the very concept of separation mandates a recognition of a sovereign God." . . .

Conceptually, what you're telling me, or telling others, is that you have a separation of church and state, but not necessarily separation of religion and state or God and state most importantly. The Constitution doesn't mandate the separation of God and State, it just mandates the separation of church and state.

Moore: Right.

Thompson: And that [is] what really is happening here in that at the top you have the sovereignty of God and God Himself creates the separation of church and state— So you wouldn't have separation of God.

Moore: That's exactly right.

Thompson: So what we're talking about here is, both the state and the church fall under the sovereignty of God.

Moore: Right.

Thompson: And in fact, from what I've read and what I think you're saying, you really couldn't have the state unless you had God.

Moore: Right, exactly.[27]

Melchior, somewhat stunned by the lengthy inquiry from the judge, took a moment to collect his thoughts and then resumed questioning me, only to be interrupted again by Judge Thompson.

Thompson: So what you're saying then is, getting back and embellishing a little bit on what I was trying to understand [about] what you believe and why you believe it, [is] that the Judeo-Christian God is at the top. And He gives the freedom of conscience that in fact allows people to worship allegedly other gods.

Moore: That's right.

Thompson: And without the Judeo-Christian God up there, you wouldn't have the freedom of conscience to worship

God or gods or pursue other religions or other duties that may be defined by Scripture.

Moore: That's right.[28]

An array of expert witnesses followed, the most impressive of whom was Michael Novak of the American Enterprise Institute. He was a scholar on religion, philosophy, and public policy, specializing in the relationship between religion and culture. An interesting discussion ensued between the judge and Novak about Alexis de Tocqueville's *Democracy in America*. Alexis de Tocqueville found that religion was a vital part of the American experiment during his visit in the 1830s and that from America's churches burned the spirit of liberty. Citing de Tocqueville and others, Novak supported my position on the subject of religion and early American life.[29]

The plaintiffs also had experts, such as a professor from the University of Tulsa who told the court that the use of "God" by English jurists, such as Sir William Blackstone in his *Commentaries on the Laws of England*, was mere "window dressing" thrown in for various and sundry reasons.[30] When asked by my attorney about references in his own writings to other English jurists such as Henry de Bracton, the expert suddenly was unable to recall any of de Bracton's writings or in which century de Bracton wrote.[31] The professor from Tulsa testified that many of our forefathers such as Thomas Jefferson and Benjamin Franklin were Deists and that the Declaration of Independence was an Enlightenment document.[32]

At the end of the sixth day of trial, after all the experts had testified, my attorneys called me to the stand to rebut the ridiculous assertions of some of the plaintiffs' experts. I was happy to counter the outlandish statements that were not justified either by history or the law. Such deception is spewed from liberal schools today without any basis in fact or law, and I had just heard from one of those liberal professors.

I explained that Sir William Blackstone was a renowned jurist who summarized the Common Law of England in his *Commentaries* from 1765 to 1769. Blackstone demonstrated that the entire history of western jurisprudence proceeded from an understanding of the nature of God. I added that, to say Blackstone's references to God were "window dressing" is to undermine the entire law on which our forefathers relied for understanding. Furthermore, for the plaintiffs' expert to use Henry de Bracton's name in his work and then deny any knowledge of de Bracton's writings or the era in which he wrote was an obvious fraud.

I had brought to the trial a copy of one of de Bracton's works because I often referred to it in making my historical and legal arguments. As "the father of the Common Law," de Bracton wrote in Latin in 1256 his *On the Laws and Customs of England*, or *De Legibus Et Consuetudinibus Angliae*.[33] I testified that de Bracton defined "natural law" as "that which nature, that is God Himself, taught all living things."[34] De Bracton, in describing how a civil action was instituted, referred to Deuteronomy, Job, and Chronicles.[35] These passages clearly showed that references to God were not "window dressing," but that God was recognized as a foundation of legal doctrine some five hundred years before Blackstone.[36]

With regard to so-called "Deists" such as Jefferson, who was the primary author of our cherished Declaration of Independence, the quote on Jefferson's memorial in Washington, D.C., refuted the expert's claim that Jefferson believed that God had no part in the affairs of men. Jefferson was objecting to the extension of slavery to the northwest territory when he said, "Can the liberties of a nation be thought secure when we have removed their only firm basis, a conviction in the minds of the people that these liberties are of the gift of God, that they are not to be violated but with his wrath?"[37] In query 18 of his *Notes on Virginia*, Jefferson made it clear that the Almighty had no attribute that could side with those who disregarded His laws.[38]

In 1776, when a great seal was being proposed for the United States, both Thomas Jefferson and Benjamin Franklin suggested designs that indicated their belief that God directs the affairs of men. Jefferson's proposal depicted Moses leading the children of Israel through the wilderness, guided by a pillar of fire by night and a cloud by day.[39] Franklin's design showed Moses standing next to the Red Sea dividing the waters.[40]

A well-known address by Franklin before the Constitutional Convention, recorded by James Madison, demonstrates Franklin's belief in a providential God. I repeated in court Franklin's words as he stood before a divided assembly on June 28, 1787, and pled for unity:

> In this situation of this Assembly, groping as it were in the dark for political truth and scarce able to distinguish it when presented to us, how has it happened, Sir, that we have not hitherto once thought of humbly applying to the Father of Lights to illuminate our understandings? In the beginning of the Contest with Great Britain, when we were sensible of danger, we had daily prayer in this room for the divine protection. Our prayers, Sir, were heard, and they were graciously answered. All of us who were engaged in the struggle must have observed frequent instances of a Superintending providence in our favor. To that kind providence we owe this happy opportunity of consulting in peace on the means of establishing our future national felicity. And have we now forgotten that powerful friend, or do we imagine we no longer need His assistance? I have lived, Sir, a long time, and the longer I live, the more convincing proofs I see of this truth—that God governs in the affairs of men. And if a sparrow cannot fall to the ground without His notice, is it probable that an empire can rise without His aid? We have been

assured, Sir, in the sacred writings, that "except the Lord build the House they labour in vain that build it." I firmly believe this; and I also believe that without His concurring aid we shall succeed in this political building no better than the Builders of Babel: We shall be divided by our little partial local interests, our projects will be confounded, and we ourselves shall become a reproach and bye word down to future ages. And what is worse, mankind may hereafter from this unfortunate instance, despair of establishing Governments by Human Wisdom and leave it to chance, war, and conquest.[41]

Those are not the words of a Deist, but of a man who knew Scripture and believed that its divine Author could come to America's aid. Certainly, God had come to my aid by enabling me to recite from memory Franklin's speech without interruption by attorneys or the court. The plaintiffs did not attempt cross-examination, and I was satisfied that the plaintiffs' expert had been impeached.

After a full week of trial we were ready for closing arguments. We gathered together in a small conference room before entering the courtroom, confident that we had done our job. We had explained our position well. Had a jury been present, they probably would have ruled in our favor. The case, however, was not before a jury, but a liberal federal judge. Even so, at least he had appeared to understand my position. We had done our duty; the result was with the Lord.

During closing arguments, Judge Thompson touched upon a key argument in our case, the definition of religion. Throughout, we had asserted that the term *religion* had to be defined and had clearly been defined not only in Supreme Court jurisprudence but by our founding fathers as well.

Now to our surprise, one of the plaintiffs' attorneys proceeded to argue to Judge Thompson that the U.S. Supreme Court "had wisely declined to adopt a specific definition of religion."[42] The court even asked counsel, "You don't think its necessary for me to define 'religion' in order to resolve this dispute?"[43] The attorney started to answer, but Judge Thompson interrupted, "Do you think it's wise?" The attorney responded, "It's certainly not wise for anything, with all due respect. It's not wise for any federal court to put on the philosopher's hat and attempt to define a concept like religion for any reason. But particularly when important fundamental rights are at stake."[44]

My attorneys and I were shocked; we felt sure that the court could not agree with such a ridiculous argument. The entire law is based on words that have defined meanings. In his closing argument, Melchior emphasized this point: "The definition of religion is *so* important, your Honor. . . . They [the founding fathers] used words because words have meaning. Not only did they use those words, but they defined those words."[45]

We were left at the end of the case with a favorable impression from Judge Thompson's own mouth when he said, "I think that is basically it. You know, I would almost think I would have to start my opinion that way. The issue is: Can the state acknowledge God? I think you [Melchior] said it. And I think in many ways I doubt the plaintiffs will disagree with you on that."[46]

We believed that if Judge Thompson understood the central issue in the case—as this comment indicated he did—then surely the answer would inevitably follow that, of course, the state could acknowledge God. We always had recognized God in the Alabama State Constitution, in our history, and in our law. Even the United States Supreme Court had made that perfectly clear in many cases. Nothing about the First Amendment or the Bill of Rights had changed. But there was nothing left to do but wait for Judge Thompson's answer to that important question.

18

JUDICIAL SUPREMACY

On November 18, 2002, less than a month after the trial ended, we were notified of Judge Thompson's ruling. The monument was declared to be unconstitutional! The court followed what other federal courts had been doing for years in removing acknowledgments of God from the public square.

During the course of the trial I came to believe that Judge Thompson would see that such rulings contradicted the plain language of the First Amendment of the United States Constitution, but I was wrong. His ruling left no doubt where he stood on the central issue in the case: "[W]hile the Chief Justice is free to keep whatever religious beliefs he chooses, *the state may not acknowledge the sovereignty of the Judeo-Christian God and attribute to that God our religious freedom.*"[1]

Judge Thompson correctly identified the issue in closing argument and now answered his own question, "Can the state acknowledge God?" He said no! And then he went even further by stating that the state could not attribute to God our religious freedom, therein contradicting the United States Supreme Court in *United States v. Macintosh*,[2] and the opinion our founding fathers expressed in numerous writings and proclamations. George Washington in his first presidential proclamation of October 3, 1789, specifically thanked God for our "civil and religious liberty with which we are blessed."[3]

Following the court's ruling, the media spread the news across the state[4] and in major national outlets.[5] The federal district judge gave me thirty days to remove the monument, stating, "If the monument is not removed within thirty days, the court will then enter an injunction requiring Justice Moore to remove it within fifteen days thereafter."[6] Most articles and editorials continued to focus on the Ten Commandments, a monument, or religion in general, and not on the issue of recognizing a sovereign God.

But the court specifically identified the issue in the opening paragraphs of the opinion:

> The question presented to this court is whether the Chief Justice of the Alabama Supreme Court violated the Establishment Clause when he placed a slightly over two-and-a-half ton granite monument—engraved with the Ten Commandments and other references to God—in the Alabama State Judicial Building with the specific purpose and effect, as the court finds from the evidence, of *acknowledging the Judeo-Christian God* as the moral foundation of our laws.
>
> ***
>
> [I]n announcing this holding today, *the court believes it is important to clarify at the outset that the court does not hold that it is improper in all instances to display the Ten Commandments in government buildings;* nor does the court hold that the Ten Commandments are not important, if not one of the most important, sources of American law.[7]

Even Judge Thompson recognized that the issue was not about the Ten Commandments or a monument to the Ten Commandments. The issue was and still is the acknowledgment of the Judeo-Christian God, the One who gave us the Ten Commandments.

Some media outlets continued to talk about the monument as an endorsement of "religion," so I tried to explain that Judge Thompson himself said that he "lack[ed] the expertise to formulate [his] own definition of religion for First Amendment purposes,"[8] and that he stated, "it is unwise, and even dangerous, to put forth, as a matter of law, one definition of 'religion' under the First Amendment."[9] How he could say that I was endorsing and establishing something he could not define was confusing at best.

We should be alarmed when judges who are sworn to interpret the law cannot even define words in the law. Judge Thompson used the words *religion* or *religious* more than 150 times in a seventy-nine-page opinion, but then said he could not define the term. This is a ridiculous and illogical position.

In our culture today, too many people have been misled to believe that words are "relative" and need no definition. The error of such reasoning in law is shown by a simple illustration that I often use. A man, while walking near a stream, picks up a stick lying on the ground. A game warden sees him and issues him a citation for fishing without a license. When the man appears in court, he explains to the judge that he was in no way "fishing." He did not have a line, weight, hook, or bait— only a stick. Furthermore, he was there with his small child to enjoy the view of the water, and he had not cast anything into the stream to "fish."

But the court levies a stiff fine against the man and sentences him to jail for sixty days, explaining that he, the judge, lacked the expertise to define *fishing* and thought it was unwise and even dangerous to define the word. As justification for his order, the judge explains that he "felt" strongly that the stick could be used to kill a fish and therefore he had no option but to impose the maximum penalty under the law. The judge in this example did not interpret the law, but made a law of his own. He usurped the powers belonging to the legislative branch, basing his ruling on his own feelings and opinions.

A short story entitled *Through the Looking Glass*, written by Lewis Carroll, vividly illustrates the problem we have in the federal courts in America today. As Alice spoke to Humpty Dumpty, Humpty exclaimed,

"There's glory for you!"

"I don't know what you mean by 'glory,'" Alice said.

Humpty Dumpty smiled contemptuously. "Of course you don't—till I tell you. I meant 'there's a nice knock-down argument for you!'"

"But 'glory' doesn't mean 'a nice knock-down argument,'" Alice objected.

"When I use a word," Humpty Dumpty said in rather a scornful tone, "it means just what I choose it to mean—neither more nor less."

"The question is," said Alice, "whether you *can* make words mean so many different things."

"The question is," said Humpty Dumpty, "which is to be master—that's all."[10]

When federal courts assume the power to redefine words, or avoid definitions altogether, they usurp the power of the legislature as the lawmaking branch. Their edicts then become self-made law based on their own feelings and predilections. Such a situation occurred in *Dred Scott v. Sandford* in 1857 when the United States Supreme Court held that slaves were "property" under the Constitution of the United States. In his dissent, Justice Benjamin Curtis explained that a basic principle underlying all law was that in order to properly understand the Constitution we must recognize that words have meaning:

[W]hen a strict interpretation of the Constitution, according to the fixed rules which govern the interpretation

of laws [definitions], is abandoned, and the theoretical opinions of individuals are allowed to control its meaning, we
have no longer a Constitution; we are under the government
of individual men, who for the time being have power to
declare what the Constitution is, according to their own
views of what it ought to mean.[11]

With regard to the First Amendment to the Constitution, federal
courts are making their own laws by refusing to define their words. A
monument becomes a "law," and the mere act of displaying a monument becomes an "establishment." Without definitions, judges have no
recourse but to use feelings and opinions as a basis for their decrees.

This is precisely what Judge Thompson did. Unable or unwilling to
define words, he turned his own biased opinions into a judicial order.
Three times in his opinion Judge Thompson wrote that the monument's sloping top and "religious air" or appearance "call to mind an
open Bible resting on a lectern."[12] In his personal inspection of the
monument, Judge Thompson stood within three feet of it and could
plainly see that it was not a Bible. And even if it was a Bible, that
would not be grounds to declare something unconstitutional.

Have we now been reduced to appearance as the basis for the constitutionality of a display? If that were the case, we would no longer be
able to display the Declaration of Independence or the Constitution of
the United States on a sloping platform for fear of offending some federal
judge. If the monument has a "religious air," then so does the Declaration
of Independence, which contains not only references to the law of God,
but also to our "Creator God," the "Supreme Judge of the World," and
"Divine Providence." Would that treasured document offend Judge
Thompson because of its "religious air"?

Straining the bounds of credibility even further, Judge Thompson
claimed that the Ten Commandments monument appeared to him to

have an "overwhelming sacred aura," an "ineffable but still over-whelming holy aura," and even something "more sublime" than the "solemn ambience of the rotunda" of the judicial building. "There was the sense of being in the presence of something not just valued and revered (such as an historical document) but also holy and sacred."[13]

Perhaps the most revealing sentiment Judge Thompson expressed in his opinion was that my definition of "religion" was "simply put, incorrect and religiously offensive."[14] Nevertheless, "my" definition of religion was the same definition of religion given by the United States Supreme Court in 1878 and 1890.[15] The definition used by the United States Supreme Court was now religiously offensive to Judge Thompson. In fact, the definition of religion contained in the *Memorial and Remonstrance*, and attached to a dissent in the 1947 case of *Everson v. Board of Education*,[16] stated that religion is "the duty which we owe to the Creator and the manner of discharging it."[17]

Judge Thompson simply could not accept the definition given by the United States Supreme Court. He stated, "Perhaps in the early days of the Republic these words were understood to protect only the diversity within Christianity, but today they are recognized as guaranteeing religious liberty and equality to the infidel, the atheist, or the adherent of a non-Christian faith such as Islam or Judaism."[18]

But Judge Thompson erred in reaching this conclusion. The understanding that God is the Author of religious freedom was recognized not only by the U.S. Supreme Court, but is still recognized by many state constitutions, including Arkansas, Illinois, Kansas, Kentucky, Louisiana, Maryland, New Jersey, North Dakota, Pennsylvania, Rhode Island, South Dakota, and Wyoming. Most other state constitutions simply refer to God as the guarantor of liberty in general.[19]

The definition of religion once used by the U.S. Supreme Court itself recognizes the Creator God who gives to all people the freedom to worship Him according to the dictates of their consciences. The thoughts and opinions of men are simply outside the reach of government. In speaking of the First Amendment, Thomas Jefferson said that he believed that "religion is a matter which lies solely between Man and his God" and that man "owe[d] account to none other for his faith or worship."[20] Jefferson continued by saying that "the legislative powers of government reach actions only and not opinions."[21] Therefore, people are entitled to believe or not believe in God as they wish because God gives them that right and government is precluded from interfering with this right.

In 1878, the United States Supreme Court reiterated that principle in *Reynolds v. United States*[22] by explaining that to allow a civil magistrate to intrude into our opinions and restrain the profession or propagation of opinions because they supposedly have an ill tendency is a dangerous fallacy. Not only is religious liberty destroyed, but the civil magistrate or judge will make his opinions the rule of judgment and he will approve or condemn the sentiments (beliefs) of others only as they identify with his own.

Judge Thompson ruled according to his own opinions and not by law. In denying the sovereignty of God, he rejected not only my beliefs but the beliefs of the people of the state of Alabama as well. Alabamians had clearly stated in the preamble to the state constitution that "to secure the blessings of liberty to ourselves and our posterity," they invoked the "favor and guidance of Almighty God."[23]

We lost our case, but we were successful in bringing to the attention of the court and the general public the issue that had avoided scrutiny for the past forty or fifty years. Since the 1960s, federal courts have consistently removed all acknowledgments of God from the public sector, whether denominated as prayer, Bible reading, displays, mottos, or historical references. Written opinions of courts no longer reference a belief in the sovereignty of God. Even references to God in our national laws are disparaged and tolerated as "ceremonial deisms."

For example, Judge Thompson stated in his opinion that "similarly, 'ceremonial deisms,' such as legislative prayers or opening Court sessions with 'God save the United States and this honorable Court,' are different from public acknowledgments of a sectarian God."[24] These attempts to discriminate against a sincere belief in God were reflected earlier in the writings of Supreme Court Justice William Brennan, who stated in *Marsh v. Chambers:*

> I frankly do not know what should be the proper disposition of features of our public life such as "God save the United States and this Honorable Court," "In God We Trust," "One Nation Under God," and the like. I might well adhere to the view expressed in *Schempp* that such mottos are consistent with the Establishment Clause, not because their import is *de minimis*, but because they have lost any true religious significance.[25]

In other words, according to William Brennan, we can legally continue to acknowledge God only so long as we do not really mean it.

A monument to the Ten Commandments was placed in the Alabama Judicial Building. This monument ultimately identified the hypocrisy of the courts and forced the federal judiciary to confront the true issue. Now that the district court had ruled, we were ready to take the issue up on appeal.

Soon after the release of Judge Thompson's order, I began to speak publicly of appeal, stating that "federal district courts have no jurisdiction or authority to prohibit the acknowledgment of God that is specifically recognized in the Constitution of Alabama."[26] Several groups came to my support. American Veterans in Domestic Defense rallied at the state capitol on December 16, 2002. About four hundred veterans who had served their country affirmed their oath to protect the

Constitution "against all enemies foreign *and* domestic." Veterans of wars abroad recognized that those who wanted to remove God from our public life were enemies to our Constitution.

Before the week ended, Judge Thompson gave a deadline of January 3, 2003, to move the monument. It did not look like it would be a very merry Christmas. But on December 23, 2002, he temporarily delayed the effect of his own order in response to my filing of a notice of appeal with the Eleventh Circuit Court of Appeals in Atlanta, Georgia. My attorneys and I enjoyed a peaceful Christmas, knowing that the monument remained in the Alabama Judicial Building and that our notice of appeal had been duly filed.

On January 20, 2003, after Christmas break, I administered the oath of office to the new governor of Alabama, Bob Riley, who had pledged his support in the battle. I was delighted to be able to discuss these issues with him. I was grateful for the opportunity to explain the importance of a united stand against the unlawful order of the federal district court. By early March, even the Alabama legislature had come to my aid, passing a proposed amendment allowing the posting of the Ten Commandments in public schools 89–0 with 6 abstentions.

The Court of Appeals held their hearing in Montgomery on June 4, 2003, and issued a ruling within one month—on July 1, 2003—upholding Judge Thompson's decision. The three-judge panel concluded that if they adopted my position,

> [I] would be free to adorn the walls of the Alabama Supreme Court's courtroom with sectarian religious murals and have decidedly religious quotations painted above the bench. Every government building could be topped with a cross, or a menorah, or a statue of Buddha, depending upon the views of the officials with authority over the premises. A crèche could occupy the place of honor in the lobby or

rotunda of every municipal, county, state, and federal building. Proselytizing religious messages could be played over the
public address system in every government building at the
whim of the official in charge of the premises.[27]

The appeals court used their own feelings to justify their illogical
opinion. By their own ridiculous logic, if the plaintiffs win simply
because they are offended at the mention of God, then every mention
of God can be removed from public life to include "in God we trust"
on our money, "so help me God" in our oaths, and "one nation under
God" in our Pledge of Allegiance. Of course, that is exactly what is
happening and what the ACLU and Americans United would like to
do. The federal district courts seem happy to comply.

The Eleventh Circuit Court of Appeals joined Judge Thompson in
judicial hypocrisy by stating that references to God on our money, our
national anthem, national holidays like Thanksgiving, and the opening
of court sessions with references to God serve a legitimate secular purpose and "are immune from Establishment Clause challenges 'because
they have lost through rote repetition any significant religious content.'"[28] I did not then, nor do I now, think that it is the place of any
court or judge to tell people that they may continue a long-standing
practice simply because it is insignificant and meaningless.

There was enormous public support, as indicated by a survey
released in August of 2003, which found that at least 77 percent of the
people of Alabama supported my position.[29] Even the United States
House of Representatives voted 260–16 for an amendment to the
Judiciary Bill to allow no funds to enforce any decision by federal
courts to order me to remove the monument.

Speaking in Mobile at Dauphin Way Baptist Church, I said, "No
amount of intimidation" would stop me from doing my job and uphold-

ing my duty.[30] I intended to take my appeal to the United States Supreme Court.

The Eleventh Circuit Court had stated, "We do expect that *if he is unable to have the district court's order overturned through the usual appellate processes, when the time comes Chief Justice Moore will obey that order.* If necessary, the court's order will be enforced. The rule of law will prevail."[31] It appeared from a plain reading of the order that the higher court indicated that the "stay" Judge Thompson had imposed would remain in effect until the appeals process was completed.

But then the unexpected happened. Judge Thompson, without any motion made by the plaintiffs and in apparent contradiction to the appeals court, lifted the stay previously imposed and gave me fifteen days to move the monument. I was now faced with a decision of momentous proportions. The federal judge decided to test my resolve even before my time to petition the U.S. Supreme Court for a writ of certiorari expired. Tom Parker, deputy director of the Administrative Office of Courts, called Judge Thompson's order "judicial tyranny" intended to intimidate me.[32]

I knew that the decision to disobey the order of Judge Myron Thompson would be sharply criticized, but what other choice did I have? I considered his order to be unlawful for several reasons. To follow an unlawful order would violate my oaths to both the United States Constitution and the Alabama Constitution. What did the rule of law require?

19

THE RULE OF LAW

At the entrance to Washington Hall, the main dining facility for cadets at the United States Military Academy at West Point, New York, is "Constitution Corner." Located adjacent to a statue of George Washington riding a magnificent stallion, Constitution Corner reminds visitors and cadets of the purpose of the academy: To provide leaders "of principle and integrity so strong that their oaths to support and defend the Constitution will unfailingly govern their actions."[1]

The plaque on Constitution Corner, entitled "Loyalty to the Constitution," informs all who visit there that the "United States boldly broke with the ancient military custom of swearing loyalty to a leader. Article VI require[s] that American Officers thereafter swear loyalty to our *Basic Law*, the Constitution."[2] Article VI of the Constitution is not only binding on officers in the military, but also on all executive, legislative, and judicial officials of both the state and federal governments.

Article VI provides that "this Constitution, and the Laws of the United States which shall be made in Pursuance thereof . . . shall be *the supreme Law of the Land; and the Judges in every State shall be* bound thereby."[3] In other words, the Constitution is our basic law, and all judges are bound to its clear meaning and its express terms. It is our "rule of law," and no judge can alter or disregard that law.

That is exactly why all judges, including the justices of the United States Supreme Court, take an oath to uphold and support the Constitution of the United States. Likewise, the express provisions of each state constitution that do not conflict with provisions of the U.S. Constitution also become a "rule of law" to which judges and other state officials in that state are bound.

Judge Myron Thompson's order to remove the Ten Commandments monument because it acknowledged the Judeo-Christian God was clearly unlawful. The express purpose of the First Amendment to the U.S. Constitution was to allow the freedom to worship God *and* to prevent the federal government (including the federal courts) from interfering with that right of the states and the people. As I have previously stated, all states acknowledge God in their own state constitutions, and Alabama is no exception. In fact, in the Alabama Constitution, the recognition of God is the basis of its justice system.

When Judge Thompson ordered me to remove the Ten Commandments monument, he not only issued an unlawful order; he also ordered me to do something that violated my conscience and my oath to the Constitution of the United States and the constitution of the state of Alabama. Judge Thompson placed himself above the law.

As a cadet at West Point, and later as a company commander in Vietnam, I knew the importance of following orders. The success or failure of a mission and the lives of others depend on strict adherence to the chain of command. That principle of obedience to superiors is also crucial to the proper functioning of a court system. Nevertheless, the principle of obedience to superior officers is based on the premise that the order given is a lawful one.

In the court-martial trial of Lieutenant William Calley, a unit commander at My Lai in Vietnam who killed more than one hundred innocent civilians, Calley defended himself by claiming that he was just following the orders of his superior, Captain Ernest Medina. Nevertheless, Lieutenant Calley was court-martialed. The military tribunal that considered his appeal rejected his defense by saying that an order to kill civilians, even if given by a superior officer, did not excuse Calley's conduct because such orders are clearly unlawful.[4]

That is exactly the principle stated on the plaque at Constitution Corner at West Point. It states: "Our American Code of Military Obedience requires that should orders and the Law ever conflict, our officers must obey the law. Many other nations have adopted our principle of loyalty to the basic law."[5] Lieutenant Calley's conviction confirmed that the basic law remained intact.

When people who are sworn to support the law disregard it and issue orders which they think are "the law," we are governed by the rule of man, not the rule of law! The United States did break boldly with ancient customs and practices on July 4, 1776, when it declared independence from Great Britain and established a nation under the authority of the "Laws of Nature and of Nature's God."

In 1776, the American colonies knew well the history of tyrannical rule in England. On June 15, 1215, on the field of Runnymede, King John was forced to sign the Magna Charta, which consisted of a preamble and sixty-three clauses that bound the king to observe certain rights and liberties of the people.[6] Not long afterward, in 1256, a noted legal scholar and judge, Henry de Bracton—who is considered the "Father of the Common Law"—explained that "the king must not be under man but under God and under the law, because law makes the king."[7] De Bracton continued, "Let [the king] therefore bestow upon the law what the law bestows upon him, namely, rule and power for there is no *rex* [king] where will rules rather than *lex* [law]."[8]

This principle is displayed even today. Carved in stone above Langdell Hall at Harvard University are the words *Non sub Homine sed sub Deo et lege* ("not under man but under God and law"), to remind us that the governing authorities, whether king or president, are not under man, but under God and law.

In 1644, a great Scottish Presbyterian pastor, Samuel Rutherford, wrote *Lex Rex*,[9] translated "Law is King," a work that made both biblical and philosophical arguments against the divine right of kings and declared that even a king is subject to the law.

In 1689, an act declaring the rights and liberties of the English people known as the English Bill of Rights provided the primary foundation on which the government rested after the "Glorious Revolution" of 1688 in which the throne of James II was given to William of Orange and his wife Mary. Although "it purported to introduce no new principles but merely to declare explicitly law," its main purpose was to declare various practices of King James II illegal, and to provide freedom from arbitrary government.[10]

The long history of the English people provided a good foundation for the resistance of our American forefathers to the tyranny of King George III. When Thomas Jefferson and other founders boldly proclaimed in 1776 that "the History of the present King of Great Britain is a history of repeated Injuries and Usurpations all having in direct Object the Establishment of an absolute Tyranny over the States," they were stating that King George III had placed himself above the law and had become a tyrant.[11]

The authors of the Declaration of Independence then enumerated in that document violations committed against the colonies, most of which were violations of the laws of England or the law of God. With no other authority on earth to which they could appeal, the founders appealed to the "Supreme Judge of the World for the Rectitude [righteousness or correctness] of [their] intentions."

Thus, the "rule of law" was the very basis on which our founding fathers rejected the rule of King George and declared independence from Great Britain. They recognized that the biblical admonitions of the thirteenth chapter of Romans required obedience to authority, but they also recognized that no man, no king, no prince, and—I might add in my case—no federal judge could place himself above the law. In fact, the motto that Benjamin Franklin chose to accompany his proposed seal for the new United States in July 1776 was "Rebellion to tyrants is obedience to God."[12]

Today, some well-meaning Christians argue that we must obey governing authorities even when they mandate that we cannot publicly acknowledge God. But historically, Christians have known better! In 1750, only twenty-six years before the signing of the Declaration of Independence, a Congregationalist minister and Harvard graduate, Jonathan Mayhew, published a sermon entitled "A Discourse Concerning Unlimited Submission and Non-Resistance to the Higher Powers." In this sermon he addressed the issue of obedience to a higher authority as required by Romans 13. This was several years before hostilities with Great Britain, and even before King George III became king.

In his published sermon, Mayhew stated that "no civil rulers are to be obeyed when they enjoin things that are inconsistent with the commands of God. . . . All commands running counter to the declared will of the supreme legislator of heaven and earth, are null and void: And therefore *disobedience to them is a duty, not a crime.*"[13] Mayhew continued:

> From whence it follows, that as soon as the prince sets
> himself up above the law, he loses the king in the tyrant: he
> does to all intents and purposes, unking himself, by acting
> out of, and beyond, that sphere which the constitution
> allows him to move in. And in such cases, he has no more
> right to be obeyed, than any inferior officer who acts beyond
> his commission.[14]

That principle was true in 1776, and it is true today. When a military commander, a president, or a federal judge sets himself above the law, he has no right to be obeyed; he, in effect, "unkings" himself. Or, in the case of a federal judge like Myron Thompson, he loses his judicial mantle and becomes a tyrant. Not only did Judge Thompson's order run contrary to both the United States Constitution and the Constitution of Alabama, but his unlawful order commanded me to remove the monument because it acknowledged God.

That is exactly why I could not remove the monument: It would violate my oath and my conscience. To deny God would be to recognize man as sovereign and would be a violation of the first commandment (see Exod. 20:3) as well as the First Amendment.[15] Judge Thompson's order, running counter to the declared will of the Supreme Judge of the world, was null and void; disobedience was a duty, not a crime.

When the Eleventh Circuit Court of Appeals refused to reverse Judge Thompson's unlawful decree, I stated:

> The rule of law must prevail in this case! That rule is
> found in our organic law, the Declaration of Independence,
> and preserved in the "religion clauses" of the First
> Amendment of the United States Constitution, which
> states: "Congress shall make no *law* respecting an establish-
> ment of *religion* or prohibiting the free exercise thereof.[16]

But other people disagreed. The associate justices of the Alabama Supreme Court eventually ordered the monument removed to preserve what they called "the rule of law." Attorney General Bill Pryor prosecuted me on ethics charges because, he said, I violated the "rule of law." Governor Bob Riley turned his back on the case because I supposedly violated the "rule of law." Noted religious leaders such as Richard Land, executive director of the Ethics and Religious Liberty Commission of the Southern Baptist Convention, and Jay Sekulow, head of the American Center for Law and Justice, joined in the chorus, saying that my refusal to obey Judge Thompson's order was a violation of the "rule of law."

Even some newspaper editors began to repeat this false accusation. The day after the monument was moved from public display, the *Birmingham News* published an editorial, "Moving Day—Monument's move is victory for rule of law."[17] The editorial stated, "The rule of law prevailed. . . . In the end, the pivotal question in this dispute wasn't whether the monument was wrong or right, but whether Moore would obey a court's command."[18]

Finally, I would stand before the Court of the Judiciary and hear Judge William Thompson (no relation to Myron Thompson) proclaim, "In defying [the federal court's] order, the Chief Justice placed himself above the law . . . [and] no man in this Country is so high that he is above the law."[19]

But the law—the true law—was clear. Nearly everyone recognized that the federal court had no basis in law to order the monument's removal. My fellow justices on the Alabama Supreme Court even stated in their brief to the federal court in a related case:

> The associate justices submit their Motion and Brief
> notwithstanding the belief of many, if not all of them, that it
> is constitutional for public officials to acknowledge God in
> public spaces and to display the Ten Commandments in
> courthouses. They all believe themselves bound, however, by
> a Final Judgment and Injunction issued by a federal court
> that has not been stayed. . . . The associate justices believe
> themselves to be bound by that injunction notwithstanding
> their personal beliefs.[20]

What my fellow justices asserted in their brief to the court was that no matter how wrong the order of a federal court might be, they were bound by blind obedience to follow it, even if it contradicted their own interpretation of the law and their beliefs.

After I was removed from office, one of the associate justices, Champ Lyons, distributed a document to attorneys in Alabama to explain his position in this case and to address his reasons for voting with the rest of the justices to remove the monument. He stated:

> No intellectually honest legal scholar can say that the framers of the First Amendment to the United States Constitution, when they chose the words "Congress shall pass [sic] no law respecting an establishment of religion or prohibiting the free exercise thereof," intended that a monument depicting the Ten Commandments in the lobby of a United States Courthouse would violate its provisions. . . . I am dismayed by the precedent from the United States Supreme Court that yields the conclusion that the Chief Justice's display of a monument in the rotunda of our building constitutes prohibited state action in the form of "a law respecting an establishment of religion."[21]

Champ Lyons, like the other justices, *knew that Judge Thompson's order was wrong!* To believe that the First Amendment prevented the display of a monument, he implied, would be intellectually dishonest.

Justice Lyons continued his thoughts by claiming that "[the judicial] oath carries with it the obligation, no matter how distasteful, to support the Constitution as interpreted by the United States Supreme Court under the doctrine of judicial review."[22] In other words, he confessed that his idea of "judicial review" was to obey the Constitution according to someone else's interpretation and not his own, no matter how wrong or misguided that interpretation might be. As if to leave no doubt about what he was saying, Justice Lyons admitted that he had "complied with a court order which, in [his] opinion, is inconsistent with the text of the United States Constitution but which [he is] bound by oath to obey."[23]

Lyons admitted he willfully obeyed an order that he knew to be unlawful. The fallacy of such logic is evident in the result—blind obedience to whatever other people might say, even though it violates the words of the law that all judges (including Champ Lyons) are sworn to uphold. This is the rule of men and not the rule of law, despite Justice Lyons's claims to the contrary.

How did we get to such a misunderstanding—that we follow the Constitution as the law unless and until a federal judge issues an order contrary to the law by which we are bound? The unwillingness of judges to follow the Constitution according to its express meaning and clear interpretation is precisely the problem in our government today.

To make sure that the government of the newly formed United States of America was "a government of laws and not of men," as the Massachusetts Constitution of 1780 indicated, the framers of our Constitution established a separation of powers. This applied to the legislative, executive, and judicial branches of government. They also established a system of federalism that divided power between the federal government and state governments.

Just two years after ratification of the Constitution, a Bill of Rights was enacted as a supplement to the Constitution to further protect the people from possible government abuse of power. The framers of the Constitution insisted on including what they called these "external devices"—the separation of powers and the Bill of Rights—in the Constitution. As James Madison said, it is

a reflection on human nature, that such devices should
be necessary to control the abuses of government. But what
is government itself but the greatest of all reflections on
human nature? If men were angels, no government would be
necessary. If angels were to govern men, neither external nor
internal controls on government would be necessary. In
framing a government which is to be administered by men
over men, the great difficulty lies in this: you must first
enable the government to control the governed; and in the
next place oblige it to control itself. A dependence on the
people is, no doubt, the primary control on the government;
but experience has taught mankind the necessity of auxiliary
precautions.[24]

Madison meant that if people were "angels" we would not need
anything to control our behavior. But because we have a fallen nature,
controls like the separation of powers are needed. The framers recognized that people in power are prone to abuse it, so they sought to
"bind [them] down from mischief by the chains of the Constitution,"
as Thomas Jefferson put it.[25] But federal judges no longer feel restrained
by the "chains of the Constitution," issuing orders that, as Lyons stated,
are inconsistent with the "text" of the Constitution.

*The Constitution signifies to the world that the United States is to be
governed by the rule of law, not of man.* It leaves no doubt on this point
by declaring—as Constitution Corner reminds us—that "[t]his
Constitution . . . shall be the supreme Law of the Land; and the Judges
in every State shall be bound thereby."[26]

The long and short of it is that our written Constitution—this
nation's fixed, fundamental law—is synonymous with the rule of law.
Enumeration of the powers of the federal government in the

Constitution shows that those powers are "few and defined," as Madison stated, holding the government accountable to the people, who can point to the written Constitution for proof of government abuses of power.[27]

One way people hold the government accountable to the law is by going to court to vindicate their rights when they are violated. Indeed, the power of the courts to declare laws passed by Congress and the state legislatures void if such laws are deemed to violate the Constitution is known as "judicial review." It exists because the Constitution holds us to the rule of law. Chief Justice John Marshall stated in *Marbury v. Madison* that "the government of the United States has been emphatically termed a government of laws, and not of men. It will certainly cease to deserve this high appellation, if the laws furnish no remedy for the violation of a vested legal right."[28] Marshall was explaining that, if Congress or the state legislatures could pass laws on any subject even if the Constitution forbids such laws, then we would live by the rule of men.

Marshall noted in *Marbury* that if the courts are to determine whether certain acts by government officials are legal or illegal, "there must be some rule of law to guide the courts" in making such a determination.[29] That "rule of law" is the Constitution. The Constitution is a document of fixed law; it applies generally over the entire country, declaring that it is "the supreme Law of the Land." It is specific both in the powers it grants and forbids to the federal government. Thus, "the particular phraseology of the constitution of the United States," Marshall wrote, "confirms and strengthens the principle supposed to be essential to all written constitutions, that a law repugnant to the constitution is void; and that *courts*, as well as other departments, are bound by that instrument."[30]

Judicial review was originally intended as a tool to *restrain* the federal government and to keep it within the boundaries set out by the

Constitution (similar to other checks and balances in the system like veto power and impeachments). But the federal courts have turned that tool into a license to rewrite the Constitution to say whatever they want it to say.

In *Cooper v. Aaron* in 1958, the United States Supreme Court boldly but erroneously claimed for the first time that *Marbury* stood for the proposition that "the federal judiciary is supreme in the exposition of the law of the Constitution."[31] From that point forward, the federal courts have presumed that their rulings were equivalent to the Constitution—whatever federal judges say is "the supreme law of the land." For the most part, lawyers and laymen throughout the country have accepted this as the truth.

But what Chief Justice Marshall actually said in the *Marbury* case could not be further from the Supreme Court's self-serving characterization. Marshall stated that "it is apparent, that the framers of the constitution contemplated that instrument *as a rule for the government of the courts*, as well as the legislature. Why otherwise does it direct judges to take an oath to support it? . . . *How immoral to impose* [*the oath*] *upon* [*judges*], *if they were to be used as the instruments, and the knowing instruments, for violating what they swear to support!*"[32]

In other words, the Constitution is the rule of law for the courts just as much as it is for Congress and the state legislatures. Judges cannot be above the Constitution that they are sworn to support. As Chief Justice Marshall noted, all judges take an oath to the Constitution, *not* to the Supreme Court. It would be *immoral* for a judge to knowingly violate the Constitution by refusing to follow its commands or through unfaithfully interpreting its words. Thus, Myron Thompson's order in my case would have been considered immoral by Chief Justice Marshall.

Attorney General Bill Pryor said in 2003 that "the rule of law means that when courts resolve disputes, after all appeals and arguments, we all must obey the orders of those courts even when we disagree with those orders. The rule of law means that we can work to change the law but not to defy court orders."[33] But the rule of law in this country is the United States Constitution, *not* the courts. This means that if the Constitution says one thing and a federal court says something else, a federal or state official who is sworn to support the Constitution must follow the Constitution. To do otherwise is to disregard the rule of law.

If, as Pryor suggests, what the federal courts say really is the supreme and final word on what the Constitution means, then the courts, not the Constitution, are supreme law. Abraham Lincoln said, "If the policy of the government, upon vital questions affecting the whole people, is to be irrevocably fixed by decisions of the Supreme Court, the instant they are made, in ordinary litigation between parties in personal actions, the people will have ceased to be their own rulers, having to that extent practically resigned their government into the hands of that eminent tribunal."[34] Even before that time, Thomas Jefferson observed, "[W]hatever power in any government is independent, is absolute also," and if the federal judiciary is wholly independent, "[t]he constitution, on this hypothesis, is a mere thing of wax in the hands of the judiciary."[35]

When a handful of people are given the power to override the words of the Constitution and to impose their agenda upon the nation simply because they carry the title of "federal judge," and no dissent is permitted from their opinion on the Constitution, then we no longer live by the rule of law. We live rather by the rule of men because it is not the Constitution—but those who interpret it—who govern us.

Under the guise of interpreting the Constitution, the federal courts have violated every principle of the rule of law. The law, particularly in the area of constitutional rights, no longer has permanence or stability. One need look only as far as the law on abortion to see that this is the case. For nearly two hundred years no "right" to an abortion existed, but in 1973 the United States Supreme Court invented one in *Roe v. Wade*.[36] Similarly, for the last five thousand years of civilization homosexual sodomy has been shunned by society and the law. But the Supreme Court in 2003 "discovered" that a right to engage in such acts was protected by the Constitution in the infamous case of *Lawrence v. Texas*.[37] The court had come to the exact opposite conclusion seventeen years earlier in *Bowers v. Hardwick*.[38]

The Constitution itself has not changed in these areas over the last two centuries, but the ideology of the Supreme Court and lower federal courts certainly has. Because we have exalted the Supreme Court as the gatekeepers of our laws, our fundamental law has changed with them. Consequently, there is no permanence to our law. The Supreme Court and lower federal courts make decisions *based on their feelings* rather than the words of the Constitution, defying the meaning of "the rule of law" and making judicial decisions nearly impossible to predict.

Some people have forgotten the vital point that judges' decisions are *opinions* on the law, not the law itself. A person's opinion on a particular topic carries weight only if it is supported by the facts. Likewise, the "opinion" or ruling of a court deserves obedience only if it is supported by the law. A court decision not grounded in the Constitution does not merit the respect we owe to the law. Such a decision is nothing more than a judge's opinion based on a whim, not on the law that "we the people" agree to be governed by as a nation.

What are the consequences when state officials such as my fellow justices on the Alabama Supreme Court obey a federal court order that is not consistent with the Constitution?

First, by assenting to a ruling that is not based on a plain reading of the constitutional text, the state official agrees that it is the federal courts and not the Constitution and the laws that govern the country. While this may be the practical reality in many areas of the law today, just because it is happening does not mean it is right. If this point is surrendered, then we have no Constitution, no fundamental law, and no fixed authority to appeal to when those judges make mistakes. Judges, like everyone else, make mistakes. Without a standard to which judges are held accountable for their mistakes, our rights are at their mercy.

Second, obedience to such a ruling means that the state official has violated his oath to support the Constitution. An oath is a solemn promise before God and the people whom the official serves. Violating such a promise is not something that should be taken lightly. Indeed, if the state official is willing to violate such a solemn promise for the sake of avoiding conflict with federal authorities, we have to wonder if he can be trusted on any other issue.

One might ask, How can the court system function properly if a lower court judge refuses to obey the orders of a higher court? It is quite simple. A higher court may always order a different result in a particular case, but it cannot order the lower court judge to violate his oath to the Constitution or his conscience.

In my case, Judge Thompson could have ordered the Ten Commandments monument to be removed by commanding a ministerial officer (one not sworn to uphold the Constitution) to carry out the order. But he did not have the authority to order me to remove the monument. In carrying out that order, I would have violated both my oath of office and my conscience. Had Judge Thompson ordered a ministerial officer to remove the monument, it still would have been an unlawful order, but a violation of the oath of office would not have been implicated. This method of resolving such disagreements between a higher court and a lower court judge preserves the integrity of the Constitution, our rule of law.

We as Americans must recognize that the federal courts are now *making* rather than *interpreting* the law, that those courts are not the supreme and sole arbiters of the law, and that surrendering to such tyranny affirms the rule of man rather than the true rule of law on which America was founded. If we fail to do that, we will suffer grave consequences. Indeed, men are not angels. Unchecked power cannot remain in their hands for too long before it is abused.

The prophet Zechariah listed the failures of previous generations of Israelites. He warned his generation that unlike the earlier generations, "they should hear the law" (Zech. 7:12). Because the previous generations had failed to adhere to the law, God "scattered them with a whirlwind among all the nations. . . . Thus the land was desolate after them, that no man passed through nor returned: for they laid the pleasant land desolate" (Zech. 7:14).

If we do not adhere to the true rule of law and instead blindly follow judicial orders that veer from the Constitution and our moral foundation, we as a nation may also be scattered to the whirlwind, having made this pleasant land desolate.

20

A MOVEMENT OF GOD

During the end of July and into the first week of August of the summer of 2003, I was busy presiding over the Alabama circuit and district judges annual summer conference in Gulf Shores, Alabama. This was generally a relaxing and pleasant time to enjoy the fellowship of other members of the bench and to learn of recent developments in the law. But this year was different as the situation in Montgomery began to change rapidly.

On Monday, August 4, 2003, Judge Myron Thompson requested a telephone conference with counsel for both sides of the Ten Commandments case. He sought any additional comments they might have before he made a decision on whether to lift the stay of his order and force the removal of the Ten Commandments monument. We had already decided to take our appeal to the United States Supreme Court, but first we had to file a petition for writ of certiorari (asking permission to appeal).

The order of the Eleventh Circuit Court of Appeals seemed clear enough: If I was "unable to have the district court's order overturned through the usual appellate processes, *when the time comes*, Chief Justice Moore will obey that order."[1] We had not completed the usual appeals process by petitioning the U.S. Supreme Court. I believed the Eleventh Circuit Court had clearly indicated that I would not have to remove the monument until we had completed all appeals.

We immediately filed a short, two-paragraph response to Judge Thompson, stating that the court did not have "jurisdiction, power, or authority to remove the public acknowledgment of God, which is authorized in the Constitution of the State."[2] Not only had the Eleventh Circuit Court indicated that we should be able to complete the appeals process before the time came to obey the order, but the Tenth Amendment to the United States Constitution states clearly that "the powers not delegated to the United States by the Constitution, nor prohibited by it to the states, are reserved to the states respectively, or to the people."[3]

One of those powers that belongs to the state is the establishment of a justice system which the Constitution of Alabama plainly indicates was "established" by invoking the "favor and guidance of Almighty God." The federal court had no authority over the justice system of Alabama in this case or over the basis of our justice system—a recognition of God. Consequently, Judge Thompson had no authority or jurisdiction to order a monument moved because it acknowledged God.

Nevertheless, Judge Thompson was determined to force the issue. On August 5, 2003, he ordered me "to remove, by no later than August 20, 2003, the Ten Commandments monument at issue in this litigation from the non-private areas of the Alabama State Judicial Building."[4]

Judge Thompson did not stop with just an order to remove the monument. He further directed that his order be served on the governor, attorney general, treasurer, state comptroller, administrative director of courts, and the eight associate justices of the Alabama Supreme Court. In an act calculated to intimidate Alabama's elected officials, he threatened heavy fines of "perhaps $5,000 a day for the first week . . . with the amount of the fine perhaps to double at the beginning of each and every week thereafter . . . until there is full compliance with the order."[5]

It was clear to me that Judge Thompson, fearing that I would not obey his order, decided to threaten other state officials and force them to remove the monument if I did not do so. A threat of heavy fines was his way of coercing obedience to that order. In fact, Judge Thompson stated that it was "the obligation of the State of Alabama" rather than any federal official, "to remove [the monument]."[6] The Eleventh Amendment to the United States Constitution prevents an action by any citizen against a state. Yet the federal court was in effect converting this suit to one against the state of Alabama by forcing other state officials not named in the suit to comply with his order.

Furthermore, the federal court had no authority to order a constitutional officer to violate his oath of office. The plaintiffs made a significant error when they failed to include in the suit a ministerial officer, such as a building manager or other property official, so there would be a proper defendant to whom the court could direct such an order. Judge Thompson, not wanting to be embarrassed at this stage of the proceedings, decided to disregard the Tenth Amendment and the Eleventh Amendment to the Constitution in addition to ignoring the plain meaning of the First Amendment.

Judge Thompson's threats worked on my colleagues. Justice Gorman Houston approached me on August 13 with a form for me to sign that would authorize him to act in my place in removing the monument. I declined his offer.[7] I knew that my refusal to relinquish my authority would place me in a precarious position. But by signing that form I would also avoid my responsibility, and the people did not elect me to do that. It was my duty regardless of the cost to uphold and support the Constitution. My oath was to the law, not to a power-hungry federal judge who chose to disregard the law. I could not turn and run for any man. I could not forsake my duty.

On Thursday, August 14, 2003, I announced my decision to uphold my oath to the Constitution of the United States and to the Constitution of Alabama. I would not move the monument. God had been with me at other difficult times in my life—West Point, Vietnam, as a deputy district attorney, and during my trials and tribulations over the Ten Commandments plaque in my courtroom in Etowah County. I knew that He would see me through this, as well.

I announced publicly that "I have no intention of removing the monument of the Ten Commandments and the moral foundation of our law."[8] Then I stated, "To do so would, in effect, result in the disestablishment of our system of justice in this state. This I cannot and will not do."[9] I concluded, "I intend to uphold my oath to the Constitution of the United States as well as to the Constitution of the State of Alabama. I have maintained the rule of law. I have been true to the oath of my office. I can do no more and I will do no less. So Help Me God."[10]

No court or judge has the authority to tell anyone what he can or cannot think. But that is exactly what this federal judge was trying to do to me. Judge Thompson had said that the monument itself was not a violation; rather, it was what I said the monument represented—the acknowledgment of God—that made it unconstitutional.

The number of media inquiries about this conflict became overwhelming. During this time, a media public relations consultant, Jessica Atteberry, was referred to me by Reverend Rick Scarborough. She agreed to become my new spokesperson. Not long after that, I appeared on *Hannity and Colmes*, and enjoyed meeting both Sean Hannity and Alan Colmes. Discussions of this issue with them on their national radio programs helped inform the public about my case.

Soon, other nationally known programs such as *Bill O'Reilly*, the *Today* show, and various CNN broadcasts discussed the case. Ms. Atteberry did a superb job in coordinating with both local and national media to explain what the issue was about. I always attempted to show that it was less about a monument or a chief justice than the right of every American to publicly recognize God and His importance to our nation without interference from the federal courts.

But even my fellow justices were confused about the issue. For example, Justice Houston vowed to "take whatever steps are necessary" to ensure that state and federal laws are followed in order that the state does not have "to pay fines threatened by a federal judge and to ensure that everyone follows the law."[11] Houston even called a meeting of the other justices on the afternoon of my announcement, ironically "to assure that the State of Alabama is a government of laws and not of men."[12]

In my presence, along with some of the other justices, Gorman Houston announced that he had already spoken to Attorney General Bill Pryor about this matter. I also knew that the attorney general, whose office was supposed to be representing me, had spoken to the governor about this situation.

I was growing concerned because it had become apparent that Pryor's nomination for a federal judgeship had created a personal dilemma for him that was recognized by others. Jess Brown, a political science professor from Athens State University, explained in a newspaper article that Pryor's chances for a federal judgeship could be damaged by his response or non-response to a federal judicial order in the Ten Commandments case.[13] Brown stated, "If [Pryor] is viewed in Washington as an Attorney General helping Moore or the state keep [the Ten Commandments] in the building he'll hurt himself."[14]

My concern proved to be justified as I watched Pryor work "behind the scenes" to convince state public officials to stand together in opposition to my position. I was not the only one who recognized this fact. For his efforts, Pryor drew praise from Morris Dees of the Southern Poverty Law Center, who said, "Pryor's actions 'behind the scenes' to orchestrate the state officials handling these things saved Alabama from constitutional crisis."[15]

The *Washington Post* observed that Pryor was "trying to keep alive his nomination for a federal appeals court judgeship, which ha[d] been blocked by Senate Democrats who accused him—among other things—of blurring the lines between church and state."[16] The orchestration of events by Pryor "behind the scenes" would continue.

On August 15, the day following my announcement that I would challenge the authority of Judge Thompson to strip the people of Alabama of their right to publicly acknowledge the sovereignty of God, I filed an emergency writ with the United States Supreme Court in an effort to stop Thompson's order.

On Saturday, August 16, 2003, more than two thousand people flocked to the Alabama Judicial Building to view the monument. Alabama Supreme Court Chief Marshal Willie James remarked, "I'm getting a counter first thing Monday morning because this (pen and paper) ain't getting it done."[17] This represented only a portion of the people who gathered that afternoon on the steps of the state capitol to hear noted speakers such as Alan Keyes, Jerry Falwell, Howard Phillips, and Rick Scarborough of Vision America (which organized the rally).

Again, as in 1997, buses brought people from as far away as California and Illinois. It was an extraordinarily hot August day as an enthusiastic but orderly crowd gathered to sing, read poetry, and pray for our state and nation.

Alan Keyes, always the eloquent orator, set the tone when he said that the "lawless acts of federal judges are attempts to wrest from Americans their right to live in communities with laws that reflect our beliefs. What we are faced with now is an effort to set the stage for religious persecution."[18] I spoke briefly following Dr. Keyes's message, urging the crowd to remember that "it is not about me; I will pass away as every politician and every pastor will, but the laws of God will remain forever."[19]

David Hall brought a group from Texas known as the Associated Conservatives of Texas. They delivered a facsimile of the Liberty Bell to open the rally. Hall stated that "Alabamians helped us at the Alamo. We're kind of coming back to Montgomery to show support for the stand by Alabamians."[20] He was referring to one particular Alabamian,

Col. William Barrett Travis, who helped to mount the famous defense of the Alamo in the winter of 1836.[21] The bravery of the men at the Alamo saved Texas from being taken by Mexico, and "Remember the Alamo" became a symbol of pride and resistance.

On August 16, 2003, and during the two weeks that followed, another symbol of pride and resistance emerged. People flocked to Montgomery day after day without invitation or summons to stand for their inalienable right to acknowledge the sovereignty and omnipotence of Almighty God.

On Monday, August 18, 2003, Judge Thompson denied our request to stay his injunction. An immediate appeal of Judge Thompson's denial was filed the next day in the Eleventh Circuit Court. This was also rejected. On Wednesday, August 20, we again petitioned the United States Supreme Court to stop Judge Thompson's order, but to no avail. The die had been cast. I would have to disobey an order from an overbearing federal judge that was clearly unlawful.

Rev. Patrick Mahoney, director of the Christian Defense Coalition, and Rev. Rob Schenck of the National Clergy Council, both of whom are headquartered in Washington, D.C., said they would block the removal of the monument. Others began to kneel in and around the monument in protest. Shortly after the Supreme Court's rejection of our emergency appeal, twenty-two people were arrested in the rotunda of the Alabama Supreme Court.[22]

I was not present. I intentionally stayed away from the crowds because I did not want to appear to be leading a resistance. God had brought His people from places far and near. This was His movement, not mine. People old and young, black and white, rich and poor, stood in defiance of the unlawful court order. It was time for God to work because men had made void His law (see Ps. 119:126).

Karen Kennedy had been diagnosed with various forms of cancer and Parkinson's disease. Although she was confined to a wheelchair, she came with her husband Wayne to protest the removal of the monument. Both Karen and Wayne were arrested, handcuffed, taken to jail, and charged with trespassing. By now the crowds were constantly growing. More than one thousand people assembled at the entrance of the judicial building. They remained throughout the night, preventing the removal of the monument from the building.

On Thursday morning, the deadline had passed, the monument remained, and I had not given in to judicial tyranny. I awoke early that morning at my home in Gallant, Alabama, where I had gone to prepare for the funeral of Kayla's grandmother, Lucille Freeman. At approximately 6:30 a.m. I was notified by my security officer, Leonard Holifield, that someone had placed a curtain around the monument to shield it from public view. Additionally, the building had been closed to public traffic.

I was infuriated! I found out later that some of the associate justices of the Alabama Supreme Court had not only compromised the principles that had been so pronounced when they ran for office, but they also had the audacity to hide the Word of God from public view just to appease a federal court judge.

I immediately called Gorman Houston, informing him that I was returning to Montgomery and that the curtain should be moved before I arrived or I would do so personally. The conversation was not friendly. I expressed my disappointment at his hypocrisy and that of some of his fellow justices for their actions in shielding the Word of God from public view. On the two-hour trip to Montgomery, I also spoke with another associate justice, Harold See, advising him of my intentions.

By the time I reached Montgomery, the curtain had been removed. Houston was quoted by the press as saying, "The building manager may have erected it" to comply with Thompson's order until the associate justices acted.[23] Trying to avoid responsibility, Houston implied that the building manager, Graham George, had acted on his own accord without any direction from him or the other associate justices.

The idea that the building manager would act without the authority of the justices in such a tense situation was ridiculous. Houston knew he had done something wrong and was trying to cover it up! I was satisfied that nothing would hide God's law and that the monument remained. That same day, I was notified that the justices had voted to move the monument, but no date for its removal was announced.

On Thursday afternoon, August 21, 2003, I addressed the large crowd and numerous media people assembled on the steps of the Alabama Judicial Building. I expressed my disappointment with my judicial colleagues, stating that I would "never deny the God upon whom our laws and our Country depend."[24] I stated, "I will not violate my oath, I cannot forsake my conscience, I will not neglect my duty," and "to do my duty I must acknowledge God. That is what this case is about."[25]

By the close of business on Friday, August 22, the Judicial Inquiry Commission (JIC) filed a complaint with the Court of the Judiciary (COJ), thereby disqualifying me from acting as a judge until the matter could be addressed by that body.[26] The original complaint filed with the JIC had been lodged by Stephen Glassroth, a plaintiff in the original federal case.[27] Not satisfied with having the federal court enter an order to remove the Ten Commandments monument, they now wanted to have me removed from office.

I had already left the judicial building on Friday at 5:00 p.m., so I was not notified of the complaint and disqualification from my duties until later. The media reported that I had been "suspended." While this was not legally accurate, it reflected the circumstances that prevented me from entering my office the following Monday.[28] An advisory opinion just issued by Attorney General Pryor's office concluded that Gorman

Houston would now assume all the duties of the chief justice. Houston had requested the opinion on Friday, the day I had been suspended.[29]

I was perplexed about how Houston had the "foresight" to request an opinion regarding the extent of his authority as acting chief justice even before I had been informed of the complaint disqualifying me from my duties. It seemed clear that the attorney general and Justice Houston were acting in concert.

Despite the plaintiffs' success and the behind-the-scenes maneuvering by other high state officials, God continued to rally His people. On Sunday, August 24, 2003, the *Mobile Register* reported that the protesters were not going away.[30] The crowds continued to pour into Montgomery from across the state and nation, standing for hours in the hot sun and remaining overnight on sleeping bags and blankets on the steps of the judicial building.

On Monday, I publicly criticized the actions of the officials of the state of Alabama who had chosen to obey a federal judge at the expense of their own oath of office to the law. I said, "We should be offended when the elected representatives of this State, the governor, the attorney general, and the justices of this Court fail to acknowledge God as the basis of our justice system."[31] In response, protesters assailed the attorney general's office, and the governor was bombarded with telephone calls and e-mails.

Finally, on the morning of August 27, 2003, five days after I had been "suspended," the Ten Commandments monument was moved to a storage room inside the judicial building about sixty feet from where it had been on display for more than two years. Not willing to risk the protests of the public, the justices decided to place the monument in a room within the building out of sight from the public. I responded, "It is a sad day in our Country when the moral foundation of our laws and the acknowledgment of God has to be hidden from public view to appease a federal judge."[32]

On Thursday, August 28, 2003, more than twelve hundred people gathered to hear Dr. James Dobson of Focus on the Family and Dr. Alan Keyes. They came to Montgomery to voice their concern over the removal of the Ten Commandments. Dobson said that people should send a message to Congress that the federal courts need to be "reined in. . . . Let the Congress know this is not going to continue," he urged.[33] Dobson warned the crowd that "the liberal elite and the judges at the highest level and some members of the media are determined to remove every evidence of faith in God from the entire culture. They are determined to control more and more of our private lives, and it is time that we said, enough is enough."[34]

In temperatures well above ninety degrees with a heat index of more than one hundred, Keyes told the crowd that the battle over the Ten Commandments in Alabama should be the start of a nationwide movement to curb the power of the federal courts.[35] The crowd responded enthusiastically.[36] Keyes also expressed his dismay over the failure of other state officials to step forward in my defense, stating, that "[f]or those who have made their reverence for law the enemy of their reverence for God I say to them: The Constitution does no such thing."[37]

The crowds continued to gather as August turned to September. Night after night they listened to speeches given by pastors, political figures, and national leaders. On Wednesday, September 3, court officials placed barricades across the plaza, telling the people that a cleanup was being done and that the sidewalk was the only area where they could assemble. A rally planned for Wednesday evening was canceled as yellow tape blocked entry to the stone-tiled plaza where for more than two weeks thousands had gathered.[38] After that, people returned to their homes.

Things soon returned to normal. The steps of the Alabama Judicial Building no longer resonated with the preaching, singing, and musical drama which had occurred during that period from August 20—the day the monument was to be moved—until September 3, when the last rally was held. To some of the state officials, especially those feeling another kind of heat, it was a relief that the gatherings which had drawn so much attention in Alabama and throughout America were finally over.

But what they thought had ended had only just begun. The sparks of hope and faith from those impromptu rallies on the steps of the Alabama Judicial Building ignited a fire that continues to burn across this land. Those who came to Montgomery to protest the removal of a monument were witnesses to another movement, a movement of God. When the key was turned on the lock after God's law was stored away, another key was turned to open the hearts and minds of the American people.

In the eyes of the world I had lost, but I had stood for the God who never loses and the law I had sworn to uphold. It was not over. I would soon stand before another court that would decide whether I would continue to serve as chief justice of the Alabama Supreme Court.

21

COURT OF THE JUDICIARY

The Court of the Judiciary, composed of private citizens, lawyers, and judges, is a politically appointed body chosen to oversee the ethical standards of judges in the state of Alabama. The COJ has the power to suspend a judge with or without pay, and even to remove a judge from office, for violation of the Canons of Judicial Ethics. Historically the power to remove an elected official from office rested solely with the legislative branch through impeachment, but in 1973 an amendment to the Constitution of Alabama created the Court of the Judiciary. The COJ has legitimately punished wrongdoing by Alabama's judges, but in many cases it is used as a political tool.

Only three judges had been removed from office during the entire history of the COJ.[1] I knew this case was a threat to my job because of the political opposition I had encountered during the battle over the acknowledgment of God. I had committed no criminal act. I had not behaved in a manner generally considered unethical conduct. I certainly had done nothing for which I was ashamed. I had simply refused to obey an unlawful order of a federal district court judge who placed himself above the law.

Even Judge Thompson had not found me to be in contempt of his court. Because no contempt hearing was held, I had not had a chance in a court of law to explain my reasons for refusing to obey the federal district court's order. I looked forward to the opportunity to present my case to the COJ because I knew that *no judge in Alabama had ever been removed from office for disobeying a court order.*

A November 12, 2003, trial date was set for the ethics trial before the COJ. My attorneys for the trial included Terry Butts, a highly respected member of the Bar and a former Alabama Supreme Court Justice; Jim Wilson, a well-known former U.S. attorney; and Mike Jones, a local attorney who proved to be an outstanding litigator. Together we were determined to mount a strong defense predicated on my oath of office to uphold the Constitution of the United States and the Constitution of Alabama, both of which permitted the recognition of a sovereign God. But we knew that because the COJ was a political creature, it would not be an easy fight.

Certain public officials of Alabama began to realize they had suffered politically during the controversy over their failure to support the law of God. With his 1.2 billion-dollar tax plan facing an uphill battle, Governor Bob Riley knew he needed public support. On September 9, 2003, within a week of the last rally, Governor Riley, with the advice and assistance of Attorney General Pryor, decided to display a copy of the Ten Commandments in the state capitol. He did it "the right way," as he put it—surrounded by other historical documents, including the Bill of Rights and the Magna Charta.[2]

David Azbell, spokesman for the governor, said these historical documents were added to make the display "legally" defensible. "We want the Ten Commandment to stay in the Capitol, and in order to achieve that goal we had to hang them in a way that judges and court rulings have instructed," he explained.[3]

Richard Cohen, president of the Southern Poverty Law Center, stated that they would have no objection to such a display if it was done for purely *"historical purposes,"* but he indicated that he would wait to see what Governor Riley said about the display before making a final judgment. He claimed that "[t]eaching history by state officials is not unconstitutional. Promoting religion is."[4]

David Azbell's remarks, together with those of Richard Cohen, were revealing. What they were actually saying is that if we recognize God purely in a historical context we are acting "legally," but if we assert that a sovereign holy God exists today, we are doing something religious that is unlawful. When high state officials fall prey to such warped logic, they allow courts and judges to dictate what they can do by what they think. And more importantly, they violate the first commandment, which forbids putting anything above the Lord.

They are saying you can acknowledge God only so long as you do it in the manner in which the federal courts say that it can be done. They are bowing to the federal courts before they bow to God. Moreover, they are violating—and causing America to violate—the third commandment by ruling that we may acknowledge God only when it is done as mere ceremony without any religious significance. Such "ceremonial deism" takes the Lord's name in vain.

In February of 2004, the eight associate justices of the Alabama Supreme Court followed the governor's example by placing a version of the Ten Commandments in the rotunda of the Alabama Supreme Court, surrounded by historical documents sufficient to "secularize" God's law.[5] Just like the governor, the justices tried to appease the ACLU, the SPLC, and AUSCS by placing their own Ten Commandments display in the rotunda where the Ten Commandments monument had been. Richard Cohen said that the new display seemed "acceptable." "Unlike Moore's monument, it does not appear to have the purpose or effect of promoting religion," he said.[6]

The justices told the public they had "returned the Ten Commandments to the Judicial Building."[7] I have often wondered how supposedly intelligent people can so easily discount the intelligence of their constituents! The people could see their hypocrisy. Indeed, one of the justices was up for reelection in 2004. My longtime associate Tom Parker ran against her for a seat on the Alabama Supreme Court. In the Republican primary, held in June of 2004, Tom beat the incumbent justice and won the nomination.

This was a difficult accomplishment, particularly because his opponent spent more money in the campaign and had the backing of several special-interest groups as well as the other justices of the Supreme Court. But the voters of the state knew that this justice had been a party to the removal of the Ten Commandments monument from the rotunda of the Alabama Judicial Building. They expressed their disapproval at the polls.

The approval by the Southern Poverty Law Center of the display set up by the associate justices but its objection to the Ten Commandments monument made me wonder: *What was the difference between a display of the Ten Commandments surrounded by historical documents and another inscribed on a granite monument locked in a storage room just sixty feet away?* The answer is simple—politics. The historical display recognizes God as just a part of history, deceiving the public about their belief in the sovereignty of God. The granite display acknowledges the sovereignty of God. To be "politically correct," we must effectively deny the sovereignty of God if we serve in public office. And most politicians willingly comply!

On September 16, 2003, one week after the historical display was put up by the governor, I decided to offer to the United States Congress the Ten Commandments monument that had remained in a storage room in the Alabama Judicial Building.

I visited Washington, D.C., where I spoke with an assembly of approximately thirty congressmen. Then I drafted a letter to the leadership of both houses of Congress, stating that the placement of the Ten Commandments monument would "restore the balance of power between the branches of government and would send a message to the federal judiciary that we, the people, have the final word on our inalienable right to acknowledge God."[8]

The placement of a monument in the U.S. Capitol by Congress could never logically be said to be "Congress making a law." Alabama Senator Richard Shelby and Congressman Robert Aderholt supported my efforts.

On September 26, 2003, I filed an appeal with the United States Supreme Court regarding the federal case about the monument. But my most immediate concern was the upcoming ethics trial on November 12. My attorneys filed numerous motions. One by one, they were denied. A request to question each member of the COJ was denied in spite of the fact that many on the COJ were not judges and would sit in effect as jurors in my case. Their relationship to various other people in the litigation was relevant.

Sue McInnish of Montgomery and Sam Jones of Mobile, the two non-lawyers on the COJ, were serving terms that had expired on January 31, 2003. They continued to serve on the court after obtaining a favorable advisory opinion from Attorney General Pryor, who was now, ironically, the lead prosecuting attorney in the ethics trial.

As for the attorney general, he had a pronounced conflict of interest and should never have prosecuted the case. We filed a motion to have Pryor removed from the case. There were many reasons for our objection.

One of these was that he had already recused from the earlier ethics trial in 1999 when he was asked to do so by the ACLU. Moreover, Pryor's office had defended me through appointed counsel in the underlying Ten Commandments case, and Pryor himself had represented the state on my behalf during the earlier trial over the Ten Commandments plaque in my Etowah County courtroom. Pryor had even taken part in strategy sessions with me and former Governor Fob James about the issues in my case.

Former Governor James submitted a written statement to the COJ, stating that Pryor's actions in prosecuting my case were "utterly contrary to the political and legal convictions which [Pryor] expressed" when Governor James appointed him to be attorney general.[9] But perhaps the greatest conflict was that Pryor had participated in private, attorney-client, privileged-moot-court arguments in preparation for the appeal of the federal Ten Commandments case.

Adding to the litany of reasons why Pryor should not have been involved in the ethics trial was the timing of the prosecution. Less than a week before my trial, the United States Senate again failed to bring to a vote Pryor's nomination as a judge for the Eleventh Circuit Court of Appeals. Needing sixty votes to break a filibuster, the vote had failed 51 to 44 on November 6, 2003.[10] Senator Jeff Sessions observed that "[a] few Democrats were impressed by Pryor's handling of the politically sensitive dispute over the Ten Commandments monument . . . but probably not enough to reach the 60 votes needed to end a filibuster."[11] Even so, the political possibilities for Pryor were certainly such as to call his objectivity into question.

In short, Pryor's participation in this case was highly improper, as was his working "behind the scenes to orchestrate the state officials," as Morris Dees had stated.[12]

Every trial before the Court of the Judiciary is required by law to be a "public" trial. When the court denied our motion to allow television cameras in the courtroom so the public could see for themselves the hypocrisy of the court, I was disturbed. Then the court restricted the trial to the limited seating capacity of the Alabama Supreme Court courtroom (approximately two hundred) and a small conference room nearby instead of a larger venue as I had requested. But when the court decided to allow one television camera in to record the reading of their final decision,[13] I knew that things had been prearranged. My attorneys and I were convinced that I would not receive a fair trial under these circumstances.

In a statement submitted to the COJ, my attorney Terry Butts wrote, "Moore's legal team advised him that in light of the rulings of the COJ denying him his basic legal rights, that an adverse ruling from the COJ is inevitable, which may well include his immediate removal from office."[14] Justice Butts did an admirable job of preparing my case and filed many valid motions before the court, but politics had taken control.

Things could not get worse—or so I thought. On Monday, November 3, 2003, just nine days before the trial, the United States Supreme Court denied my request for appeal of Judge Thompson's order and the Eleventh Circuit Court's opinion affirming that order.[15] This would certainly increase the odds of the COJ ruling against me. Now they knew that my ability to question Judge Thompson's un-lawful order would never be heard by the highest court of the land.

I stated publicly that I believed the members of the COJ had already made up their minds that I had violated the Canons of Judicial Ethics when I refused to obey Judge Thompson's order.[16] When asked if I would resign, I replied, "I certainly intend to go through the trial so that people know what this case is all about . . . I did not move the monument in accordance with the judge's order. *These officials don't want you to know why I didn't move it.*"[17]

The day before the trial, Attorney General Pryor filed the prose-cution's brief which demanded that I be removed from office. The trial itself, held on November 12, 2003, was relatively short. I was the first and only witness called to the stand. The Attorney General questioned me directly.

Pryor: And your understanding is that the Federal Court ordered that you could not acknowledge God; isn't that right?

Moore: Yes.

Pryor: And if you resume your duties as Chief Justice after this proceeding, you will continue to acknowledge God as you have testified that you would today?

Moore: That's right.

Pryor: No matter what any other official says?

Moore: Absolutely. Without—let me clarify that. Without an acknowledgment of God, I cannot do my duties. I must acknowledge God. It says so in the Constitution of Alabama. It says so in the First Amendment to the United States Constitution. It says so in everything I have read. So—

Pryor: The only point I am trying to clarify, Mr. Chief Justice, *is not why*, but only that, in fact, *if* you do resume your duties as Chief Justice, you will continue to do that without regard to what any other official says; isn't that right?

Moore: Well, I'll do the same thing this court did with starting with prayer; that's an acknowledgment of God. Now, we did the same thing that justices do when they place their hand on the Bible and say, "So help me God." It's an acknowledgment of God. The Alabama Supreme Court opens with "God save the state and this honorable court." It's an acknowledgment of God. In my opinions, which I have written many opinions, acknowledging God is the source—a moral source of our law. I think you must.[18]

Pryor effectively eliminated the only issue in my case—*why* I had not obeyed the federal court order. He said in effect that he did not want to know *why*, but only *if* I would continue to acknowledge God. In a trial about the ethics of my action, the prosecution did not even care about the reasons for my disobedience. In every court in Alabama, before a defendant can be punished for disobedience of a court order— that is, be held in contempt—he is entitled to a hearing to determine why he disobeyed.

In my case, I was never cited for contempt by the federal court. In spite of this, and without any inquiry about why I disobeyed, I was removed from my position as chief justice of Alabama—a punishment that even the federal court could not have handed down. I disobeyed because I was ethically bound to do so by my oath of office that forbade me from following an unlawful order. The *why* is crucial because we are bound to obey only *lawful* orders and to disobey those orders that are not lawful. That is the distinction between the rule of law and the rule of man.

When the chief judge in my case, Bill Thompson, began reading the final judgment, I could sense his nervousness. The decision announced that the court deemed me guilty of violating the Alabama Canons of Judicial Ethics. Judge Thompson declared that I had shown "no contrition for my actions," and that I had given them no assurance that I would not do the same thing again. Because of this, the COJ voted to remove me from the office of chief justice of the Alabama Supreme Court.

I wondered how one could ever show "contrition" for acknowledging God? According to *Webster's Dictionary*, *contrition* is defined as "sorrow for and detestation of sin with a true purpose of amendment, arising from a love of God for His own perfections (perfect contrition) or from some inferior motive, as fear of divine punishment (imperfect contrition)."[19] Even the word *contrition*, according to *Webster's*, acknowledged God. The only thing I ever said I would do again was to acknowledge God, just as Thompson himself had done when he opened the ethics trial with prayer at the request of my attorney, Terry Butts.

From the very beginning, I knew that officially recognizing the sovereignty of God was the issue, and that removal from office was a possibility if I did not "bow down" to the whim of the federal courts. But I was at the moment astonished that it actually happened. I had come to know Judge Bill Thompson well over the last few years. He also professed Christianity and seemed to support my position. Even so, I was removed from office. This was the first time such a thing had happened in Alabama to a judge for disobeying a court order or for acknowledging God as the judicial oath required.

Immediately after the trial, I was asked to address a group of reporters assembled on the sidewalk outside the judicial building. I stood in the halls of the judicial building surrounded by attorneys and close friends and my wife Kayla. She had never wavered in this battle to preserve the right to openly acknowledge God. Even before the ethics trial began, Kayla understood that regardless of the consequences, we could never deny God. After Pryor's questioning of me, Kayla told me she had perfect peace, knowing that God would continue to bless us no matter what happened.

When I addressed the media, I told them, "I have absolutely no regrets. I have done what I was sworn to do. It's about whether or not you can acknowledge God as a source of our law and our liberty. That's all I've done."[20]

The day after my removal, Gorman Houston, using his authority as acting chief justice, fired two of my closest assistants, Rich Hobson, a sixteen-year veteran of the court system, and Tom Parker, general counsel for the Unified Judicial System.[21] I called the dismissals exactly what they were—"exemplary of the vengeful political agenda of those who have long desired the removal of the Ten Commandments and the acknowledgment of God from the rotunda of the Alabama Judicial Building."[22] Parker and Hobson had been "steadfast in my support and courageous in their defense of our religious liberties," and they "deserve[d] better treatment than being fired because of their loyalty and devotion to God and this State."[23]

Plaintiff Stephen Glassroth and the Southern Poverty Law Center were equally vengeful, declaring that they would file a complaint with the Alabama State Bar requesting that I be disbarred from the practice of law. John Giles declared that this maneuver was designed "to keep [Roy Moore] off the bench at any level in the future."[24] True to their word, a complaint requesting disbarment was later filed before the Alabama State Bar.

The following week some of my supporters filed federal lawsuits in Montgomery and Mobile, claiming that the removal of a duly elected official by a non-elected body was a violation of the right to vote that is guaranteed all citizens.[25] These actions named as defendants the remaining members of the Alabama Supreme Court, the state attorney general, and members of the Judicial Inquiry Commission.[26] Eventually these suits were dismissed. Supporters of the Ten Commandments were frustrated, and those organizations dedicated to removing God from our public square rejoiced. They had achieved their objectives. Not only had the Ten Commandments been removed, but I had been removed from office as well.

Despite some powerful opposition, the people of Alabama continued to stand with me. More than 60 percent of the respondents in a statewide poll conducted by the *Mobile Register* and the University of South Alabama did not think I should have been removed from office.[27]

After the ruling by the COJ, my appeal had to be directed to the Alabama Supreme Court, the same body on which I had served as chief justice and which had voted to remove the Ten Commandments monument from public display. I realized that Associate Justice Houston would have to recuse (excuse himself from the case) because he was now the acting chief justice, and reversal of the COJ's decision would result in a loss of his own power.

Furthermore, he had fired my close associates, Hobson and Parker, and had transferred my office personnel to different jobs within the judicial building, showing a personal bias against me. I wanted to let the other justices have an opportunity to explain their blind obedience to Judge Thompson's unlawful order, so I only petitioned for the recusal of Justice Houston.

Nevertheless, all of the justices chose to excuse themselves from hearing the case to avoid addressing the issues. Even Justice Houston recused, but *only after he helped select an alternate court* of retired appellate justices. My attorney, Phillip Jauregui, noted the irony: "[R]ather than rule on our motion to disqualify Justice Houston, the Court let him lead the charge in selecting new justices to hear the appeal."[28]

The process of selecting the alternate court, in which the governor of Alabama participated, was not in accordance with the law, which required the governor to select from a panel of lawyers from the Alabama Bar Association. The contrived selection process in which Houston participated resulted in the selection of two justices with obvious conflicts of interest.

I had previously relieved Justice Janie Shores from her position with the Alabama Supreme Court following her retirement—a decision with which she had publicly and strongly disagreed. Another retired judge selected for the court was Braxton Kittrell, who had been the chairman of the JIC when it investigated me years before. Some time later, I learned that another judge, Harry Wilters, was the brother-in-law of Janie Shores.

We filed recusal motions requesting that Janie Shores and Braxton Kittrell step down because of their obvious conflicts of interest, but again my motion was denied. Thus, in my appeal I would stand before judges and justices, some of whom had indicated a prior prejudice against me, and all of whom believed that the rule of man and the rule of law were one and the same.

Jim Zeigler, chairman of the League of Christian Voters, summarized the situation perfectly when he said, "It's just very hard for voters who supported Judge Roy Moore to feel confidence" in the selection process for the special justices.[29]

My attorney, Phillip Jauregui, did an outstanding job of arguing my case before the special court on Wednesday, February 25, 2004. Jauregui forcefully argued that "the Chief Justice didn't take an oath to support a regime of judges who are warring against the Constitution. He took an oath to support the Constitution."[30] Charles Campbell of the attorney general's office represented the state after Bill Pryor finally obtained his coveted federal judgeship through a recess appointment (without confirmation by the U.S. Senate) by President George W. Bush, only days before my appeal was heard.

Campbell argued that under my view of the oath every man would become a law unto himself.[31] Of course, he missed the critical issue. The law is the Constitution, and every person taking the oath is entitled to his own interpretation. This in no way interferes with the authority of the higher court that can always order the final result in a case. But no judge is permitted to tell another judge what he must think or believe. If an act (like the removal of a monument) is to be performed according to the judgment of a higher court, then that court may order a lower ministerial officer to perform the act. But he can never order another constitutional officer to violate his conscience or his oath.

The special court released its decision on Friday, April 30, 2004. It, like the COJ, also refused to examine the threshold issue of whether Judge Thompson's order had been lawful. The court said the case was simply about "a public official who took an oath to uphold the Constitution of the United States and then refused to obey a valid order of a United States District Court."[32] But I had maintained throughout that the order was not valid because it was not lawful, and it was my duty to disobey. The court assumed that the order was valid without considering the possibility that it was not.

When judges blindly follow the unlawful edicts of another judge, which they believe to be unlawful, they violate their own consciences and consequently the oath they took to uphold the law. Judicial tyranny exists because activist judges put themselves above the law. This philosophy of judicial supremacy must be stopped if we are to preserve the rule of law in America.

I appealed my removal from office to the United States Supreme Court, arguing that the state violated my First Amendment rights because it removed me because of my sincere belief in God. I was not surprised that the decision by the special Alabama Supreme Court was unanimous. I had threatened the philosophy of judicial supremacy. Those who sat behind benches wearing black robes and wielding gavels did not want to be reminded that there is a God, or, for that matter, a Constitution that they were sworn to uphold. Judicial restraint gave way to judicial tyranny, and a new law reigned—the rule of man.

22

THE BATTLE CONTINUES

F ollowing my removal from office, I was very busy. During the next twelve months I spoke in more than thirty states and in many states three or four times.

The Birmingham-based Foundation for Moral Law, headed by Dr. Mel Glenn, did an excellent job raising money for my attorneys' fees, but more than three hundred thousand dollars still remained to be paid. Glenn is a devout Christian who knows and understands the importance of God's law to American society. When he was only twelve years old, he lived only a few blocks from the Sixteenth Street Church in Birmingham. This church was bombed on September 15, 1963, killing four children. On January 5, 2001, Mel's son, Melford Glenn Jr., was murdered.

Mel found strength from God to cope with these tragedies. They motivated him to become involved in spreading the knowledge of the Ten Commandments among young people. The Foundation for Moral Law was created to assume the responsibilities of the Ten Commandments Defense Fund and to fight to preserve the moral foundation of law.

A decision was made in January of 2004 to move the Foundation for Moral Law to Montgomery. Rich Hobson, the former administrative director of courts for the state of Alabama, became the new president of the organization, replacing Reverend Phillip Ellen, who remained on the board of directors. Glenn continued to serve as executive director of the foundation, and my daughter, Heather, who had worked for him part time, stayed on as the foundation's secretary.

The staff was also increased by the employment of attorneys and other personnel who had been fired from the Alabama Supreme Court after my removal from office. Included among these was Leonard Holifield, who provided security services for the foundation. The legal staff consisted of Tom Parker, former head of the legal department of the Administrative Office of Courts, Drew Dill, Ben DuPré, and eventually Greg Jones, all of whom had worked for me while I was chief justice. They soon became involved in fighting other religious liberty cases besides my own. Their exceptional knowledge of the First Amendment and constitutional jurisprudence was a great asset in representing others who had been sued for their religious beliefs and in submitting *amicus curiae* briefs in cases across the country.

Volunteers like Daniel Monplaisir and Noah Stansbury came forward to help the Foundation for Moral Law achieve its mission of preserving our moral and religious heritage and exposing the grievous error of the federal courts' interference with our basic right to worship and acknowledge God.

I was honored to be named chairman of the board of directors in February of 2004. I continue to serve today in that capacity without pay as an advisor and assistant to the foundation. The mission of restoring the moral foundation of law and halting the growing apostasy in our land is a worthy goal.

As I spoke to various groups across America, I could see that my case had touched a nerve. The federal courts were out of control, and people were aware that something had to be done. Our Constitution itself was in jeopardy. Decisions like the United States Supreme Court's ruling in *Lawrence v. Texas*,[1] on June 26, 2003, indicated that the federal courts believed they were no longer restricted by the

Constitution they were sworn to uphold. In 1986, in *Bowers v. Hardwick*,[2] a Georgia case involving sodomy, the high court ruled there was no right to sodomy under the United States Constitution. But seventeen years later in *Lawrence*, the court declared that such a right existed based on "values we share with a wider civilization."[3] A new right to privacy had emerged, created by the court out of thin air. Increasingly, the Supreme Court has turned to "international law" and "foreign precedents" as a basis for their decisions.

In a speech to the Southern Center for International Studies in Atlanta, Georgia, on October 28, 2003, Justice Sandra Day O'Connor said of their decision in *Lawrence*:

> Solicitude [concern] for the views of foreign and international courts also appeared in last term's decision in *Lawrence v. Texas*. In ruling that consensual homosexual activity in one's home is constitutionally protected, the Supreme Court relied in part on a series of decisions from the European Court of Human Rights. I suspect that with time, we will rely increasingly on international and foreign law resolving what now appears to be domestic issues, as we both appreciate more fully the ways in which domestic issues have international dimensions, and recognize the rich resources available to us in the decisions of foreign courts.[4]

About eighteen months earlier, Justice O'Connor said, "Because of the scope of the problems we face, understanding international law is no longer just a legal specialty. It is becoming a duty."[5]

A fellow justice of the United States Supreme Court, Stephen Breyer, in a speech to the American Society of International Law on April 4, 2003, in Washington, D.C., agreed with Justice O'Connor: "[W]e find an increasing number of issues, including constitutional issues, where the decisions of foreign courts help by offering points in comparison. This change reflects the 'globalization' of human rights."[6] Justice Breyer continued, "When I can, I like to remind audiences that I love the American Bar Association with their 600,000 members and 800,000 committees because it is in those committee meetings, through discussion and debate, that law is created. The same, I should add, is true today of much international or trans-national law. Is it not?"[7]

Our Constitution does not need foreign law to interpret its meaning. And our laws are not made by bar association committees or foreign courts; they are made by the state legislatures and the Congress of the United States. These remarks by Justice O'Connor and Justice Breyer demonstrate that some of the justices of the highest court in our land no longer feel bound by the Constitution they are sworn to uphold, and they believe that law originates from a source other than the American people.

But an even greater danger exists when judges feel that whatever they say is the law. Quoting the constitution of the nation of Bahrain, Justice O'Connor sang the praises of that Arab nation's commitment to the rule of law principle, stating that Bahrain's own constitution provides that *"no authority shall prevail over the judgment of a judge, and under no circumstances may the course of justice be interfered with."*[8] Justice O'Connor concluded that "it is in everyone's interest to foster the rule-of-law-evolution."[9] She urged that these principles be taught in law schools, high schools, and universities across America.[10]

This "evolution" in "the rule of law" is nothing more than a glorified rule of man, which is contrary to our constitutional system. A commitment to the U.S. Constitution must be preserved if we are to retain the true rule of law.

The ACLU is familiar with this new trend toward international law. In a recent conference in Atlanta, Georgia, on "Human Rights at

Home: International Law in U.S. Courts," held from October 9–10, 2003, Anthony Romero, executive director of the ACLU, said that their goal is "no less than to forge a new era of social justice—one where the principles enunciated in the Universal Declaration of Human Rights are recognized and enforced in the United States."[11]

And indeed, it is a new era when rights are declared to be given by an international declaration and not from God. Those rights found in the Universal Declaration of Human Rights come not from God but from man. While the standards of man change from one generation to the next, God's standards never change. Moral standards based on a recognition of God seem unacceptable to our courts today because they represent an authority to which even the courts must answer; therefore, the acknowledgment of God must be prohibited by judges. Judge Myron Thompson understood this quite well. That is the same logic underlying his ruling that the Ten Commandments monument was unconstitutional—because it acknowledged God.

Judge Myron Thompson was a featured speaker at this conference hosted by the ACLU despite the fact that, at that very time, ACLU attorneys had pending before his court a petition for attorneys' fees in my case. Despite this obvious appearance of impropriety, which has long dictated recusal (removal) from a case, Thompson continued to preside over this one. A new era of social justice has been forged in which the ethical standards historically recognized by the courts have been discarded and a new standard of right and wrong has been established.

To address the problems of a "run away" federal judiciary, Herb Titus and I drafted the Constitution Restoration Act (CRA) of 2004, after consulting many people, including Howard Phillips, chairman of the Conservative Caucus, who was instrumental in facilitating the suggestions of others into the process of drafting the legislation. The CRA would protect from federal court interference any public official's acknowledgment of God as the sovereign source of law, liberty, or government.

The CRA also provides that those federal judges who choose to base their opinions on constitutions, decrees, directives, judicial decisions, executive orders, administrative rules, or policies of any foreign state or international organization can be impeached and removed from office.

Immediately after the CRA became public, opponents sought to disparage the CRA by claiming that we were trying to "strip" the courts of their power and authority. This was not an attempt to strip the courts of anything they had a right to, but to deny them the jurisdiction they had taken away from state governments. It is the right—indeed, the duty—of the Congress to regulate the jurisdiction of the federal courts under Article III of the United States Constitution when the courts exercise jurisdiction they do not have under the Constitution. It is a provision of "checks and balances" to maintain the separation of powers essential in our form of government.

The lead sponsors of the CRA are Senator Richard Shelby in the U.S. Senate and Representative Robert Aderholt in the House of Representatives. Aided by their cosponsors, Senators Zell Miller, Sam Brownback, Lindsey Graham, Wayne Allard, Daniel Inhofe, and Trent Lott, and Representative Mike Pence, they caused the proposed act to receive immediate support, which led to subcommittee hearings in both the House and the Senate. Although the Senate considered the CRA in a hearing addressing the larger issue of religious liberty, the House of Representatives heard testimony on September 13, 2004, about the specifics of the CRA.

As I sat before a subcommittee of the House of Representatives judiciary committee, I was happy to know that this legislation had garnered the attention of many in the Congress. I worked diligently to promote the CRA at grassroots levels in nearly thirty states during the past year. Many organizations gave their support independently of my actions. I attribute the popularity of the CRA of 2004 to its simplicity and obvious necessity. It is a constitutionally sound approach to the correction of the problem of an "out of control" federal judiciary.

There are other checks and balances available to Congress, of course, such as impeachment, cessation of funding, and even reduction of the number of district and/or appellate courts. But the first step should be an attempt to remind the federal courts that they are not above the Constitution and should remain within the jurisdiction they were assigned under the law.

Federal courts are not the masters of their own jurisdiction; Congress is. The Constitution provides that even Congress—much less the federal courts—does not have authority over the states in matters of religion. It is certainly true that the Congress cannot establish a national church, but it is equally true that no branch of the federal government can prohibit the acknowledgment of God under the First Amendment. Many states already have provisions in their constitutions that prevent an establishment of religion, but all states acknowledge God.

In his last days in office, our first president, George Washington, who had served as president of the Constitutional Convention which framed and drafted the Constitution, voiced his concern over attacks on the authority of the Constitution and our form of government. He said, "Toward the preservation of your government and the permanency of your present happy state, it is requisite not only that you steadily discountenance irregular oppositions to its acknowledged authority, but also that *you resist with care the spirit of innovation upon* [*the Constitution's*] *principles, however specious the pretexts.*"[12]

There are attacks upon our Constitution today from a most unlikely source—the federal courts that are sworn to uphold and support its authority. Turning to foreign law and international authority or even one's own feelings to interpret the Constitution's principles is something like asking a total stranger to direct the affairs of your household. It is a dangerous proposition, especially when this stranger has no regard for the values and principles upon which your family has prospered. The Supreme Court of the United States and lower federal courts of this land have demonstrated their disdain for the fundamental morality upon which our country was established by creating "rights" granted by man and not by God.

The acknowledgment of God and His sovereignty is the foundation for the liberty, justice, and freedom of conscience enjoyed by Americans over many generations. "One Nation under God, with liberty and justice for all" is more than a nice phrase. It is the embodiment of all that we hold dear. The right to be treated equally in a court of law exists because we are judged on our actions and not our thoughts, opinions, or beliefs.

It doesn't matter what you believe or don't believe about God when you stand before a human judge. That relationship is reserved for God, and man is prohibited from interfering with it. A person's beliefs are irrelevant when he commits a criminal act because courts are precluded from analyzing one's beliefs. It is no more right to kill or steal for money than it is to kill or steal because of your beliefs about another person. The end result is still death or loss of property, and all such offenses are punished equally. That is justice.

Likewise, liberty of conscience is secured because the powers of government are supposed to regulate actions only, and not opinions. A person's form of worship or articles of faith are outside the jurisdiction of government. The First Amendment secures that principle for the states and the people. The recognition that these rights are given by God remains the foundation for liberty and justice for all. It is the principle on which our Constitution and the First Amendment stand.

Federal courts have not only stood in opposition to the authority of the Constitution by turning to international law and foreign authority; they have also undermined the principles upon which the Constitution was begun—a belief in the fallibility of man and the sovereignty of God. The Constitution Restoration Act is appropriately titled because it seeks to restore our recognition of a higher authority and to curb the government's authority. This is exactly what the Constitution does.

As citizens, we must be aware of attempts to subvert our law and government. An understanding of our history is crucial to a vision of our future. No longer can we afford to ignore attempts to destroy our culture and our heritage by efforts to create a new world by divorcing ourselves from God.

But the question is not a new one for nations that have been blessed by God. During the reign of King Ahab, the people of Israel turned to worship of false gods. Ahab's wife Jezebel, a Phoenician princess, introduced into Israel the worship of the Phoenician god Baal and corrupted the nation and the people with idolatry. Elijah, a prophet of God, challenged 450 prophets of Baal on Mount Carmel, where he defied their false worship with a trial by fire from heaven. Before the people who assembled on Mount Carmel, Elijah asked, "How long halt ye between two opinions? if the LORD be God, follow him: but if Baal, then follow him" (1 Kings 18:21).

That question could be asked of the American people today. From our humble beginnings, God has blessed and protected our nation as no other in history. In 1892, the United States Supreme Court, in *Holy Trinity Church v. United States*,[13] said that we were a "Christian nation," a "Christian people, and the morality of the Country is deeply ingrafted upon Christianity."[14] As late as 1931, in *United States v. Macintosh*,[15] the Supreme Court recognized this truth, stating that "we are a Christian people." Today, detractors often ask, "But which God?" The United States Supreme Court in 1892 had no problem with such a question.

From the commission of Christopher Columbus, to the first charter of Virginia granted by King James I in 1606, to the Mayflower Compact in 1620 and the Fundamental Orders of Connecticut in 1638–39, the court covered the history of early-America Christians.[16] Jumping to the mid-1700s, the *Holy Trinity Church* court cited the Declaration of Independence, the constitutions of the various states, and even references in the United States Constitution to show that ours was a Christian nation.[17]

In *Updegraph v. Commonwealth*,[18] the Pennsylvania Supreme Court concluded that "Christianity, general Christianity, is, and always has been a part of the common law of Pennsylvania . . . not Christianity with an established church and tithes and spiritual courts, but Christianity with liberty of conscience to all men."

We should have no problem today saying who God is and affirming our faith in Him to refute those who attack the moral basis of our society. That is exactly why the Ten Commandments has had such a recent impact in America. There is no question who the God of the Ten Commandments is and what His impact has been on our nation.

Those who grew up under the teaching that the God of the Bible is the God on whom America was founded should be concerned at the modern attempts to make us deny that truth. That truth was known from the time the Pilgrims left the Mayflower, to the time when our nation began more than 150 years later, through the Civil War, World War I, World War II, Korea, and Vietnam, and until only recently—when it has become politically correct to ask whose God is the foundation of America.

During the summer and early fall of 2004, American veterans organized to take the Ten Commandments monument on a tour across the country. On September 15, 2004, *USA Today* reported that more than "two dozen lawsuits" over the display of the Ten Commandments were pending in state and federal courts. The story featured a picture of the Ten Commandments monument and Jim Cabaniss, who led the veterans organizations.[19]

My final appeal to the United States Supreme Court was rejected on October 4, 2004.[20] They did not want to hear the truth about the First Amendment and the acknowledgment of God. But my efforts to acknowledge God had sparked a fire across America. I knew that the Supreme Court would eventually have to address the issue.

Exactly eight days later, on October 12, 2004, the United States Supreme Court announced its decision to address not one but two Ten Commandments cases: *Van Orden v. Perry*,[21] from Texas and *ACLU of Kentucky v. McCreary County*,[22] from Kentucky. The media immediately called to get my opinion. It is natural to ask why the United States Supreme Court refused to consider the case of a Ten Commandments monument in a Supreme Court Judicial Building placed there by the chief justice of Alabama and backed with solid legal precedent, then decided to consider other Ten Commandments displays. The real reason is to avoid the legal issue!

I told the media that, in both *Van Orden* in Texas and *McCreary County* in Kentucky, those who defended the display of God's law did so on the basis that the displays were merely historical in nature. In the Texas case, the state had argued that the "Decalogue . . . is displayed in a museum setting."[23] And the Fifth Circuit Court of Appeals upheld the six-foot-high and three-and-one-half-foot-wide monument dedicated by the Fraternal Order of Eagles in Texas in 1961 partly on the basis that it was "part of a display of seventeen monuments, all located on grounds registered as a historical landmark."[24]

In Kentucky, three counties—McCreary, Harlan, and Pulaski—placed similar depictions of the Ten Commandments in either their courthouses or classrooms. After the ACLU filed complaints, the counties modified their displays by placing other "secular historical and legal documents" around the Ten Commandments in hopes that the displays would be considered a historical acknowledgment acceptable to the federal district court.[25] In spite of the counties' efforts, the federal district court concluded that the modified displays failed to meet its secular requirements, and ordered the displays removed "immediately."[26] The counties proceeded to modify their displays still further by placing other items around the Ten Commandments such as the full text of "The Star Spangled Banner," together with a paragraph statement explaining how the documents related to the Ten Commandments.

Again, the federal district court declined to accept the counties' attempts to "secularize" the display and ordered the Ten Commandments removed "immediately."[27]

The difference between these cases accepted by the United States Supreme Court for review and my case is simple. Those cases in Kentucky and Texas deny the sovereignty of God while my case was predicated upon that acknowledgment. Unfortunately, the Supreme Court did not want to confront the truth that the recognition of God was never denied by the First Amendment until the court began in the 1960s to turn away from the truth and from the law. The acknowledgment of God was the very object of that amendment.

Today, Christians have been convinced that they must first bow down to the gods of this world (such as the federal courts) before they can recognize the one true God in heaven. That is exactly what is being done in both the Texas and Kentucky cases by trying to justify a display of God's law as only secular in nature and in no way representative of the true God.

Such hypocrisy and lack of faith will never be rewarded. Daniel was prohibited from bowing to any other god by the order of King Darius, but he defied the king. With his shutters open, he prayed to the one true God (Dan. 6:10). Likewise, Shadrach, Meshach, and Abednego were never denied the right to worship their God as long as they bowed down to the golden idol of Nebuchadnezzar (Dan. 3:15). Like Daniel, they answered the king in this matter, stating, "We will not serve thy gods, nor worship the golden image which thou hast set up" (Dan. 3:18).

The rulings by the United States Supreme Court will ultimately be a devastating loss for America regardless of whether the displays of the Ten Commandments are removed or allowed to remain. If the Ten Commandments are removed, it will be because they are too "religious." But if they are permitted to stay, it will be because they are "historical" and have little or no religious value. In either event, the precedent will be set and the United States Supreme Court will have set themselves above the law and above God. You can never reach the right result when you start from the wrong premise!

And yet, there is reason for hope. God has never forsaken His people. From Alabama to Kentucky and Texas, from Georgia and Louisiana to Oregon and California, the people of God are coming forward to defend their inalienable right to worship God. They are tired of the arrogance and hypocrisy of judges who open their courts with "God save the United States and this Honorable Court" and take their oath "so help me God" but then deny that God exists as soon as they put on their black robes.

People are demanding to know the truth. And the truth is that we need to return to the knowledge of God upon which America and our laws were founded. We must stand courageously for God. Like Daniel, David, and Paul of the Scriptures, we must be willing to stand. A woman named Esther stood against an unjust law to save her people. Knowing that her defiance could cost her life, she risked all when she declared, "If I perish, I perish" (Esth. 4:16). Her boldness and courage saved her people.

After her release from jail on bond, Karen Kennedy returned home with her husband Wayne. Though confined to a wheelchair and restricted by the constant administration of oxygen, she had been arrested and handcuffed during her peaceful protest over the removal of the Ten Commandments monument on August 20, 2003. Charged with trespassing, she was convicted in the Montgomery County District Court in Alabama, but she continued to fight. While awaiting a jury trial on appeal, Mrs. Kennedy's long battle against various forms of cancer finally ended when she died quietly at her home in Prattville, Alabama, on August 28, 2004.

She died one year and one day after the monument was removed from the rotunda of the judicial building, but she lived to see the movement of God in the hearts of His people. Her attorney, Jim Zeigler of Mobile, was quoted as saying, "She has won her case from a higher seat of judgment."[28]

Like Karen Kennedy, America is fighting a long battle against a cancer that has sapped our strength, restricted our freedom, and confined us as a people. The removal of our right to publicly acknowledge God is a cancer that will slowly take the life of our nation, and it must be stopped! Karen's courage, faith, and commitment in her fight to defend God's law is an example to all of us. It has been said that the battle is not to the strong alone; it is to the vigilant, the active, and the brave. May we stand with Karen Kennedy when our battle on earth has ended and proudly proclaim that we fought the good fight, we finished our course, we kept the faith.

There is a spiritual battle raging across our land—a battle between good and evil, right and wrong, light and darkness. This is a struggle between those who acknowledge Almighty God and those who deny His sovereignty. Every man, woman, and child is engaged in this warfare, "for we wrestle not against flesh and blood, but against principalities, against powers, against the rulers of the darkness of this world, against spiritual wickedness in high places" (Eph. 6:12). A poem I wrote illustrates this spiritual conflict:

CAN HE COUNT ON YOU?
Today we face another war
Fought not upon some distant shore,
Nor against a foe we can see
Yet one as ruthless as can be.

He'll take your life and children too
And say there's nothing you can do.
He'll make you think that wrong is right
'Tis but a sign to stand and fight.

And though we face the wrath of hell,
Against those gates we shall prevail.
In homes and schools across our land
It's time for Christians to take a stand.

And when our race on earth is run
The battles over, the victory is won,
When through all the earth His praise will ring
And all the heavenly angels sing.

'Twill be enough to see the Son
And hear Him say, "My child well done,"
You kept the faith so strong and true;
I knew that I could count on you.[29]

Will you, like David, stand against the giant of disbelief that threatens our nation and our culture? Let us proclaim with the loudest voice and clearest exposition, as David did, "*Is there not a cause?*" (1 Sam. 17:29, emphasis added). Let us take up the banner of our God and go forth to do battle, that "all the earth may know that there is a

God in [America], and all this assembly [of people] shall know that the LORD saveth not with sword and spear: for the battle is the LORD's" (1 Sam. 17:46–47).

There is indeed a cause, and God is waiting for His people to stand in faith—to let their light shine in the darkness that threatens to engulf us. Can He count on you?

In the end, that's all that really matters!

NOTES

Chapter 2

1. General Douglas MacArthur, speech upon his acceptance of the Sylvanus Thayer Award (West Point, N.Y., May 12, 1962).

Chapter 3

1. Roy S. Moore, deputy district attorney, November 20, 1980.
2. "Etowah deputy D.A. to seek repeal of good time law," *Gadsden Times*, January 7, 1979.
3. "Deputy D.A. lists court problems," *Gadsden Times*, December 2, 1979.
4. Ibid.
5. Official transcript, meeting with Etowah County judges, October 15, 1981, 5.
6. Ibid., 7.
7. Ibid., 18.
8. Ibid., 19.
9. Ibid.
10. Julius Swann, letter to William H. Morrow Jr., general counsel, Alabama State Bar, October 26, 1981.
11. Ibid.
12. Alabama State Bar, letter to Roy Moore regarding ASB 81-355, May 7, 1982.
13. Roy S. Moore, deputy district attorney, letter to W. W. Rayburn, district attorney, June 21, 1982; see also, "Deputy DA seeks election as judge," *Gadsden Times*, June 22, 1982.
14. "Stewart defeats Moore for Circuit Judge," *Gadsden Times*, September 29, 1982.
15. "Etowah judges strike back, file complaint," *Birmingham News*, December 19, 1982, letter reply to judge's complaint.
16. Ibid.
17. Circuit judges Julius Swann, Cyril Smith, Hobdy Rains, and William Cardwell, letter to William H. Morrow Jr., October 20, 1982.
18. Ibid.
19. General Council William H. Morrow Jr., report regarding Disciplinary Complaint 82-188-M, February 1983, 10.
20. "Defeated but not forgotten by his enemies," *Anniston Star*, December 5, 1982.

Chapter 5

1. Roy S. Moore, in memory of my father at Christmas, December 2, 1980.
2. 449 U.S. 39, 41, 42 (1980).
3. Webster's *American Dictionary of the English Language*, 1828 ed., s.v. "table."

4. Ibid., s.v. "religion."

5. George Washington, Farewell Address, September 17, 1796, reprinted in *The Founders' Constitution*, ed. P. Kurland and R. Lerner (Chicago: Liberty Fund, 1987), 684.

6. Reaffirmation, reference to "one nation under God" in the Pledge of Allegiance, Pub. L. No. 107-293, 116 Stat. 2057 (2002).

7. Art. 3, Northwest Ordinance of 1789, reprinted in William J. Federer, *America's God and Country* (Coppell, Texas: FAME Publishing, Inc., 1994), 484 (emphasis added).

8. George Washington, first inaugural address, April 30, 1789, reprinted in *Documents of American History*, 9th ed., vol. 1 (Englewood Cliffs, N.J.: Prentice-Hall, Inc. 1973), 152.

9. John Locke, *Great Books of the Western World: Second Treatise of Civil Government*, ed. Robert Gwean (Chicago: *Encyclopedia Britannica*, 1991), chap. 3, p. 28.

10. *Everson v. Board of Education*, 330 U.S. 1 (1947).

11. Ibid., 18.

12. President Dwight D. Eisenhower, speech confirming the Act of Congress that added the phrase "under God" to the Pledge of Allegiance, June 14, 1954, reprinted in William J. Federer, *Treasury of Presidential Quotations* (St. Louis: Amerisearch, Inc., 2004), 313–14.

13. Senator Burke, statement concerning resolution on Pledge of Allegiance, *Congressional Record* 8563, daily ed., June 22, 1954.

14. *Engel v. Vitale*, 370 U.S. 421 (1962).

15. Ibid., 422.

16. *Abington v. Schempp*, 374 U.S. 203 (1963).

17. *Wallace v. Jaffree*, 472 U.S. 38 (1985).

Chapter 6

1. Thomas Jefferson, "A Bill for Establishing Religious Freedom," June 12, 1779, reprinted in *The Founders' Constitution*, ed. P. Kurland and R. Lerner (Chicago: Liberty Fund, 1987), 77.

2. Preamble, Alabama Constitution, 1901.

3. *Ex parte State ex rel. James*, 711 So. 2d 952, 954 (Alabama 1998).

4. 811 F. Supp. 669 (N. D. Ga. 1993).

5. John Quincy Adams, *The Jubilee of the Constitution* (N.Y.: Samuel Colman, 1839), 13–14.

6. Mayflower Compact, reprinted in *Founders' Constitution* 1, 610.

7. William Bradford, *Of Plymouth Plantation*, ed. Morris & Knopf (New York, 1997), 61.

8. "ACLU may challenge prayer in courts," *Gadsden Times*, June 20, 1994.

9. Robert C. Cottrell, *Roger Nash Baldwin and the American Civil Liberties Union* (New York: Columbia Univ. Press, 2000).

10. William Blackstone, *Commentaries on the Laws of England* 1, University of Chicago Press Facs. ed. (1765), 125.

11. "Use of prayer in courtroom has Moore experiencing legal fight," *Gadsden Times*, December 12, 1994.

12. "Ministers support Etowah Judge, condemn ACLU over prayer issue," *Birmingham News*, August 3, 1994.

13. Ibid.

14. 370 US. 421, 439 (1962) (Douglas, J., concurring).

15. George Washington, first inaugural address, April 30, 1789, *Documents in American History*, chap. 5, sup. n. 7.

Chapter 7

1. Roy S. Moore, circuit judge, December 14, 1993.

2. The Tenth Amendment provides: "The powers not delegated to the United States by the Constitution, nor prohibited by it to the states, are reserved to the states respectively, or to the people" (U.S. Constitution).

3. "Judge faces lawsuit for religious stance," *Gadsden Times*, January 18, 1995.

4. Ibid.

5. *Alabama Freethought Association v. Moore*, 893 F. Supp. 1522 (N.D. Ala. 1995).

6. "ACLU files lawsuit against Judge Moore," *Gadsden Times*, April 1, 1995.

7. Ibid.

8. Ibid.

9. Ibid.

10. U.S. Constitution, amend. 1

11. *America's God and Country*, chap. 5, sup. n. 6, 163.

12. U.S. Constitution, art. 6, par. 3.

13. Judiciary Act of 1789, currently codified at 28 U.S.C., sec. 453.

14. "Judge cheered at rally," *Birmingham Post-Herald*, April 11, 1995.

15. "Flag-waving throng cheers for Moore," *Gadsden Times*, April 11, 1995.

16. "James backs state judge who prays in courtroom," *Birmingham Post-Herald*, April 14, 1995.

17. Ibid.

18. *Ex parte State ex rel. James*, 711 So. 2d, 956–57.

19. Ibid., 957.

Chapter 8

1. Thomas Jefferson, *Writings*, ed. Merrill D. Peterson (New York: The Library of America, 1984), 744.

2. Names of subscribers, *Commentaries on the Laws of England* 4 (Philadelphia: Robert Bell, 1771).

3. Edmund Burke, *The Spirit of 76: The Study of the American Revolution by Participants*, ed. Commanger and Morris (New York: Castle Books, 2002), 134.

4. Ibid.

5. *Blackstone's Commentaries* 1, 38–39.

6. James Madison, *The Federalist 43*, ed. George W. Carey and James McClellan (2001), 229.

7. *Blackstone's Commentaries* 1, 42.

8. Ibid.

9. Ibid.

10. John Locke, *Second Treatise of Civil Government* in *Great Books of the Western World*, ed. Robert Gwean (Chicago: Encyclopedia Britannica, 1991), 56.

11. James Wilson, *Wilson's Works*, 2nd ed., vol. 1, ed. James D. Andrews (1896), 93.

12. Arthur J. Stansbury, *Elementary Catechism of the Constitution of the United States for the Use of the Schools*, ed. William H. Huff (1993), 43.

13. *United States v. Macintosh*, 283 U.S. 605 (1931).

14. Ibid., 625.

15. George Washington, first inaugural address, *Documents in American History*, chap. 5, sup. n. 8.

16. Benjamin Franklin, *Congressional Record*, the House of Representatives, First Session of the Thirty-third Congress (Washington, D.C.: AOP Nicholson, 1854).

17. *Webster's American Dictionary of the English Language*, preface, Foundation for American Christian Education Facs. ed. (1828).

18. Thomas Jefferson, *Notes on the State of Virginia* "Query XVIII," reprinted in *Writings*, 289.

19. George Washington, letter to Hebrew congregation of Newport, R.I., reprinted in *American State Papers and Related Documents on Freedom in Religion*, 4th revised ed., ed. William A. Blakely (Review and Herald, 1949), 172.

20. James Madison, *Memorial and Remonstrance Against Religious Assessments*, reprinted in *American State Papers and Related Documents on Freedom in Religion*, 4th revised ed., ed. William A. Blakely (Review and Herald, 1949), 114–15.

21. Thomas Jefferson, "Bill for Establishing Religious Freedom," chap. 6, sup. n. 1.

22. *McGowan v. Maryland*, 366 U.S. 420 (1961).

23. Ibid., 562–63 (Douglas, J., dissenting).

Chapter 9

1. "Governor Fob James' remarks at the Judge Roy Moore support rally held on May 16, 1995," *The Messenger*, May 24, 1995.

2. "Rallying 'round the judge," *Birmingham News*, May 17, 1995.

3. *The Messenger*, sup. n. 1.

4. *Alabama Freethought Association v. Moore*, 893 F. Supp. 1522, 1544 (N.D. Ala. 1995).

5. "Moore 1, ACLU 0," *Gadsden Times*, July 8, 1995.

6. "Judge gets OK to keep showing Commandments," *Birmingham News*, July 8, 1995.

7. "Moore suing ACLU," *Gadsden Times*, December 8, 1995.

8. James Madison, *Annals of Cong.* 1 (1789), 757, reprinted in *Founder's Constitution* 5, 93.

9. Ibid.

10. Ibid.

Chapter 10

1. "ACLU says it's ready to fight judge over religious issues," *Birmingham News*, January 9, 1996.

2. *Impact*, "Reclaiming America brings vision and people together," April 1996.

3. "Alabama Judge, ACLU wrestle over Religion," *Boston Globe*, January 14, 1996.

4. "Religion in Court sparks suits in Alabama," *Buffalo News*, January 12, 1996.

5. "Lawsuit pits Judge, ACLU in fight over religious courtroom," *Tallahassee Democrat*, January 12, 1996.

6. "Alabama Judge Goes to Court in Religious Battle," *Los Angeles Times*, January 11, 1996.

7. "Moore begins his battle in Montgomery," *Montgomery Advertiser*, September 12, 1996.

8. Ibid.

9. "Faithful follow Moore," *Gadsden Times*, September 12, 1996.

10. "Capitol Notes," *Gadsden Times*, September 15, 1996.

11. "I will not stop prayer," *Gadsden Times*, November 23, 1996.

12. Ibid.

13. Ibid.

14. Ibid.

15. "Judge Moore to defy ban on prayer before court," *Birmingham News*, November 23, 1996.

16. "Ten Commandments cases back in spotlight," *Gadsden Times*, January 9, 1997.

17. "Judge to Moore: Change Plaque," *Birmingham News*, February 11, 1997.

18. "Moore gets 10 days to change display," *Gadsden Times*, February 11, 1997.

19. "Judge faces deadline on religious display," *New York Times*, National Report, February 13, 1997.

20. Ibid.

21. "Spotlight gets bigger for Etowah Judge," *Gadsden Times*, February 22, 1997.

22. "Moore Rally at GSCC attracts overflow crowd," *Gadsden Times*, February 24, 1997.

23. Thomas Jefferson "A Summary View of the Rights of British America," July 1774, reprinted in *Writings*, 122.

24. "Poll: 88% says judge has right to display Ten Commandments," *Dothan Eagle*, March 1, 1997.

25. "U.S. House votes to back state judge on Commandments," *Birmingham News*, March 6, 1997.

Chapter 11

1. "Rally sends a message," *Birmingham News*, April 13, 1997.

2. "Rally draws thousands," *Montgomery Advertiser*, April 13, 1997.

3. "In Praise of Moore," *Gadsden Times*, April 13, 1997.

4. "Dissenters protest at rally," *Montgomery Advertiser*, April 13, 1997.

5. "Rally sends a message," *Birmingham News*, April 13, 1997.

6. "Dissenters protest at rally," *Montgomery Advertiser*, April 13, 1997.

7. "Rally sends a message," *Birmingham News*, April 13, 1997.

8. "Rally draws thousands," *Montgomery Advertiser*, April 13, 1997.

9. "Rally sends a message," *Birmingham News*, April 13, 1997.

10. "Rally draws thousands," *Montgomery Advertiser*, April 13, 1997.

11. Ibid.

12. William Singleton III, "Courting the Big Ten," *HomeLife*, August 1997.

13. "Rally draws thousands," *Montgomery Advertiser*, April 13, 1997.

14. Ibid.

15. "Nine Alabama pastors join brief opposing Judge Moore," *Alabama Baptist*, May 22, 1997.

16. Joseph Story, *Commentaries on the Constitution 2* (Boston: Little, Brown, & Co., 1851), 594.

17. "Nine Alabama pastors join brief opposing Judge Moore," *Alabama Baptist*, May 22, 1997.

18. Story, *Commentaries*, 594.

19. Statement by Senator Kennedy presenting resolution of the House of Representatives of the Commonwealth of Massachusetts, *Congressional Record* 8558, daily ed., June 22, 1954.

20. Ibid.

21. "Judge presses his case on television," *Birmingham Post-Herald*, September 11, 1997.

22. *Documentary History of the Supreme Court of the United States*, 1789–1800, vol. 2, ed. Maeva Marcus (New York: Columbia University Press, 1988), 13.

23. "Court tosses Ten Commandments case," *Gadsden Times*, January 24, 1998; *see Ex parte State ex rel. James*, 711 So. 2d 952, 962 (Alabama 1998).

24. "Court throws out Ten Commandments case," *Montgomery Advertiser*, January 24, 1998.

25. "Court tosses Commandments case," *Gadsden Times*, January 24, 1998.

26. "Court throws out Ten Commandments case," *Montgomery Advertiser*, January 24, 1998.

Chapter 12

1. "Spiritual war predicted over public posting," *Green Bay Gazette*, March 16, 1998.

2. "Decalogue Debate Back to Square One," *ABA Journal*, March 1998.

3. Ibid.

4. John Adams, letter to officers of the First Brigade of the Third Division of the Militia of Massachusetts, October 11, 1798, *The Works of John Adams-Second President of the United States: with a Life of the Author, Notes, and Illustration,* ed. Charles Francis Adams (Little, Brown, & Co., 1854), 228–29.

5. George Washington, Farewell Address, September 17, 1796, chap. 5, sup. n. 5, 684.

6. Braxton Kittrell Jr., letter, Judicial Inquiry Commission, November 25, 1996.

7. *Merriam-Webster's Collegiate Dictionary,* 11th ed. (Springfield, Mass., 2003).

8. *Columbia Encyclopedia,* 6th ed., s.v. "star chamber" (2001).

9. *Encyclopedia Britannica,* 15th ed., vol. 11 (1992), 218.

10. Stephen Melchior, letter to Attorney Rosa Davis, April 18, 1998.

11. "Young claims harassment," *Gadsden Times,* April 26, 1998.

12. Amend. 581, sec. 6.17, Alabama Constitution, 1901 (emphasis added).

13. "Judge Moore ally accuses judicial panel of persecution," *Birmingham News,* April 25, 1998.

14. "Commandments Judge claims he's target of covert probe," *Birmingham News,* October 8, 1998 (emphasis added).

15. "Moore says JIC ruling not moot," *Birmingham News,* April 6, 2000 (emphasis added).

16. "Trouble for Moore," *Gadsden Times,* June 3, 1999.

17. Ibid.

18. "Judge Moore cleared," *Gadsden Times,* September 2, 1999.

19. Ibid.

20. "Moore foe admits he was driven by revenge," *Birmingham News,* September 4, 1999.

21. "Former mayor says ethics allegation was his retaliation," *Gadsden Times,* September 15, 1999; "Ex-mayor sought revenge in filing complaint," *Pensacola News Journal,* September 5, 1999.

22. "Ethics Commission director felt used with Moore probe," *Gadsden Times,* September 16, 1999.

23. "Moore foe admits he was driven by revenge," *Birmingham News,* September 4, 1999.

Chapter 13

1. "State GOP Kicks Off 2000 Election With Judicial Candidates," *Birmingham News,* November 9, 1999.

2. "Petition urges Moore to run for Chief Justice," *Birmingham News,* November 9, 1999.

3. Ibid.

4. "Moore decides to run," *Gadsden Times,* December 8, 1999.

5. "Moore Runs for Chief Justice," *Birmingham News,* December 8, 1999.

6. "Judge Took Social Trips with Lawyers," *Gadsden Times,* December 28, 1999.

7. "Truth be told," *Gadsden Times,* December 8, 2000.

8. "Ten Commandments Judge leads in race for Chief Justice," *Washington Times,* May 2, 2000.

9. "Moore wins without a run off," *Gadsden Times,* June 7, 2000.

10. Ibid.

11. "Ten Commandments defender wins vote," *New York Times,* National Report, June 8, 2000.

12. "Moore defeats See," *Birmingham News,* June 7, 2000.

13. Ibid.

14. "Judge Roy Moore . . . Upholding the Moral Foundations of the Law," campaign flyer, Alabama Republican Party, 2000.

15. "Coat tails affect races," *Gadsden Times*, November 9, 2000.

16. Ibid.

17. "Moore Wins, Credits God," *Birmingham News*, November 8, 2000.

Chapter 14

1. "Ten Commandments judge leads in race for Chief Justice," *Washington Times*, May 2, 2000; "Ten Commandments Judge brings Veteran's Day message to Wiregrass," *Dothan Eagle*, November 12, 1999; "Pinto beans and preaching at the poor house," *Mobile Press-Register*, March 1, 1998.

2. Alabama Constitution (1901), art. 16, sec. 279.

3. *See* Alabama Constitution (1901), amend. 328, sec. 6.16.

4. Alabama Code 1975, sec. 12–2–30(7),(8).

5. Alabama Code 1975, sec. 41–10–275.

6. Rule 18.5(a), Ala. R. Crim. P., Rule 12.3 for grand jurors.

7. Henry de Bracton, *On the Laws and Customs of England*, vol. 2, ed. Samuel Thorne (Cambridge, Mass.: Belknap Press of Harvard University Press, 1968), 405.

8. Ibid.

9. George Washington, Farewell Address, September 17, 1796, chap. 5, sup. n. 5, 684 (emphasis in original).

10. *Documentary History of the Supreme Court of the United States 1789–1800*, vol. 2, ed. Maeva Marcus (New York: Columbia University Press, 1988), 284.

11. Ibid., 515.

12. *America's God and Country*, 651; John Eidsmoe, *Christianity and the Constitution: The Faith of Our Founding Fathers* (Grand Rapids, Mich.: Baker Book House, 1996), 117.

13. Blackstone's *Commentaries* 1, 235.

14. Blackstone's *Commentaries* 4, 43–44.

15. George Washington, first inaugural address, reprinted in *Documents of American History*, chap. 5, sup. n. 7.

16. "Moore will seek blessings of God," *Birmingham News*, January 16, 2001.

17. Ibid.

18. 366 U.S. 420, 562–63 (1961) (Douglas, J., dissenting).

19. House Rep. No. 1693 (1954), 2340.

20. Samuel Adams, speech concerning the Declaration of Independence, August 1, 1776, reprinted in *The World's Best Orations*, ed. Ferd. P. Kaiser (St. Louis, 1899), 93–109.

21. Blackstone's *Commentaries* 1, 41.

22. *Glassroth v. Moore*, 229 F. Supp. 2d 1290, 1331–24 (M.D. Ala. 2002) (emphasis added).

23. "Colleagues criticize Moore over monument," *Montgomery Advertiser*, August 4, 2001.

24. Ibid.

Chapter 15

1. "Moore: Cuts Unfair," *Gadsden Times*, February 13, 2001.

2. Ibid.

3. "Opposition to Moore makes strange allies," *Gadsden Times*, May 17, 2002.

4. "Chief Justice questions rush on Constitution," *Gadsden Times*, April 8, 2001.

5. *State v. Manley*, 441 So. 2d 864 (1983).

6. *Opinion of the Justices, No. 373*, 795 So. 2d 630 (Ala. 2001).

7. *Opinion of the Justices, No. 358*, 692 So. 2d 107 (Ala. 1997).

8. *Opinion of the Justices, No. 373*, 795 So. 2d 632.

9. Ibid., 644.

10. *Alabama Citizens Watch*, May/June 2001.

11. Ibid.

12. *D.H. v. H.H.*, 830 So. 2d 16, 20 (Ala. Civ. App. 2001).

13. *Williams v. State*, 55 Ala. App. 436, 438, 316 So. 2d 362, 364 (Ala. Crim. App. 1975).

14. Ibid., 438, 363.

15. *Ex parte H.H.*, 830 So. 2d 21, 34 (Ala. 2002) (Moore, C. J., concurring specially).

16. *H.H.*, 830 So. 2d 26.

17. "Chief Justice: Homosexuals unfit as parents," *Mobile-Press Register*, February 16, 2002; "Moore: Lesbian unfit as parent," *Birmingham News*, February 16, 2002.

18. Editorial, *Birmingham News*, February 20, 2002.

19. "Holmes calls for inquiry of Moore," *Montgomery Advertiser*, February 18, 2002.

20. 848 So. 2d 963 (2002).

21. 17 U.S. 122, 163 (1819).

22. *Hughes v. Hughes*, 44 Ala. 698 (1870).

23. *Ex parte Pankey*, 848 So. 2d 982 (Moore, C. J., dissenting) (emphasis in original).

24. Ibid.

25. Alabama Constitution (1901), amend. 111, sec. 256.

26. *Ex parte James*, 836 So. 2d 813 (Ala. 2002).

27. George Washington, Farewell Address, September 17, 1796, chap. 5, sup. n. 5, 683–84.

28. 550 So. 2d 986 (Ala. 1989).

29. Ibid., 993.

30. *Goodridge v. Dep't of Public Health*, 440 Mass. 309, 313, 798 N.E. 2d 941 (Mass. 2003).

31. 5 U.S. 1 Cranch 137 (1803).

32. Ibid., 177.

33. 840 So. 2d 115 (Ala. 2002).

34. *Ex parte Bayliss*, 550 So. 2d 995.

35. 847 So. 2d 331 (Ala. 2002).

36. 80 U.S. (13 Wall.) 679, 732 (1871).

37. *Yates v. El Bethel Primitive Baptist Church*, 847 So. 2d 347–48.

38. Ibid., 355.

39. Ibid., 369, emphasis added.

40. "Odd alliance lines up against Moore," *Montgomery Advertiser*, May 7, 2002; "Opposition to Moore makes strange allies," *Gadsden Times*, May 17, 2002.

41. "Opposition to Moore makes strange allies," *Gadsden Times*, May 17, 2002.

42. Ibid.

43. Ibid.

Chapter 16

1. "Moore defends new monument," *Birmingham News*, August 8, 2001.

2. Ibid.

3. "Moore defends granite display," *Montgomery Advertiser*, August 8, 2001.

4. "Moore claims duty in posting large monument," *Mobile Register*, August 8, 2001.

5. "Moore defends granite display," *Montgomery Advertiser*, August 8, 2001.

6. *The Federalist No. 37*, 185.

7. *2 Debates on the Constitution*, 404–05 (emphasis in original).

8. Herbert W. Titus, *The Constitution of the United States: A Christian Document* (Chesapeake, Va.: Titus Publications, 1997), 11–12.

9. "Moore defends new monument," *Birmingham News*, August 8, 2001.

10. "King marker blocked," *Gadsden Times*, August 29, 2001.

11. Ibid.

12. "King's speech display blocked," *Montgomery Advertiser*, August 29, 2001.

13. "King Marker Blocked," *Gadsden Times*, August 29, 2001.

14. "Holding back a monument," *Mobile Register*, August 29, 2001.

15. "Holmes rejects plaque," *Montgomery Advertiser*, September 2, 2001.

16. Ibid.

17. "Black lawmakers plan suit over MLK plaques in state Judicial Building," *Gadsden Times*, September 29, 2001.

18. "Holmes rejects plaque," *Montgomery Advertiser*, September 2, 2001.

19. "Atom Sculpture Awaits Judicial Building Spot," *Gadsden Times*, October 28, 2001.

20. Eisenhower, Senate *Congressional Record*, June 22, 1954, chap. 5, sup. n. 11.

21. "Moore: Take back our land," *Chattanooga Times Free Press*, December 3, 2001.

22. Ibid.

23. Ibid.

24. Roy S. Moore, circuit judge, July 1998.

Chapter 17

1. Morris Dees, letter to Ayesha Khan, July 16, 2002.

2. "Nut letter haunts Dees in lawsuit against Moore," *Birmingham News*, September 26, 2002.

3. Ibid.

4. "Moore's lawyers want new judge in monument lawsuit," *Birmingham News*, October 2, 2002.

5. *Glassroth v. Moore*, Bench Trial Proceedings, transcript, vol. 1, 28, 97, 61.

6. Ibid., 48.

7. Ibid., 53.

8. Ibid., 56.

9. Ibid., 29.

10. Ibid., 103.

11. Ibid., 105.

12. Ibid., 100.

13. Ibid., 152.

14. Ibid., 187 (emphasis added).

15. Ibid., 214.

16. Ibid., 228.

17. Ibid., 231, 235.

18. "Lawyers: Display bullies," *Montgomery Advertiser*, October 16, 2002.

19. Transcript, vol. 1, 216–17.

20. James Madison, *Memorial and Remonstrance*, chap. 8, sup. n. 22, 113.

21. Transcript, vol. 1, 166; *see also* "Commandments monument offended lawyer," *Mobile Register*, October 16, 2002.

22. Madison, *Memorial*, chap. 8, sup. n. 22, 112–20.

23. Transcript, vol. 2, 122.

24. Ibid., 137.

25. "Moore wants to restore Moral Foundation of Law," *Birmingham News*, October 18, 2002.

26. *Yates v. El Bethel Primitive Baptist Church*, 847 So. 2d 331 (Ala. 2002).

27. Transcript, vol. 4, 82–83, 86.

28. Ibid., 89.

29. Transcript, vol. 5, 26–34.

30. Transcript, vol. 6, 133, 137.

31. Ibid., 162–63.

32. Ibid., 148–49.

33. Henry de Bracton, *On the Laws and Customs of England*, 2 vols., ed. Samuel Thorne (Cambridge, Mass: Belknap Press of Harvard University Press, 1968).

34. Transcript, vol. 6, 263.

35. Ibid., 266–67.

36. Ibid., 268.

37. Ibid., 272.

38. Thomas Jefferson, *Notes on the State of Virginia*, chap. 8, sup. n. 20.

39. Transcript, vol. 6, 273; *America's God and Country*, 322.

40. Ibid.; Ibid., 246.

41. Transcript, vol. 6, 273–75; Report of House of Representatives, First Session of the Thirty-third Congress, Committee on the Judiciary (Washington, D.C.: A.O.P. Nicholson, 1854).

42. Transcript, vol. 7, 18.

43. Ibid.

44. Ibid., 19.

45. Ibid., 69–70.

46. Ibid., 73.

Chapter 18

1. *Glassroth v. Moore*, 229 F. Supp. 2d, 1290, 1312 (M.D. Ala. 2002) (first emphasis in original).

2. 283 U.S. 605 (1931).

3. George Washington, proclamation, a National Thanksgiving, *Messages and Papers of the Presidents* 1789–1897, vol. 1 (James D. Richardson, published by authority of Congress, 1899).

4. "Moore's Monument Must Go, says Judge," *Mobile Register*, November 19, 2002; "Judge rules Monument violates Constitution," *Birmingham News*, November 19, 2002; "Judge evicts Commandments display," *Montgomery Advertiser*, November 19, 2002.

5. "Judge's Biblical Monument is ruled unconstitutional," *New York Times*, November 19, 2002; "10 Commandments Monument must go," *USA Today*, November 19, 2002.

6. *Glassroth v. Moore*, 229 F. Supp. 2d 1319.

7. Ibid., 1293 (emphasis added).

8. Ibid., 1314.

9. Ibid., 1313, n. 5.

10. Lewis Carroll, *Through the Looking Glass (And What Alice Found There)* (Waterville, Maine: Thorndike Press, 2003), 108 (originally published in 1871).

11. *Dred Scott v. Sandford*, 60 U.S. 393, 621 (1856) (Curtis, J., dissenting).

12. *Glassroth v. Moore*, 229 F. Supp. 2d 1295, 1300, 1303.

13. Ibid., 1300, 1303, 1295.

14. Ibid., 1314.

15. *Reynolds v. United States*, 98 U.S. 145, 162–64 (1878); *Davis v. Beason*, 133 U.S. 333, 342 (1890).

16. 330 U.S. 1, 63–72 (Rutledge, J., dissenting).

17. Ibid., 64.

18. *Glassroth v. Moore*, 229 F. Supp. 2d 1311 [quoting *County of Allegheny v. ACLU*, 492 U.S. 573 (1989), quoting in turn *Wallace v. Jaffree*, 472 U.S. 38 (1985)].

19. Catherine Mallard, *The Christian Heritage of the United States of America* (Springfield, Va.: Christian Heritage Ministries, 1999), 15, 49, 64, 72, 80, 96, 127, 142, 148, 165, 172, 183, 228.

20. Thomas Jefferson, letter to Danbury Baptist Association, January 1, 1802, reprinted in *Writings*, 510.

21. Ibid.

22. 98 U.S. 145 (1878).

23. Alabama Constitution (1901), preamble.

24. *Glassroth v. Moore*, 229 F. Supp. 2d 1308.

25. *Marsh v. Chambers*, 463 U.S. 783, 818 (1983) (Brennan, J., dissenting).

26. "Moore Plans Appeal," *Montgomery Advertiser*, December 11, 2002.

27. *Glassroth v. Moore*, 335 F. 3d 1282, 1294 (11th Cir. 2003).

28. Ibid., 335 F. 3d 1301 [quoting *Lynch v. Donnelly*, 465 U.S. 668, 717 (1984)] (Brennan, J., dissenting).

29. "Survey: Most back Moore's position," *Birmingham News*, July 14, 2003.

30. "Moore offers his case for monument," *Mobile Register*, July 28, 2003.

31. *Glassroth v. Moore*, 335 F. 3d 1303 (emphasis added).

32. "Judge lifts stay on order," *Mobile Register*, August 6, 2003.

Chapter 19

1. "Loyalty to the Constitution," Constitution Corner, United States Military Academy, West Point, New York.

2. Ibid.

3. U.S. Constitution, art. 6, para. 2.

4. See *United States v. Calley*, 48 C.M.R. 19, 22 USCMA 534 (1973).

5. "Loyalty to the Constitution," Constitution Corner, USMA.

6. *New Encyclopedia Britannica*, 15th ed., vol. 7 (Chicago, 1992), 673.

7. Henry de Bracton, *On the Laws and Customs of England*, vol. 2, ed. Samuel Thorne (Cambridge, Mass.: Belknap Press of Harvard University Press, 1968), 33.

8. Ibid.

9. Samuel Rutherford, *Lex Rex, or The Law and the Prince: A Dispute for the Just Prerogative of King and People*, reprint of original 1644 ed. (Virginia: Sprinkle Publ., 1982).

10. *Encyclopedia Britannica*, 15th ed., vol. 10, Robert McHenry (1992).

11. Declaration of Independence.

12. Benjamin Franklin, *America's God and Country*, 246.

13. Jonathan Mayhew, *A Discourse Concerning Unlimited Submission and Non-Resistance to the Higher Powers*, available at: http://www.lawandliberty.org/mayhew.htm) (emphasis added).

14. Ibid.

15. "Congress shall make no law respecting an establishment of religion or prohibiting the free exercise thereof . . . .," U.S. Constitution, amend. 1.

16. Roy S. Moore, Alabama chief justice, statement, around July 4, 2003 (emphasis in original).

17. "Moving Day—Monument's move is victory for rule of law," *Birmingham News*, August 28, 2003.

18. Ibid.

19. *Moore v. Judicial Inquiry Commission*, transcript, no. 33, vol. 4 (2003), 156.

20. Associate justices, Alabama Supreme Court, brief in support of motion to dismiss *McGinley v. Houston*, 282 F. Supp. 2d 1304 (M.D. Ala. 2003), 2. Available at http://news.lp.findlaw.com/hdocs/docs/religion/mcginhstn82603oppbrf.pdf (emphasis added).

21. Champ Lyons Jr., "His Monument, My Oath, and the Rule of Law," May 12, 2004, 8, 10.

22. Ibid., 13.

23. Ibid., 24.

24. James Madison, *The Federalist No. 51*, ed. George W. Carey and James McClellan (2001), 268–69.

25. Thomas Jefferson, "Resolutions Relative to the Alien and Sedition Acts," reprinted in *The Founders Constitution* 1, ed. P. Kurland and R. Lerner (1987), 293.

26. U.S. Constitution, art. 6, para. 2.

27. James Madison, *The Federalist No. 45*, eds. George W. Carey and James McClellan (2001), 241.

28. *Marbury v. Madison*, 5 U.S. 137, 163 (1803).

29. Ibid., 165.

30. Ibid., 180 (emphasis in original).

31. *Cooper v. Aaron*, 358 U.S. 1, 18 (1958).

32. *Marbury v. Madison*, 5 U.S. 179–80 (emphasis added).

33. Attorney General Bill Pryor, official statement, August 21, 2003.

34. Abraham Lincoln, first inaugural address, March 4, 1861, reprinted in *The Essential Abraham Lincoln*, ed. John G. Hunt (New York: Gramercy Books, 1993), 218–19.

35. Thomas Jefferson, letter to Judge Spencer Roane, September 6, 1819, reprinted in *Writings*, 1426.

36. 410 U.S. 113 (1973).

37. 539 U.S. 558 (2003).

38. 478 U.S. 186 (1986).

Chapter 20

1. *Glassroth v. Moore*, 335 F. 3d 1282, 1303 (11th Cir. 2003) (emphasis added).

2. "Moore: Federal court lacks authority," *Birmingham News*, August 5, 2003.

3. U.S. Constitution, amend. 10.

4. *Glassroth v. Moore*, 275 F. Supp. 2d 1347, 1349 (M.D. Ala. 2003).

5. Ibid., 1349.

6. Ibid.

7. "Moore removed from office," *Gadsden Times*, November 14, 2003.

8. "Monumental showdown looms," *Birmingham News*, August 15, 2003.

9. "Moore to ignore order," *Gadsden Times*, August 15, 2003.

10. "Moore's decision isn't a surprise," *Montgomery Advertiser*, August 15, 2003.

11. "Moore to ignore order," *Gadsden Times*, August 15, 2003.

12. "Defiance creates rift among justices," *Mobile Register*, August 15, 2003.

13. "Bill Pryor faces dilemma," *Gadsden Times*, August 14, 2003.

14. Ibid.

15. "For Pryor, Religious, Legal Rights in Conflict," *Washington Post*, August 25, 2003.

16. Ibid.

17. "Thousands throng to display," *Montgomery Advertiser*, August 17, 2003.

18. "Capitol Rally," *Birmingham News*, August 17, 2003.

19. Ibid.

20. Ibid.

21. *Encyclopedia Britannica*, vol. 1, 15th ed. (Chicago, Ill., 1992), 200.

22. "Court won't stop monument move," *Birmingham News*, August 21, 2003.

23. "Moore disappointed with colleagues' decision, says he'll continue legal fight," *Gadsden Times*, August 22, 2003.

24. "Moore's colleagues order monument out," *Mobile Register*, August 22, 2003.

25. Ibid.

26. "Moore barred from duties," *Birmingham News/Post Herald*, August 23, 2003.

27. "Moore's colleagues order monument out," *Mobile Register*, August 22, 2003.

28. "Roy Moore Suspended," *Gadsden Times*, August 23, 2003; "Roy Moore Suspended," *Mobile Register*, August 23, 2003.

29. "Acting Chief Justice Houston to reissue monument order," *Birmingham News*, August 24, 2003.

30. "Protesters Not Going Away," *Mobile Register*, August 24, 2003.

31. "Moore blasts state leaders," *Montgomery Advertiser*, August 26, 2003.

32. "Monumental defeat," *Gadsden Times*, August 28, 2003.

33. "Dobson, Keyes urge reining in courts," *Birmingham News*, August 29, 2003.

34. "A historic occasion," *Citizens Magazine*, vol. 17, no. 11, November 2003.

35. "Dobson, Keyes urge reining in courts," *Birmingham News*, August 29, 2003.

36. "Moore supporters continue fight," *Mobile Register*, August 29, 2003.

37. Ibid.

38. "Monument rally cancelled after protesters ousted," *Birmingham News*, September 4, 2003.

Chapter 21

1. "Court to hear Moore case seldom ousts judges," *Birmingham News*, August 31, 2003.

2. "Ten Commandments on display at Capitol," *Gadsden Times*, September 10, 2003.

3. Ibid.

4. Ibid (emphasis added).

5. "Ten Commandments on display as part of documents exhibit at Judicial Building," *Gadsden Times*, February 6, 2004.

6. Ibid.

7. "The Law Has Returned," campaign flyer for Alabama Supreme Court Justice Jean Brown, May 2004.

8. "Moore will offer his monument to Congress," *Birmingham News*, September 17, 2003.

9. "Moore efforts to remove Pryor renewed," *Birmingham News*, October 24, 2003.

10. "Vote on Pryor blocked again," *Birmingham News*, November 7, 2003.

11. "GOP to push for vote on Pryor again," *Montgomery Advertiser*, November 6, 2003.

12. "For Pryor, Religious, Legal Rights in Conflict," *Washington Post*, August 25, 2003.

13. "Court orders Moore trial open to public," *Gadsden Times*, October 30, 2003.

14. "Removal may be inevitable," *Gadsden Times*, October 31, 2003.

15. "Supreme Court says 'no' to Moore," *Gadsden Times*, November 4, 2003.

16. Ibid.

17. Ibid (emphasis added).

18. Transcript, COJ trial, Jeana S. Boggs, November 12, 2003 (emphasis added).

19. *Webster's Encyclopedic Unabridged Dictionary of the English Language* (New York: Random House Value Publishing, Inc., 1996).

20. "Alabama Judge Thrown Out," *Vancouver Sun*, November 14, 2003.

21. "Two of Moore's aides fired," *Gadsden Times*, November 16, 2003.

22. Ibid.

23. Ibid.
24. Ibid.
25. "Lawsuits say Moore was illegally removed from office," *Gadsden Times*, November 20, 2003.
26. Ibid.
27. "Survey finds support for Moore," *Gadsden Times*, November 25, 2003.
28. "Seven retired judges named to hear appeal," *Gadsden Times*, December 16, 2003.
29. "Judges hearing Moore appeal are not accountable to voters," *Gadsden Times*, February 25, 2004.
30. "Moore Appeal heard," *Gadsden Times*, February 26, 2004.
31. Ibid.
32. *Moore v. Judicial Inquiry Commission of the State of Alabama*, So. 2d, slip. op. 25 (Ala. 2004).

Chapter 22

1. 539 U.S. 558 (2003).
2. 478 U.S. 186 (1986).
3. *Lawrence v. Texas*, 539 U.S. 576.
4. Justice Sandra Day O'Connor, *Remarks before the Southern Center for International Law Studies*, Keynote Address, October 28, 2003.
5. Justice Sandra Day O'Connor, *Keynote Address at the 96th Annual Meeting of the Society of International Law*, March 16, 2002.
6. Justice Stephen Breyer, "The Supreme Court and the New International Law," Speech at the 97th annual meeting of the American Society of International Law, April 4, 2003.
7. Ibid.
8. O'Connor, *Remarks* (emphasis added).
9. Ibid.
10. Ibid.
11. Anthony Romero and Ann Beeson, Program Brochure, Human Rights at Home: International Law in U.S. Courts.
12. George Washington, Farewell Address, September 17, 1796, chap. 5, sup. n. 5, 683.
13. 143 U.S. 457 (1892).
14. *Holy Trinity Church*, 143 U.S. 471 [quoting *People v. Ruggles*, 8 Johns. 290, 294–95 (New York, 1811).
15. 283 U.S. 605, 625 (1931).
16. Holy Trinity Church, 143 U.S., 465–67.
17. Ibid., 467–69.
18. 11 Serg. & Rawle 394 (Pa. 1824).
19. "More courts tackle Ten Commandments" *USA Today*, September 15, 2004,
20. *Moore v. Judicial Inquiry Commission of State of Alabama*, 125 S. Ct. 103 (2004).
21. 351 F. 3d 173 (5th Cir. 2003).
22. 354 F. 3d 438 (6th Cir. 2003).
23. *Van Orden v. Perry*, 351 F. 3d 180.
24. Ibid., 182.
25. *ACLU of Kentucky v. McCreary County*, 354 F. 3d 440–41.
26. Ibid., 444 [quoting *ACLU of Kentucky v. McCreary County*, 96 F. Supp. 2d 679, 691 (E.D. KY. 2000)].
27. 354 F. 3d 444 [quoting *ACLU of Kentucky v. McCreary County*, 145 F.Supp.2d 845, 853 (E.D. KY. 2001)].
28. "Commandments supporter dies," *Montgomery Advertiser*, August 29, 2004.
29. Roy S. Moore, chief justice, Alabama Supreme Court, May 4, 2001.